# ARTS OF WONDER

RELIGION AND POSTMODERNISM

*A series edited by Thomas A. Carlson*

RECENT BOOKS IN THE SERIES

*Secularism in Antebellum America*,
by John Lardas Modern (2011)

*The Figural Jew: Politics and Identity in Postwar French Thought*,
by Sarah Hammerschlag (2010)

*The Indiscrete Image: Infinitude and Creation of the Human*,
by Thomas A. Carlson (2008)

*Islam and the West: A Conversation with Jacques Derrida*,
by Mustapha Chérif (2008)

*The Gift of Death, Second Edition*, and *Literature in Secret*,
by Jacques Derrida (2008)

# ARTS OF WONDER

*Enchanting Secularity—*
WALTER DE MARIA,
DILLER + SCOFIDIO,
JAMES TURRELL,
ANDY GOLDSWORTHY

JEFFREY L. KOSKY

*The University of Chicago Press*
CHICAGO & LONDON

The University of Chicago Press, Chicago 60637
The University of Chicago Press, Ltd., London

Paperback edition 2016

25 24 23 22 21 20 19 18 17 16 2 3 4 5 6

ISBN-13: 978-0-226-45106-0 (cloth)
ISBN-13: 978-0-226-41180-4 (paper)
ISBN-13: 978-0-226-45108-4 (e-book)
DOI: 10.7208/chicago/9780226451084.001.0001

The University of Chicago Press gratefully acknowledges the generous support of Washington and Lee University toward the publication of this book.

Support for the publication of this book was provided by the Class of 1956 Provost's Faculty Development Endowment at Washington and Lee University.

Library of Congress Cataloging-in-Publication Data

Kosky, Jeffrey L.
Arts of wonder : enchanting secularity : Walter de Maria, Diller + Scofidio, James Turrell, Andy Goldsworthy / Jeffrey L. Kosky.
pages cm. — (Religion and postmodernism)
Includes bibliographical references and index.
ISBN 978-0-226-45106-0 (cloth : alkaline paper)
ISBN 0-226-45106-2 (cloth : alkaline paper)
ISBN 978-0-226-45108-4 (e-book)
ISBN 0-226-45108-9 (e-book)
1. Light in art. 2. Light art. 3. Art and religion. 4. Earthworks (Art). 5. De Maria, Walter, 1935- Lightning field. 6. Blur Building (Expo.02, Switzerland). 7. Turrell, James—Criticism and interpretation. 8. Goldsworthy, Andy, 1956- —Criticism and interpretation. I. Title. II. Series: Religion and postmodernism.
N8219.L5K67 2012
709.05'1—dc23
2012017785

♾ This paper meets the requirements of ANSI/NISO Z39.48-1992 (Permanence of Paper).

*To Claire Sabine Kosky and Oscar Irving Kosky*

# CONTENTS

# FIGURES

# *PREFACE*

I have long used the category "disenchantment" when teaching and writing about the modern condition. In this, I am not unusual. This interpretation of modernity has been dominant for many years. To be modern, it claims, is to share in the disenchantment of the world. This is not just a thesis about the state of our psyche or the condition of human being; it does not just say that we moderns (those moderns?) are jaded or bored, lacking in ideals or commitment, frustrated or disappointed—in short, that we are (they are?) a disenchanted lot. It is also a thesis about the world itself. In the diagnosis of modern disenchantment is contained a decision about the nature, or lack thereof, of the world and what counts as real. It is as much a concern of cosmology as of anthropology.

This book addresses these cosmologies and anthropologies, and even the theologies of modern disenchantment. It is motivated by my own disenchantment with modern disenchantment—my sense that the models of modern disenchantment are no longer enough and that we need new models of human being, the world, and the relation of each to the other. On the basis of intimate encounters with particular works of art, *Arts of Wonder* therefore poses, without embarrassment, far-reaching questions regarding the nature, or lack thereof, of humanity, the world, and even God in the wake of modern disenchantment.

* * *

"Disenchantment" as a diagnosis of modernity was employed most famously by Max Weber in his classic essay "Science as a Vocation." There Weber wrote, "The fate of our times is characterized by rationalization and intellectualization and above all by 'the disenchantment of the world.'" The increasing intellectualization and rationalization of the age means, he continued, that "principally there are no mysterious incalculable forces that come into play, but rather that one can, in principle, master all things by calculation. This means that the world is disenchanted." Mysteries having been banished, the world that remains is one we can *count on*, reliably and predictably, precisely because it is one we can *count up*, measure and compute in a calculative science. In such a world, "one need no longer have recourse to magical means in order to master or implore the spirits, as did the savage, for whom such mysterious powers existed. Technical means and calculations perform the service."[1] Thanks to the ever increasing calculative capabilities of knowledge and science, and owing to ever more effective technologies, we have the power to order and organize, make and manipulate, the world in accordance with reasons of our own.

Following Weber, disenchantment is not simply a matter of the death of God or of the gods, demons, and spirits; it is not simply a challenge to theology or religion. Rather, it concerns the dismissal of the very notion of "mystery" from our encounter with the world and with ourselves. Disenchantment, then, is a signal of healthy-minded autonomy. A good modern, the story goes, is disenchanted: he does not come under the spell of mysteries, nor is he held in thrall by the charm of unspeakable wonders. He lets his actions and decisions be organized as methodic and systematic means in pursuit of known ends, and he can, precisely because he calculates means to pursue ends "controlled by the intellect," offer a reasonable account of all he does.

And yet, however empowering the project of disenchantment and demystification might be, many today have grown disenchanted with modern disenchantment and are seeking a new story to tell about it. They sense the lovelessness of the world fostered by the calculative thinking that dominates modern economic, scientific, and philosophical logic. They feel the absence of charm and wonder as deeply enervating. And they suspect another truth, one in which the world might come to light in a far more wonderful way.

Can the spell of modern disenchantment be broken?

* * *

Taking its point of departure from Weber's thesis, *Arts of Wonder* looks to significant artwork of the late twentieth and early twenty-first centuries to stage intimate encounters with modern disenchantment. The works of art I encounter are most often thought to be representative of secular modernity and therefore to share in the disenchantment of the world, but listening to the appeal of these appealing works, I was surprised to find myself invoking a vocabulary that I had long kept at a distance. These works of art work, I found, make places where we might encounter mystery and wonder, hopes for redemption and revelation, transcendence and creation—longings traditionally cultivated and addressed in religious traditions, but that, when developed through the encounter with these works of art, are nevertheless crucial aspects of enchanting secularity.

By exploring these themes through encounters with cutting-edge works of art, *Arts of Wonder* suggests that one need not look only to traditional religion or religious traditions for refuge from the vicissitudes of human being in the world set up by modern disenchantment. A "secular" response to these challenges can also be cultivated, without fleeing the modern condition. But, having been trained in theology, I understand, too, that it is the task of religion, as much as of art, to help us creatively affirm our worlds (or not). Religion does this by offering an interpretation of the world that lets us see a god revealed in or through it—which implies that it elaborates for us an image of a god so that we might find it (or not) in the worlds where we dwell. I try in this book to do both.

Insofar as my engagement with religious texts and practices is not simply critical, I risk being taken by strident defenders of a purely secular and disenchanted modern art as a leftover from a supposedly religious past. Inversely, insofar as my response to our disenchantment with modern disenchantment is elaborated through secular works and not religious traditions, I risk being taken by the traditionally religious or religiously traditional as irrelevant, insignificant, or even profane. Let the reader read, I say. I leave it to him or her to decide: Do these religious considerations deepen and prolong our encounters with the work of art, the best criteria art writing could adopt? Do the works of art let us see an image of the divine in the world we inhabit, the best way religion has of bringing significance to today's world?

* * *

The book is organized into an introduction and five chapters, each of which revolves around an encounter with a work of art. The majority of the works treated are site-specific; many can be classified as earthworks or land art. This makes the question of place or of sacred places an important subtext of this book. It is organized almost as much around the individual artworks as around the places into which these artworks gathered me.

On the basis of intimate encounters with these places and these works of art, I test the limits and possibilities of disenchantment and enchantment by asking a type of question adopted from Michel Serres and Martin Heidegger, each of whom, in different ways, suspects that we heirs of modern disenchantment have become world-less to the degree that we don't deal with things, that we no longer experience what it means to dwell as human being to the degree that the things of a world have been reduced to our objective knowledge, representation, or picture of them. My encounters with these works have taught me the importance of this claim, even if I do not accept their theses unquestioningly.

What are the things that appear in a world? What is our model for a thing? Is it the object met in the laboratory, so easily submitted to mastery and control? Or are there richly endowed, wonderful things, provoking experiences other than mastery and control, perhaps even enchanting experiences? These latter are the things with which the artists I engage work: lightning at Walter De Maria's *Lightning Field*; clouds with Diller + Scofidio's *Blur*; the sky and light itself in James Turrell's art; and driftwood and melt, rivers and tides in the work of Andy Goldsworthy. What if we took clouds as our model for what counts as reality, not the carts we crashed together in the high school physics lab? What if we remembered the lightning flash that brought the world momentarily to light, and did not start with the lighthouse that brings ships safely ashore by harnessing and duplicating the power of the sun? The inclusion of these things in the artistic work of creation makes for a world rich with enchanting possibilities, yet one that remains a worldly work of human being in the world.

* * *

This book is the register of my journeys to these places and of my encounters with these works of art. It aims to maintain the striving and uncertainty of an encounter in which you do not always know what you want to say before you say it—very often because the effect the thing has is to give you new and unexpected words. A tentative and probing way—striving and remaining open—this is the way we proceed when we encounter something wonderful. I would like to think this book adopts a corresponding form of literary composition. That style or form is one that leaps between genre and disciplines and ventures tentative thoughts. The holes and loose ends are meant as invitations; sometimes an incomplete thought or word can be the most generous one given to a reader.

It also aims to maintain some of the intimacy of an encounter. I therefore say "I" and share my stories. If this risks putting my I on a stage populated by more abstract issues and texts from philosophy, theology, and cultural theory, it is not without some hesitation and embarrassment that I do so, but it is ultimately important to the work the book wants to do. Telling these stories is not meant to establish the unimpeachable authority of individual identity (my own, in this case) and its extratextual experience. It is rather meant to stage or perform in person, as it were, some of the conceptual concerns of the texts and theories with which I wrestle with students. On some level, this book is for them: students and former students, not necessarily my own, but anyone who remains studious in their life outside and after the university, still wondering about the world and the human being who inhabits it.

As the expertise we manufacture in the university, even in the humanities where I teach, leads to more and more specialized knowledge, and as the scope and scale of the knowledge that our microscopic specializations produce become more and more gigantic, we risk losing sight of the impact that our knowledge and the concepts we elaborate have on our lives. What does it mean, if anything, or what is it like to experience, or not, this knowledge we transmit? Is the life of the university just an abstract relation to ideas, or is our discussion in the classroom rendered sterile and alienated from itself when cut off from the person or existence of those who meet there?

Through both the records of my own experience and the questioning after things, this book is meant to convey my sense of the urgency of these ill-framed questions. It is therefore a book about clearings and the light, clouds and lightning, driftwood and melting snow, not only a book about God, Self, and World in the condition of modern disenchantment. If the critic suspects a lack of specialization and questions the possibility for expertise in chapters that draw from so many disciplines and genres, each seeming to gloss the other, without ever arriving at one and staying there comfortably, then he has experienced something of what I find wonderful in what comes or can come in the wake of modern disenchantment as it surges on.

# *ACKNOWLEDGMENTS*

This book would never have befallen me were it not for two events. One was moving to the forested foothills of Lexington, Virginia, in the Shenandoah Valley, where I came to live the need to make and hold open a sort of clearing of my own, like those I struggle to understand in this book. The power that this exercised over me as I wrote was something I was aware of. I was, however, less aware of the influence of the other event: the gift of my two children. It took more than one friend and colleague pointing out the insistence of the children in these pages for me to recognize it. One of them, wise beyond her years, described the genesis of the book when she called it "some new vision for you of the world born of your relationship with your children," and another offered the most revealing of thoughts about the book's end when he said, "One day your children will read the book and see their father contemplating the sacred places in it." Learning from friends like this what inspired the book, I have dedicated it to Claire and Oscar.

This inspiration is matched by the material support given by Washington and Lee University, where I teach. This support came, importantly, in the form of a place where I could talk and share with others, students and colleagues with whom I could think—but also in the form of several fellowships. In particular, I am grateful to the Glenn Grant and the Lenfest Summer Fellowship programs for supporting summer writing and for funding trips to many of the artworks. Special thanks is owed to June Aprille and the Office of the Provost at Washington and Lee for additional support securing permissions and the publication of this book. These programs and the individuals involved in them display the university's understanding of and commitment to providing the material conditions that make research and writing in the humanities possible.

What came over me with the two events of displacement to the hills of Virginia and the reception of Claire and Oscar would never have grown into this work if many friends and colleagues had not offered their assistance, encouragement, and insight. Liane Carlson, my student, my friend, and soon to be, if not already, also my colleague, has been an ongoing and indefatigable conversation partner; it is not the ones who stay that are the closest, but those who keep coming back. Eduardo Velàsquez was unflagging in his support; he never doubted, especially not the tone and the voice. Eduardo's support also took the concrete form of including me in several workshops he organized where I could present drafts of this work. Doug Johnson, an invaluable eye from the urban provinces, cut many pages where they needed to be cut and called me back to earth in several places; his live response framed my editing through much of the rest of the manuscript. Howard Pickett, William Robert, and Jonathan Eastwood offered insightful readings that helped me understand where the manuscript might fall within and between its various audiences. I owe an unredeemable debt to the generosity shown to me, now and for many years, by Mark C. Taylor, who read and responded to every chapter in some form or another. His ongoing interest remains an inspiration.

Perhaps one of the more unexpected gifts came from an old friend, Jim Lasko. This book would be nowhere near as beautiful as it is without Jim's know-how, and his love for the drafts I shared was an early vote of confidence that I was going in the right direction. Cynthia Hooper deserves a special thanks for having contributed her wonderful work. Eric Sawden at the Goldsworthy Studio is due my undying gratitude for giving the last hours of his day each day for a week responding to my requests. I would also like to thank Alan Thomas and Randy Petilos at the University of Chicago Press for their invaluable assistance steering this book to a place where it could see the light of day. Joel Score at the Press deserves high praise for the many ways in which he improved the manuscript. Finally, Tom Carlson. The seeds of much of this book are marginal remarks and passing references, outtakes of sorts, from the long conversations with him that have made some of the more wonderful places of my life.

Last but not least, Stephanie Hodde. A book dedicated to my children and what I receive from them cannot not also be indebted to their mother, my wife: what I receive from them I receive together with you, always, and not without you. I am mindful of that—and when I am not, I owe you even more.

# ARTS OF WONDER

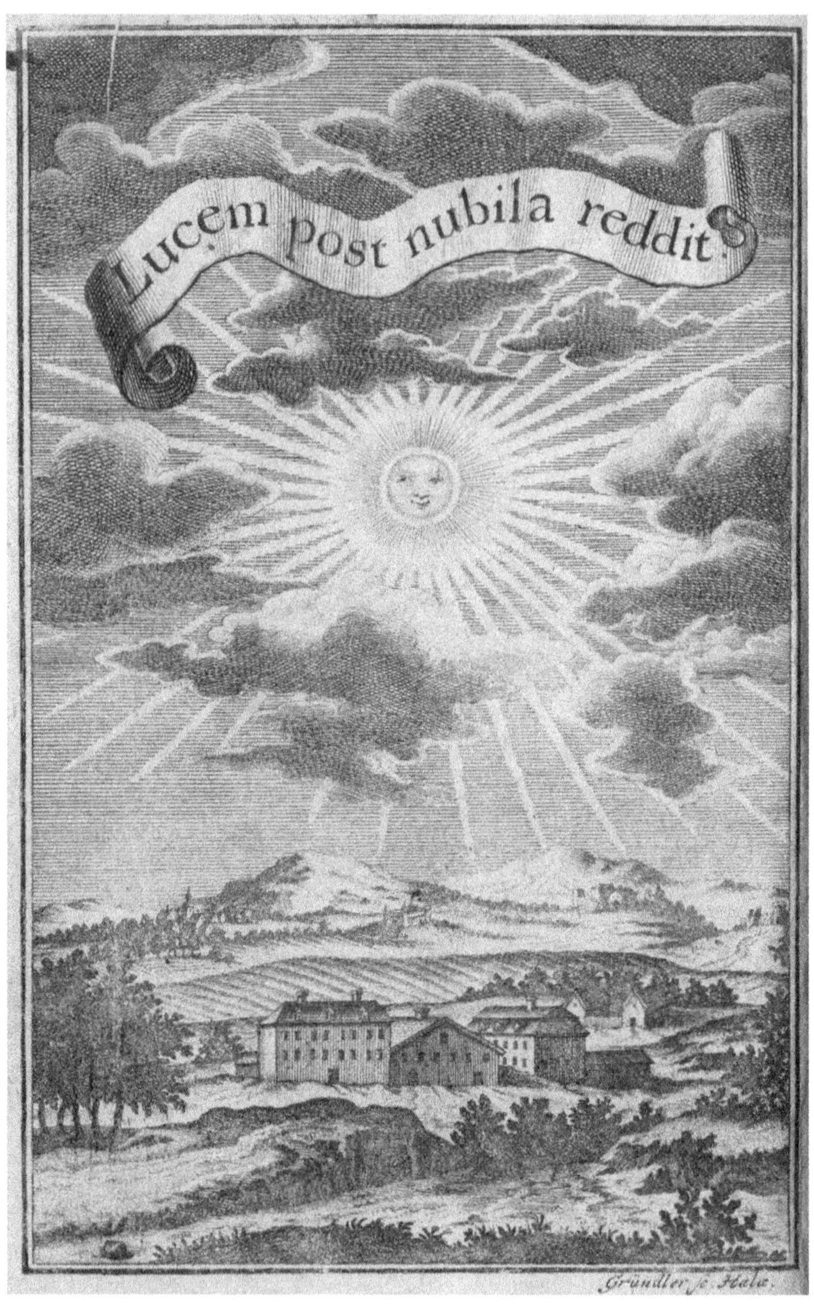


FIGURE 1. Frontispiece from Christian Wolff, *Vernünfftige Gedancken von Gott, der Welt und der Seele des Menschen auch allen Dingen überhaupt den Liebharen der Wahrheit* (1720). Rare Book Collection, University of North Carolina at Chapel Hill.

(IN PLACE OF AN) INTRODUCTION

# A Picture of Modern Disenchantment

### *Lucem post nubila reddit*

When I teach a class on modern disenchantment, I share with students a picture that has come to be a sort of obsession for me. I learned of it while reading Karl Barth, the Protestant theologian whose savage yet insightful critique of modern theology, as well as of secular modernity, proved decisive for theology in the twentieth century. Though Barth's book does not include a reproduction, I tracked it down. I thought it might serve as a picture of modern disenchantment. Perhaps it could help my students translate the abstract concepts of our discussion into things to which they could relate—and aren't things precisely what is at issue in questioning the world of modern disenchantment?

The picture is banal, ordinary. What it shows has become almost a commonplace, hardly worth remark, much less years of obsession. Here it is (fig. 1). The frontispiece to Christian Wolff's emblematic work of the European Enlightenment, *Reasonable Thoughts on God, the World and the human Soul, and All things in General. Communicated to the Lovers of Truth by Christian Wolff*. It is an image of enlightenment and of revelation—of seeing the light and seeing it according to the format of light as a cone of illuminating rays streaming from a point source. The banner unfurled above the smiling sun says, *Lucem post nubila reddit* (He/It brings back the light after the clouds). This gives voice to a certain dualism: light and dark are opposed and irreconcilable, the light coming only after the darkness and clouds have passed or been destroyed. It also gives voice to a sense of novelty or uniqueness, a break with how things have been in that dark past. And finally it implies that light, at some time, departed, if it now returns or is brought back.

Wolff's image depicts the climactic event that ends the historical struggle of opposing forces or rectifies the disastrously dark times of the past: light returns triumphant, clouds dissipate, and all there is (*God, the World and the human Soul, and All things in General*) appears distinctly in the clearing made by the one cone of light. What Wolff's frontispiece shows, then, is the dawn of a day when all things will fit into one unified world picture. We can make a picture of the world.

* * *

Look again at the picture. A smiling sun pierces a mass of clouds, bathing mountains and forests, river and town in its illuminating rays. As the clouds clear and the fog lifts, heavens and earth are drawn together in one and the same light, within the frame of one comprehensive picture. Nothing is left out; "all things in general" appear in the clearing made by the sun's radiant cone. They do not fade into the clouds, float about in an endless sky, or drift away in the running river, but stand secure, established on solid ground. In the clearing made by the sun's cone of rays, things sit on the ground. All things, each in its place, resting serenely, are gathered together in one light and make up a landscape.

This landscape is not the wild. It is an arranged, ordered, even cultivated clearing in which men have made themselves at home in some estate or manor—not exactly a castle, but nonetheless safe and secure beside the flowing river. A small town or hamlet is built there, in the clearing illuminated by the sun, and around this dwelling place the landscape rises and is gathered together in the cone of light. Everything in this world picture, it would seem, takes its stand as a part of this cultivated landscape, which is formed by the play between the sun, whose light clears away the clouds, and the home or city built there in the lit space.

The picture itself is organized in two tiers. The lower half, or perhaps third, depicts the earth, in a space that is organized in what we think of as a natural or realistic way. The whole picture opens up to the gaze of a spectator looking through its frame, as through a window, from a position outside the picture and slightly above it. From the this elevated viewpoint, feet not on the ground, the observer can look through the frame down onto the landscape, where nothing escapes or vanishes, or straight ahead into the sky, where his gaze meets face-on a smiling sun. Looking out, not up, into the clearing in the cloud cover, one sees a sky like a skin or blank sheet drawn behind the realistic scene below, limiting and binding the gaze to this horizonless world. Behind the parting clouds lies not what Blaise Pascal (1623–1662) named "the eternal silence of infinite spaces," the endless empty space of an unbounded universe that would fill us with dread, but the sheet of the sky and a smiling face. Their presence in the picture puts a stop to our gaze.

The sun itself hardly needs to have attention called to it—so corny, so utterly silly is it that serious comment seems impossible. What I nevertheless find significant about it is this: You can see here the face of what appears when the clouds dissipate; you can see the point that completes and holds together the cone of light; you can see the summit of the mountain of light that connects earth and sky. This summit awaits you with a welcoming smiling face. Wolff is very bold here, perhaps apocalyptic; the clouds or dome of the sky no longer block your gaze into the heavens or obstruct your march to the summit. There is something there to see!

* * *

When I share this picture with the students in my class on modern disenchantment, I do not tell them of its source. I point out to them that the subject of the emblematic sentence is unstated because, in Latin, it can be implied in the verb. I then ask them what they think is symbolized by the sun, who or what shines the light in which we see the world. The responses are divided. Some answer "God," identifying the point source, the apex of the cone of illuminating rays, as God himself, who acts as the cause or agent whose activity shines the light (the rays) in which the world comes to light clearly and distinctly. Indeed, the scholar Jonathan Crary, an art historian, has remarked on "how deeply theological was the notion that light was radiant (composed of rays)."[1]

Other students answer "Reason," claiming that reason shines the light in which all things appear truly. These students' interpretation is more in keeping with the setting of the image in the context of the modern enlightenment. The book in which it serves as frontispiece was, after all, called *Reasonable Thoughts on God, the World and the human Soul, and All things in General*—as if the list of things illuminated by the light of reasonable thought includes God. In the other reading of the picture, God would not be among the things illuminated but the light itself.

Yet the first group of students, the ones who put God in the position of the sun, surely give voice to a widespread and influential opinion about the nature, function, and position of God in relation to the universe: He shines the light in which objects appear truly or really, really and truly, and we can be certain of our relation to them when we see in the light he shines. This conception of God is perhaps as widespread among the avowedly religious of today, in the wake of modern disenchantment, as it is among those who reject religion or do not count themselves as religious.

What are we to make of the fact that our picture of modern disenchantment gives rise to two such interpretations—sun = God and sun = reason—both of which seem to give voice to truth? Closer consideration of Wolff and the Enlightenment project might help.

## Excursus on the theology of modern disenchantment

Few students or scholars today make a career of studying Christian Wolff (1679–1754). Nevertheless, most would agree that he is an emblematic figure of the Enlightenment, at least in Germany, where he was its leading representative before Immanuel Kant and after G. W. Leibniz. Kant wrote that "those who reject the method of Wolff . . . can have no other aim than to shake off the fetters of science altogether."[2] No small praise, even if Kant would follow with sharp criticism. Wolff is also known as "the most industrious student" or, according to others who give him more credit, the most significant colleague of Leibniz, a philosopher who is still widely studied today. Indeed, Leibniz sponsored Wolff's appointments in the academies of eighteenth-century Germany, and the two were so close that scholars, including Kant, speak of the "Leibnizian-Wolffian system."[3]

### A GOD WHO RENDERS REASONS / REASONS THAT ARE DIVINE

Wolff's close connection with Leibniz lends support to the equation of the sun with reason—after all, the central tenet of the "Leibnizian-Wolffian system" was the principle of sufficient reason or the *principium reddendae rationis* (principle of rendering reason). There are many formulations of this principle in Leibniz and Wolff, but all of them, according to Arthur Schopenhauer (1788–1860), whose thought exercised a profound influence on Nietzsche and Freud, ultimately boil down to this claim: nothing is or happens without a reason. As Wolff puts it, *nihil est sine ratione cur potius sit quam non sit* (nothing is without a ground or reason why it is rather than is not).[4] Schopenhauer could also have referred to §56 of Wolff's *Ontologia*, in which he offers the following definition of sufficient reason: "By sufficient reason, we understand that by which something is." Martin Heidegger, in his own groundbreaking discussion of the principle of reason, concludes that where the principle of reason reigns, everything that is "is itself a consequence of a reason, and that means it is by virtue and apropos of the demand to render reasons." In other words, "everything that is, is by virtue of" the reason rendered for it.[5] Nothing comes to light on its own, in a light of its own shining, as it were, but only appears in a light from another, in this case the light of the reasons illuminating it. Anything that gets into the picture of the world we hold in modern disenchantment gets there by the rendering of reasons.

What the picture *Lucem post nubila reddit* depicts is the blessed event in which the light appears and clears the way to safe and secure ground on which things come to stand. Read with the principle of reason in mind, this event is the giving of reasons. It is no great leap, then, to see Wolff's frontispiece as depicting the operation of what Leibniz called the *principium magnum, grande et nobilissimum*, the grand, powerful, and most noble principle—namely, the principle of reason. This rendering of reason (Leibniz's *prinicipium reddendae rationis*) is what is represented in the picture of the world that accompanies Wolff's metaphysics. The banner says as much: *Lucem post nubila reddit*, which could be translated as "He/It *renders* the light after the clouds."

And yet, Leibniz will also provide support for those who want to claim that the sun is God. Consider "A Résumé of Metaphysics." This text begins by asserting the principle of rendering reasons: "There is a reason in Nature why something should exist rather than nothing." Leibniz then goes on to say, "This reason must be in some real entity or cause," as if reason's role of explaining, answering "why," or providing grounds was played by the cause. And he concludes by claiming that "the ultimate reason for things is usually called by one word 'God.' There is therefore a cause for the prevalence of existence over non-existence."[6] There is, in short, "some real entity or cause" in which the reason for things resides. The entity that brings together cause and reason in this way is the one "usually called . . . 'God.'"

Importantly, then, modern disenchantment does not mean the disappearance of God or the neutralization of theology. Indeed, there is a theology of modern disenchantment: divine is whatever holds the position of the sun in this picture, the smiling source of a light that illuminates a world in which objects appear at rest under the sun. God or reason—both make for a world that appears clearly and distinctly to the man who looks at it. It is as if a certain form of enlightenment (the principle of rendering reason) shared a common structure of bringing things to light with a certain form of religion (the God who shines a light on all things). This format or way of organizing our picture of the world is modern disenchantment.

## SMILE, IT'S THE BEST OF ALL POSSIBLE WORLDS

The smile on the face of the sun, so corny and silly as to seem unremarkable, takes on added significance at this point. Surely the world picture opens with a smile and a landscape falls cheerfully into place when the god who shines a light does so indistinguishably from the reason that might lead things to their ground. A brief consideration of Leibniz's thought shows that the smiling god who serves to render reasons to the man who looks on—this god of modern disenchantment—emerges in the contest of the principle of reason with another god, one who does not render reasons and so might not be part of the setup of modern disenchantment.

Consider the most important corollary of the principle of rendering reason: the claim that this is "the best of all possible worlds." An explicit assertion of this appears in Leibniz's *Theodicy*, a work whose title means literally "justification of God": "There is an infinitude of possible worlds among which God must needs have chosen the best, since he does nothing without acting in accordance with supreme reason."[7] The term *theodicy* is in fact attributed to Leibniz, even if it refers back to a long history of thinking that, without using the term explicitly, attempts to justify or defend the attributes of God, especially his goodness, justice, or holiness, against the observation of apparent evil and suffering in the physical world. In a sense, theodicy's task is to ensure that the sun in whose light the world comes to be does indeed have a smile on its face. The claim that this is the best of all possible worlds is the answer to the theodical investigation (yes, it does smile), and the principle of reason is the guarantee that this response will be affirmative. This is indeed the best of all possible worlds when reasons rendered are rendered to the man looking on.

Commenting on the connection of the two claims, the philosopher Donald Rutherford writes:

> When presented in these terms [in relation to the principle of reason], Leibniz's theodicy is seen to be more philosophical and less narrowly apologetic, than many have supposed. Underlying this argument is an assumption concerning the unlimited scope of reason. Given the universal validity of the principle of sufficient reason, *nihil fit sine ratio*, it follows that there must be a reason why this world . . . exists rather than some other very different but equally possible world. In Leibniz's view, the only compelling account of this fact is in terms of the selection of this world by God from among an infinity of possible worlds as the best world for creation.

Rutherford's observation suggests that the smiling sun indicates more than cheery optimism or a sunny disposition. The claim that this is the best of all possible worlds does not express a subjective outlook, mood, or disposition; it is not the naïveté of one who blindly persists in the faith that he inhabits the best of all possible worlds despite all evidence being to the contrary—as with Pangloss in Voltaire's *Candide*, commonly taken to be a caricature of Leibniz and his claim. "This is the best of all possible worlds" is an assertion about reality—more particularly, about the reality that comes to light when reasons must be rendered for all the things that are or happen in the world. As a physical claim resting on a metaphysical principle, it is therefore also not equal to the claim that this is the happiest or most joyful of worlds. The persistent experience of sadness or suffering need not wipe the smile off the face of the sun.

When read this way, the smiling sun seems indifferent to the question of human joy or sadness. What it indicates instead is the openness or availability of the things it brings to light—"all things in general," according to the title of Wolff's book. More particularly, since the rendering of a reason is the price they pay for admission into the clearing where all that is comes to light, "all things in general" will be available to rational investigation. What makes this world "the best" is that it has or will have had a reason rendered to the I that knows. This means that we need not merely "acknowledge [the world's] orderly character without having it confirmed"; we can be certain: rational investigation can secure on solid grounds the order of the cosmos so that we can be certain of where things stand. The sun smiles in modern disenchantment not because the best of all possible worlds is one in which man will (somehow, somewhere, somewhen) be happy, but because, in the clearing made by its light, nature will have rendered itself "dependable and serviceable to him," by giving back its reason to the man who knows it.[9]

## LOST CAUSE, REASON RENDERED

This liberates the man of modern disenchantment from the uncertainty and unreliability of a world order grounded on what Leibniz deplored as the "absolutely absolute decree" of a God who hides his face and speaks from a cloud.[10] The "absolutely absolute decree" recalls late medieval theological positions (most often categorized as nominalist) in which an obsession with divine omnipotence and its defense came to dominate theological reflection. *Lucem post nubila reddit* imagines the triumph of rendering reasons over this "absolutely absolute decree" issued from a God who keeps his reasons to himself.

The nominalist defense of the causal power of divine omnipotence forbade the reliability or calculability of the world since a truly omnipotent power could not be limited and so hung like a threatening cloud over all that came to light in this world. In its shadow, everything can be, or at least could have been, otherwise. Even if the unlimited omnipotence of divine causal power chose to bind itself to the order it ordains by its creative act (what the theologians described as the *potentia absoluta* choosing to create an order that its power would then respect and whose limits it would obey, operating now as *potentia ordinata*), this order remained mysterious and hidden in the inscrutable choice of a divine agent. It might be reliable, but you could not be certain, nor certain what it was. Access to it required faith, without rational confirmation.

The obsession with the causal power of an omnipotent God lay under one of the seemingly most arcane but in fact deeply significant debates of medieval theology: the debate about a plurality of possible worlds. Most scholars suggest that the floodgate for speculation about a plurality of worlds was the promulgation in 1277, at the hand of Etienne Tempier, bishop of Paris, of a series of 219 condemnations of doctrines that limited or even denied the omnipotence of God. Among the doctrines condemned was the following: "§34 That the first cause (i.e., God) could not make several worlds." One cannot say that God could not make worlds other than this one because such an assertion would deny that God is truly omnipotent and his causal power unlimited. The line of thinking defended by Tempier and his council carried forward into the nominalist theologies of the fourteenth century, as in Nicholas Oresme, who affirmed, "God can and could in his omnipotence make another world besides this one or several like or unlike it."

When Leibniz asserts, "there is an infinitude of possible worlds among which God must needs have chosen the best," he should be seen as intervening in this medieval debate. The end he imagines for it would be the beginning of the age of modern disenchantment.

The claim that this is the best of all possible worlds is probably not what constitutes Leibniz's modernity, however. It is instead his justification of this claim on the assertion that "he [God] does nothing without acting in accordance with supreme reason" that will launch modernity's departure from the Middle Ages. Nicolas of Autrecourt in the fourteenth century, for instance, explored the claim that this one and only world was the best of all possible worlds, but he justified this assertion not by claiming there is a reason why something is the way it is but by asserting that God willed it to be so. The basis for Autrecourt's claim, that is, was a defense of divine omnipotence, not of God's rationality. As Hans Blumenberg puts it, "It is easy to see that this *universum perfectissimum* has nothing to do with Leibniz's 'best of all possible worlds' since any other arbitrarily chosen world, as sheer fact, would have to receive this predicate."[11] As one minimized the need of a ground for the divine will in anything other than its own maximum of causality, the contingency of the made order (it could just as well be otherwise) was maximized.

In such a cosmos, reason and rational action seem powerless to master or form a plan to alter an order whose contingency and unpredictability leave it insufficiently reliable. Far from self-assertion, the ideal human relation to nature and the cosmos would be an act of self-negation that removes the human source of the disruption of God's plan and "finds" one's place, in a providential order accessible only in a faith received without reason rendered.

Everything changes, however, when the principle of reason dominates and a disenchanted world appears in the light it shines. The "absolutely absolute decree" of a God who hides his face and clouds the world is removed and a picture of the world can be constituted, one in which a new relation to "God, the World and the human Soul, and All things in General" is possible. "All things in general" having rendered the reasons that make them reliable and calculable, the man of modern disenchantment can undertake what Blumenberg calls "the immanent self-assertion of reason through the mastery and alteration of reality."[12]

## The apotheosis of electricity

The connection between *lucem post nubila reddit* and "the self-assertion of reason through the mastery and alteration of reality" appeared to me in a second book I found in the course of preparing to teach students about modern disenchantment. One of the first titles to appear when you type "disenchant" into the catalog of the library at the university where I teach used to be Wolfgang Schivelbusch's *Disenchanted Night: The Industrialization of Light in the Nineteenth Century.*[13] Opening the book, I found a picture (fig. 2), which Schivelbusch suggestively labels "The Apotheosis of Electricity," that seemed a perfect way to picture to my students "the self-assertion of reason through the mastery and alteration of reality." Like *Lucem post nubila reddit*, it has much to say about the project of rendering the light after the clouds.

The image served as the title page for the 1882 volume of *La lumière électrique*, a journal devoted to celebrating the wonders of nascent electrical technologies. Foremost among these was doubtlessly the power to make and to control the light that would illuminate cloudy days and dark nights. Lightbulbs for the home, lampposts for the street, spotlights for the workplace, all allowed modern man to organize time independent from the natural, cosmic rhythms of the rising and setting sun. One contemporary observer from 1857 described an experiment in Lyon, France, in altering the urban reality with electric arc-lighting: "Strollers out near the Chateau Beaujou yesterday evening at about 9 p.m. suddenly found themselves bathed in a flood of light that was as bright as the sun. One could in fact have believed that the sun had risen. This illusion was so strong that birds, woken out of their sleep, began singing in the artificial daylight."[14] People thought "in all seriousness of 'turning night into day,' to cite a popular expression of the period,"[15] and many contemporaries dreamed that electric technologies would make a "second sun." Under the light of this technological second sun, a darkened nature would be altered, making a veritable paradise. One would have no need to wait on nature's sun to cause a new day to dawn. Electricity would light streetlights that dispel the darkness, where vice lurks, and spotlights that extend the workday, increasing human productivity and empowering man to do more to manufacture what had not been provided for him by God or nature.

* * *

What struck me about this image was its formal similarity to *Lucem post nubila reddit*. This suggested to me that "The Apotheosis of Electricity" could be read as a commentary on the first picture of modern disenchantment, a commentary that might lay bare the ground or truth of the first. Consider the two images side by side and you will see what struck me (figs. 2 and 3). The pictures are organized in the same way. Each has two tiers, an earth below and a sky above, and in each sky a cone of illuminating rays contends with clouds. In each, the clouds seem to be in the picture only in order to disappear as rays of light strive to illuminate or enlighten both portions and unify the two tiers. Both thus depict the dawn of a new day in which earth and sky are joined in a whole embraced by one single frame. They depict formally the same illumination that, banishing the clouds, clears a space or makes a clearing where the distinct forms of the world emerge into the safety and security of solid ground and clear skies. *Lucem post nubila reddit*—in both.

Two things distinguish "The Apotheosis of Electricity" from Wolff's image, however. First, and most noticeably, through the parting clouds neither the heavens nor a smiling sun is revealed, but rather a lighthouse and celestial factory. The source of enlightenment, the light whose illuminating rays reveal the world, is the man-made power plant, acting through the lighthouse, which belongs to the earth below. No longer dependent on the contingencies of global weather patterns or an omnipotent God who might have a reason for what he makes happen but won't render it, men have empowered themselves to light the world. Whereas the mysterious causal power of the divine will (banished by the Leibnizian-Wolffian sun = God/Reason) or the weather might send, unpredictably and uncontrollably, clouds to obscure the sun that lights the world, the celestial factory can be counted on to light the way for all ships looking for safe harbor on solid ground. Human calculative powers have produced a light of calculated effect, and this light clears the way for a world on which you can count. Characterizing nineteenth-century modernity as the age

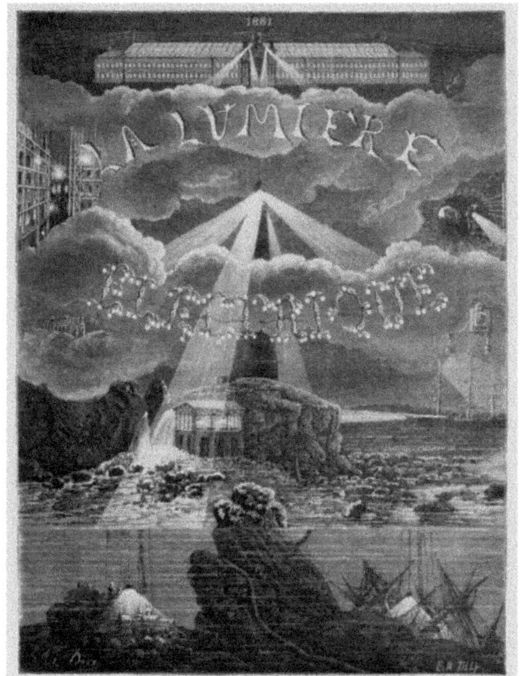

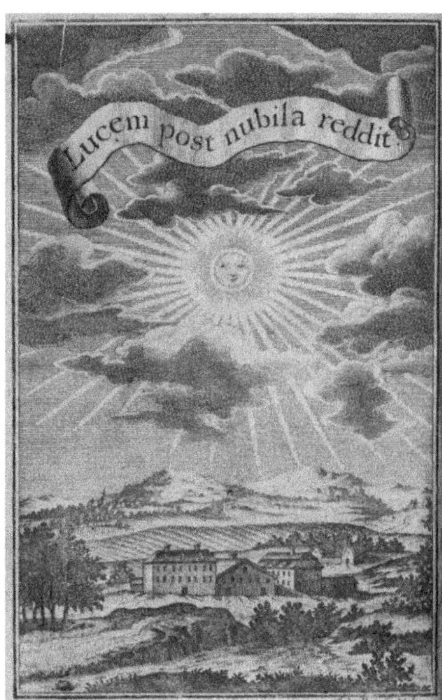


FIGURE 2. Title page from *La lumière électrique* (1882).

FIGURE 3. Frontispiece from Christian Wolff, *Vernünfftige Gedancken von Gott, der Welt und der Seele des Menschen auch allen Dingen überhaupt den Liebharen der Wahrheit* (1720). Rare Book Collection, University of North Carolina at Chapel Hill.

of "the industrialization of light," Schivelbusch describes a modern disenchantment in which men become the industrious manufacturers and calculated administrators of light, marshaling it against the darkness or opacity of a nature that surrounds and threatens them. Light serves the mastery of stormy seas.

This leads to the second major point of difference from Wolff's image: Not graced by a smiling sun, the earthly landscape has little solid ground. Dark waters and stormy seas haunt the lower tier, having already drawn at least one ship, in the lower right corner, to a watery grave. Though marginal, the shipwreck is, in fact, the catastrophic ground or disastrous background whose negation founds the "apotheosis of electricity" as a form of *lucem post nubila reddit*. That is to say, in the margins of this image, we see the declaration that the stars and suns of modern skies are not cosmic intelligences smiling on man but bodies of an indifferent nature likely to abandon him to atmospheric contingencies and leave him shipwrecked.

With the apotheosis of electricity, man need not wait to be saved from imminent shipwreck by the gratuitous event of a God in the otherworld or a sun in the skies beyond our reach. He can assert himself, calculating his own best course through stormy seas, thanks to the ever-reliable light he casts from his own lighthouse. When nature does not care for man, self-assertive man takes care of himself, struggling to push the contingencies of nature and the threat of shipwreck to the margins. And he does so most effectively, with the assistance of technologies that extend his reach and enhance his powers to such a degree that he is able to light distant reaches of the earth with a simple flick of the switch or wave of the hand. The sun in the sky becomes the electricity that clears the clouds and dispels the fog, letting things come safely to ground. Human industry here says what the god Marduk exclaims in Babylonian cosmogony: "Let the dry land appear!" If one's ship is to come in, "The Apotheosis of Electricity" tells us, this happens through self-assertive work, effort, and the struggle to master the contingencies of storm and sea.

* * *

As I read these two images together, then, what I saw illustrated was a correspondence between the landscape that appears in the light of a smiling sun and the apotheosis of man-made light powered by the electric factory. "The Apotheosis of Electricity" shows the struggle against the contingencies of a nature ruled by omnipotent or occult cause, be it a mysterious God who renders no reason for his decree or the vagaries of the weather, which likewise renders no reason. This struggle is ended by the light that appears when *lucem post nubila reddit*. What I saw then was that the chronologically later picture ("The Apotheosis of Electricity") might show the hidden background of that silly, smiling sun whose face had obsessed me. The upper tier of "The Apotheosis of Electricity" is what that sun made possible, while its lower tier is what it struggled with and triumphs over. Cause operates reasonably in the world when the world has been altered by modern technologies. And inversely, technology alters the world when cause has been made to operate reasonably.

Pursuing the thoughts suggested by the similarity of the two images led me to see a strange inversion in the logic ordering them. The apotheosis of electricity, its ascent to the skies, which it will clear of clouds, becomes the hidden ground of the smiling sun in Wolff's image of enlightenment. The sun is depicted as smiling on man because the technoscientific project of calculation has already taken aim at reorganizing nature into the landscape that rests on solid ground. The clearing in which all things come to stand in the light of a smiling sun is a clearing made by the apotheosis of electricity—that is, by modern technologies. Technology clears the clouds so that the sun can shine a cone of light that illuminates the earth below. The unstated subject of *Lucem post nubila reddit* (the implied but unstated "He" or "It" who brings back the light after the clouds) is modern technology.

We moderns (those moderns?) are devoted to these technologies that, we believe, can hold open this illuminated clearing or this clearing for illumination—technologies that reveal a world for us in such a way that what they light up can be secured for "the immanent self-assertion of reason." The divine is whatever holds the position of the factory whose light makes the clearing: God, the sun, the electric generator. And our devotion to it takes as many and as various forms: the prayers and rituals of the religious, our addiction to modern technologies of light and speed, and so on.

# 1 : Walter De Maria, *The Lightning Field*

## SEEING A FLICKERING LIGHT

### Darkling

Devoted to the technologies that make and hold open the illuminated clearing, we have inherited the clear and distinct world of things revealed by the apotheosis of electricity. Indeed, the light that once made a modest clearing in which human beings could build their abode on solid ground now reaches worldwide. Just look at the unearthly photos of our world taken by orbiting satellites and you will see the planetary deployment of modern illumination: the illuminated clearing where man sets up house alongside the things that sustain him has become the sprawl of the global city; darkness and clouds have been banished, along with forests and wildlife. Nothing now escapes the light.

The dream of enlightenment, in apparently fulfilling itself, has arrived at a strange inversion—one that is stated well by Pantope, a character in Michel Serres's beautiful meditation *Angels: A Modern Myth*: "They say that cities developed out of clearings in forests; now these 'clearings' appear like 'darklings' in between the cancerous growths of light from the city."[1] The clearings are now dark spots, and, even worse, these darklings have been lost and forgotten amid the global omnipresence of the light administered by human industry. Heir to the sun of the enlightenment and the electric factory, our daily life seem to know no night, no dark in the sprawling omnipresence of illumination—and so we know no place to see the light and the clearing it makes. This lends support to the suspicion felt by some of us that the enlightened world and the objects it presents to our grasp is increasingly deserted, as all dissolves in the glare of too much light.

We must, I suspect, go to the darkling to find the clearing.

Not content with leaving the "darklings" to be lost in all the light, those disenchanted with modern disenchantment dream of sparing them from oblivion and thereby saving the things that come to light there. Like the mystics and ascetics of another age, these disenchanted moderns go into

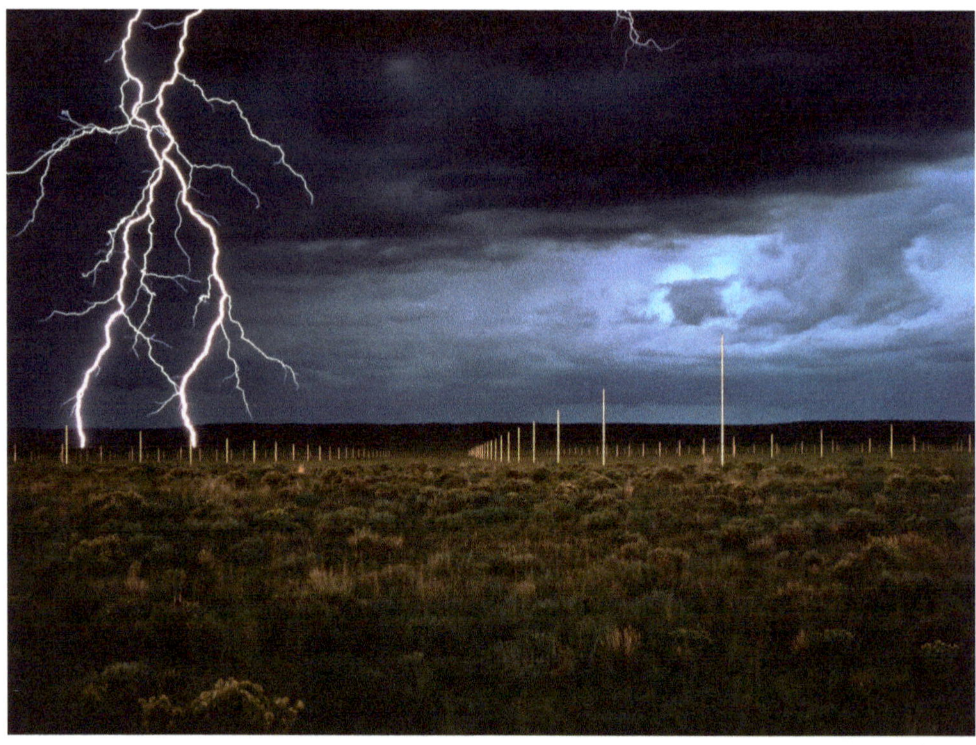

FIGURE 4. Walter De Maria, *The Lightning Field* (1977). Permanent earth sculpture: 400 stainless steel poles arranged in a grid array measuring one mile by one kilometer; average pole height 20 feet 7 inches, pole tips form an even plane. Quemado, New Mexico. Photograph by John Cliett. © Dia Art Foundation, New York.

the desert to see another light. What they seek is the darkness in which they might see the light. "The light," after all, "shines *in* the darkness." It does not shine where there is full or total light, and the shining does not extinguish the darkness without obscuring the light itself.

A third image (fig. 4), therefore, to add to the first two: *The Lightning Field* by Walter De Maria, a work that the art critic Kenneth Baker has praised as "the ultimate work of Land Art."[2]

## THE LIGHTNING FIELD

The lightning field itself covers a parcel of ground one mile wide by one kilometer long. Four hundred polished and sharpened steel poles, spaced at intervals of 220 feet, emerge from the earth in a desert plain in New Mexico, making a grid twenty-five poles wide by sixteen poles long. The length of the poles varies with the surface of the earth so that all rise to the same height above sea level, making for a "smooth visual recession that allows you to see the poles imposing a framework of pictorial perspective on the terrain viewed through them.... *The Lightning Field* coordinatizes a part of the plain.... A network of locations, *The Lightning Field* gives the impression that the natural reality of the plain has become observable in a new way, even in a sense for the first time."[3] Perspective is the way to organize the space of a picture, something an artist does to open or clear a space for the figures and shapes he will then create. It is a preliminary to creating the picture and the placement of things within it. Finding a perspectival grid and a network of orienting coordinates here in the barren vastness of the remote desert is surprising, because one does not often look to the desert as an organized place. The presence of such a grid here, on a plain that extends some thirty miles beyond to the Datil Mountains, make this place one where we encounter the barest minimum, the inchoate emergence of the organization of space into a human world. One comes here to attend the very opening of a world, the moment of its flashing into being amid the empty, indifferent void of the "natural" plain and homogeneous desert.

The poles all rise to the same height so that one can imagine, De Maria says, a plane of glass (I think, too, of the sky) touching each of the points, its weight evenly distributed and borne aloft. The artificial flatness of this plane works to lift up or bring forward the contour of the contrasting natural earth below. Or do the poles penetrate the earth, sinking under the weight of a descending sky? Here, it is difficult to decide if you are witnessing the creation or the destruction of a world: do the poles rise and measure an opening that separates earth and sky, or are they pressed down as the distance between earth and sky collapses apocalyptically, leaving only these "emblematic relics of the world," the faintest traces left of its having been, "daring you to think of them as all there is left of the world"?[4] Is this the dawn of a habitable clearing or its twilight? The Pueblo peoples of the surrounding land, which include most notably the Zuni and the Hopi, are also sensitive to this ambiguity. They identify many places in this region as sites where their ancestors crawled from the caves and depths of the earth in which they had been made and emerged onto the earth's surface, where they breathed air under the sky—and equally many places as sites where one can make the reverse passage, out of this world and into the other.

As De Maria's title suggests, the steel poles are powerful attractors of lightning strikes in an area that was carefully chosen not only for its isolation and expansive view, but also for the power and energy frequently manifested there in severe climatic effects. Extremes of atmospheric moisture, wind, and temperature are accompanied by heightened electrical activity. Strong winds of thirty to fifty miles an hour are said to blow steadily for days sometimes in the spring; only eleven inches of rain fall each year; thunderstorms can be seen from the field on an average of one in six days throughout the year; and on one out of every ten days a lightning storm passes directly over the field. Though not common, lightning strikes are unusually frequent in the area, charging the experience of being there with the promise of great power, but also with the unmistakable threat of destruction by the very energies that the poles seem to invite.

* * *

Look again, now at the three images together (figs. 5, 6, and 7).

Like Wolff's *Lucem post nubila reddit* and "The Apotheosis of Electricity," the picture of *The Lightning Field* is organized in two tiers: an earthly landscape below and clouds above. But unlike the clouds that, in the earlier images, show themselves in order to be banished, the clouds above *The Lightning Field* show no sign of dispersing; they make no opening or clearing for the otherworldly, supernatural, or transcendent to reveal itself. Indeed, they are likely gathering, forming a lid that closes over the whole scene. All of this gives the picture a great horizontal emphasis but little sense of vertical movement and a corresponding absence of feeling of possible ascent or escape.

There is one possible exception, an exception that flashes within this still closed picture.

*The Lightning Field* differs from the previous two images in that here the light shines when the clouds do not part. The smiling sun and the celestial electric factory have yielded to the wild flash of lightning—which in its jagged flickering creates momentary and momentous visions, the striking presence of these poles. In fact, this light flashes *only* when clouds and darkness remain in the picture. The schematic geometry of point, line, and cone cannot account for how this work of illumination brings a world to light. There is no cone of rays emanating in straight lines from a depicted point source, gathering all together and holding it in an illuminated clearing. There is no single point or source from which the rays emerge, seeming as they do to come from beyond the frame of the picture, lost in the unrepresentable darkness of the clouds. This is a fluctuating light, a swerving, forking, bifurcating zigzag that brings things into the picture only momentarily and resists being pinned down in one particular place. "Capricious," in the words of Camille Flammarion, "it is impossible to assign it any rule. . . . As many strikes as extravagances. . . . [It] does not give any explanation; it acts, that's all."[5] We can speak of its effects with more certainty than of it itself.

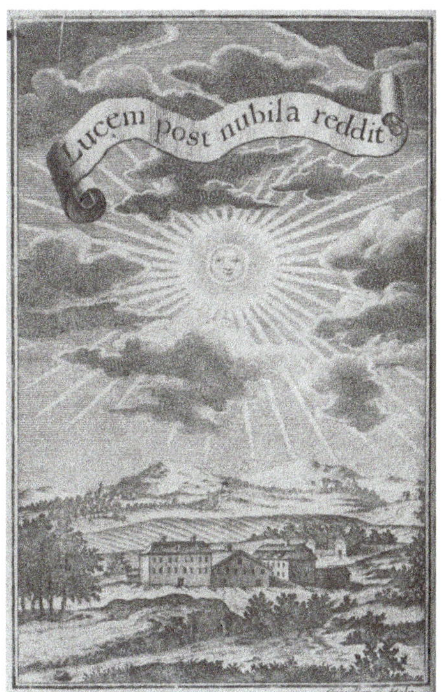


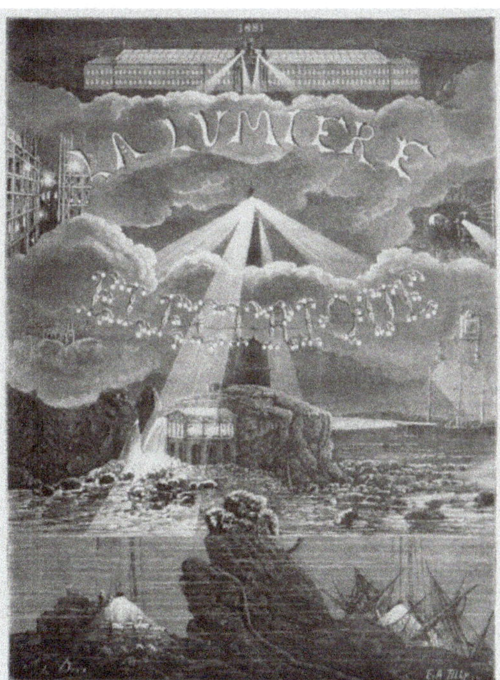


FIGURE 5. Frontispiece from Christian Wolff, *Vernünfftige Gedancken von Gott, der Welt und der Seele des Menschen auch allen Dingen überhaupt den Liebharen der Wahrheit* (1720). Rare Book Collection, University of North Carolina at Chapel Hill.

FIGURE 6. Title page from *La lumière électrique* (1882).

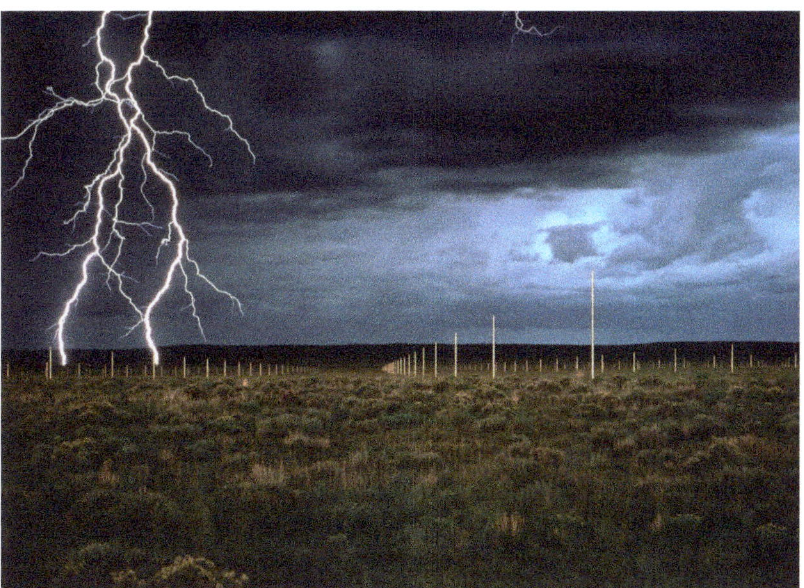

FIGURE 7. Walter De Maria, *The Lightning Field* (1977). Photograph by John Cliett. © Dia Art Foundation, New York.

This recalls the description Michel Serres once offered of the chaotic cloud of falling atoms out of which the cosmos was born, according to the ancient philosopher Lucretius. "The lightning, in its oblique flight, crosses the rays of the rain. Now here, now there; ripped from the clouds, the thunderbolts flash from everywhere.... Obliqueness of a lightning strike against a parallel field."[6] Very nearly a description of the scene in which scientists once believed life emerged, when a lightning strike sparked catalytic processes in a primordial soup. As in Lucretius, the zigzagging motion we see in *The Lightning Field* crosses with its randomness the law-governed, linear trajectories of objects falling through clear and empty space, and in this unexpected flash, the connections and conglomerations of the things that make up a world fall into place: momentously and momentarily, the poles form constellations.

Writing in a special issue of the journal *Antigone*, a literary review of photography, the noted art historian and philosopher Georges Didi-Huberman commented on the difficulties faced by those who have wanted to make a picture of the world that includes lightning. "How can one fit the trace obtained in the photograph into a perspectival scheme?... The evidence for the relation form/ground that the image of the lightning gives is part of a long tradition of hypotheses and recurrent questioning about the exact *place* of what one does nevertheless see so distinctly outlined against the ground of a stormy night." Is the lightning shaped like a helix whose projection only seems in our photograph to be a line (as nineteenth-century German meteorologist Ludwig Kaemtz hypothesized)? Or are the lines we see only the irregular edges of a thick dark cloud behind which the lightning truly flashes (as his English contemporary Michael Faraday supposed)?[7] Out of what depths does the lightning strike? Where is this thing we see so distinctly in the picture? What edge defines its place? Recalcitrant to being depicted clearly and distinctly in a picture of the world, lightning is not represented so much as presented. The "nonrepresentable" presents itself, as the lightning flash is the light in which it itself is portrayed; there is no need for the flash produced by our high-tech cameras to open a clearing prior to its appearance, and in fact, such a flash often causes the lightning to vanish. "The lightning is itself light's writing 'which imprints itself by itself on the sensitive film,' detaching itself from a dark night." "The instrument of this revelation... was photography."[8] The photographic film, its dark negative, is the sole place where this presentation is revealed in a picture.

What comes to light in such a picture of the world? What comes to light when the lightning flashes in the desert darkling? There is no permanent place to rest or home to lay your head, nothing that abides permanently alongside you granting you the felt stability of an anchor on solid ground.

It is as if the sea and flowing river of *Lucem post nubila reddit* and "The Apotheosis of Electricity" have returned as the shifting sands of the desert. On this impermeable surface, there is little ground for building or laying a foundation. Few things have come to stand constantly and permanently here in the clearing momentarily illuminated by the lightning flash. You see not solid and stable objects, but ephemera, poles that happen in a flash and vanish. The lightning brings things to light not so much by leading them to solid ground but by making them flash and flow and flow away, like waves rising and crashing.

Hardly the dawn of a new day, yet it is where one goes to see the world flash into light.

* * *

Each summer from May to September, hundreds of supposedly disenchanted moderns go to the desert in groups of no more than six at a time harboring sometimes faint, sometimes strong hopes that lightning will strike on the day they have chosen to be there. They pay no small fee and devote a large amount of supposedly scarce time and energy in the expectation of no greater compensation than a glimpse of flashing light.

The light they seek is the light that comes when the clouds do not part.

The vision they seek is solicited by the lightning poles.

The visions they receive are things that happen and, happening, flow away.

## Into the land of enchantment: In search of lost causes

In the summer of 2004, I joined the disenchanted moderns (moderns disenchanted with modern disenchantment?) and made a journey to the provinces of New Mexico looking for *The Lightning Field*. Reminded by the license plates that New Mexico is "the land of enchantment," I wandered off into the darkling of the desert to see the light. What had awakened this desire to seek the darkling and spare its clearing from oblivion is hard to say. It was a time of fullness for me. Things were finally falling into place. All things, or at least many of the things, I had most wanted (but thought had drifted away) were now rendering themselves to me. I had just completed the first year of a new job, the long sought and anxiously awaited tenure-track position as a college professor. My first child had been born a little over a year before. And sometime in the three months between the birth of my daughter and the beginning of my job, I had bought my first house. After some dark years, everything was looking bright. My ship had come in.

I was not the first comfortable but disenchanted modern to stray into these deserts. One of the more interesting of those who preceded me was Aby Warburg (1866–1929), widely recognized as one of the founding fathers of the modern discipline of art history. Those profoundly influenced by Warburg include Erwin Panofsky and Ernst Gombrich, both of whom would go on to give the discipline its modern shape. The influential philosopher Ernst Cassirer also participated in seminars hosted by Warburg at the institute he founded in Hamburg.

Warburg reports on his journey to New Mexico in an unusual format: the transcript for a slide lecture given while a patient at Ludwig Binswanger's Kreuzlinger Sanatorium, where he had been committed on account of schizophrenic delusions that led him to threaten his wife and children at home with a kitchen knife immediately following the military collapse of Germany in 1918. There is also a record of unpublished notes for this lecture, excerpts of which appear in various publications. What attracted me to Warburg was not only the fact that he too had come to this "land of enchantment" but the fact that we would both be caught under the spell of the lightning. In Warburg's case, this would take the form of a fascination with the Pueblo raindance, which is really a lightning dance summoning, through the ritual handling of serpents, what most of us try to avoid. The very first picture Warburg presented at Kreuzlingen conveys what held him under its spell (fig. 8).

This is a sand painting that appeared on the floor of an altar where the raindance was performed. The lightning falls from the clouds in the form of snakes, which were manipulated with hand and mouth during the performance of the ritual. At a crucial moment the snakes were thrown violently from the hands of the Indian onto the sand painting, where they twisted and writhed, erasing the image and becoming themselves clothed in the lightning depicted therein. These snakes were then sent into the wild, where they were intended to cause the lightning to come and fertilize the fields. Thus the existence of the Indian's world depended on the lightning, which alone would keep the fields open for cultivation.

Another picture also sparked Warburg's interest (fig. 9). This one, made by schoolchildren, comes near the end of his lecture. Toward the end of his stay among the Pueblo, Warburg asked the children to illustrate a fairytale he recounted to them in which a terrible storm strikes with lightning and thunder. In their pictures, the children, already attending an American school, draw two houses according to geometric and perspectival rules (so-called realism), but when the moment came to depict the unplaceable, unrepresentable, but nevertheless real lightning strike in a picture of the world, the children reverted to symbols

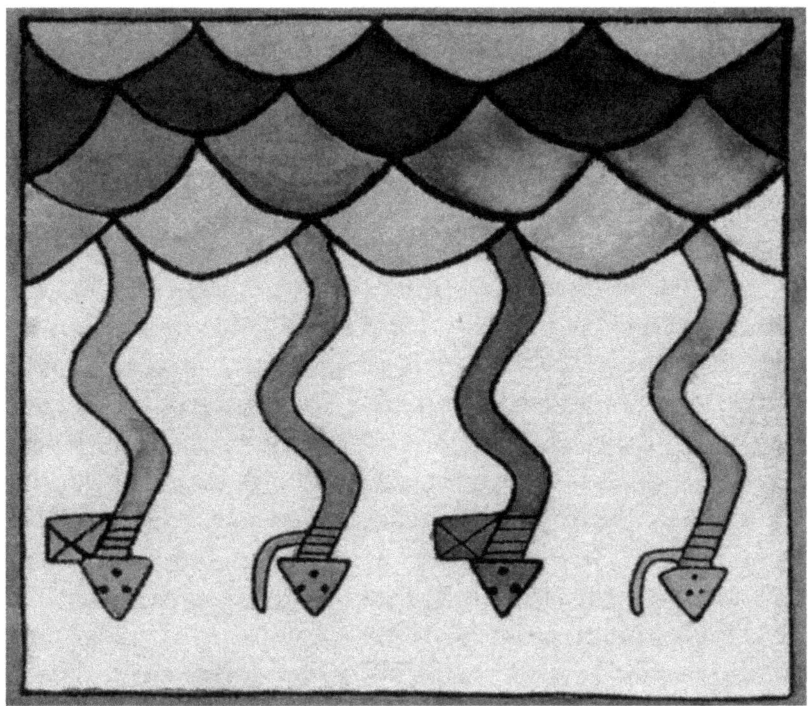

FIGURE 8. Anon., Serpent as lightning. Reproduction of an altar floor, kiva ornamentation (n.d.). Courtesy of The Warburg Institute, London.

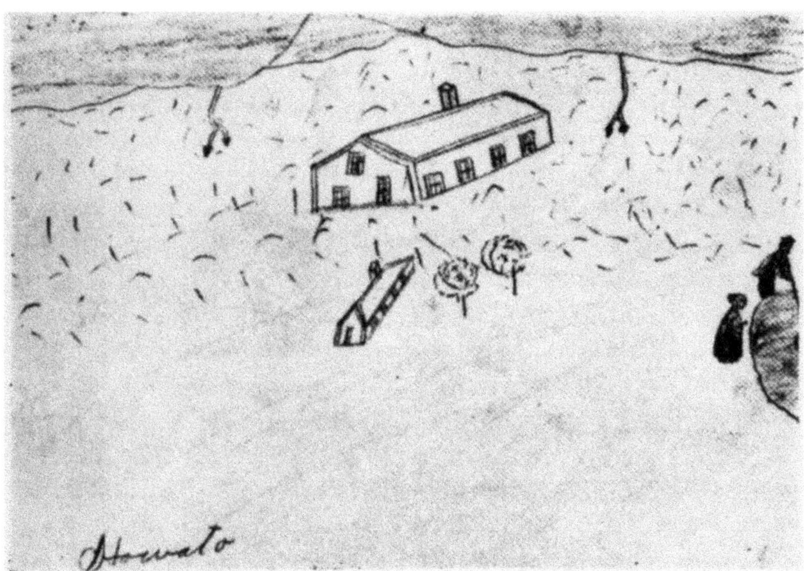

FIGURE 9. Anon., Hopi schoolboy's drawing of a house in a storm with lightning (n.d.). Courtesy of The Warburg Institute, London.

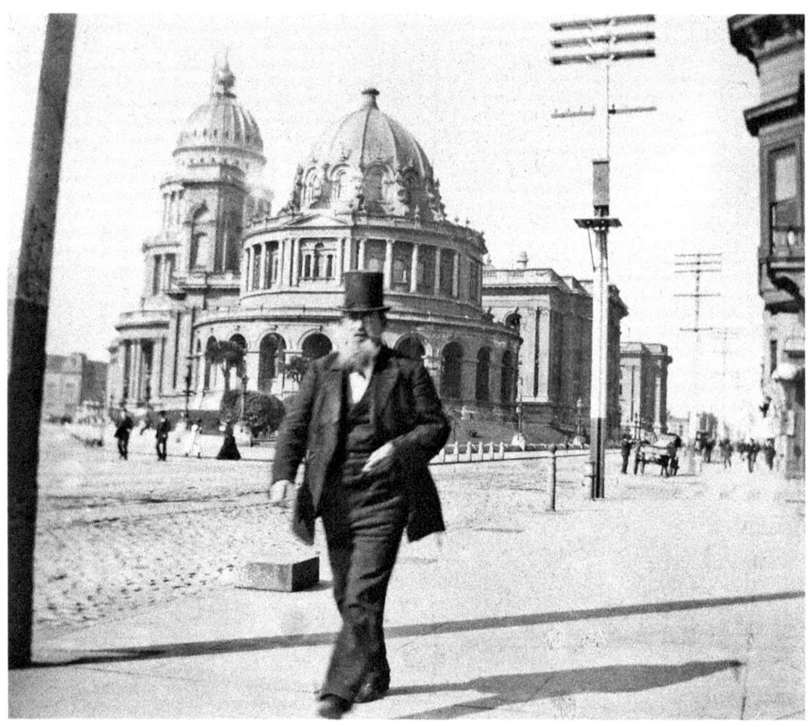

FIGURE 10. Anon. (Aby Warburg?), "Uncle Sam" (n.d.). Courtesy of The Warburg Institute, London.

and drew serpent-headed zigzags placed in uncertain and indefinite positions.

A final picture, taken in the streets of San Francisco, at the farthest edge of the west, connects Warburg's interests with my own interest in *Lucem post nubila reddit* and "The Apotheosis of Electricity." It is a picture of "Uncle Sam in a stovepipe hat," whose westward expansion displaced and decimated the Indians and the world Warburg discovered while living among them (fig. 10).

Warburg meets the apotheosis of electricity in person in this man on the street. Calling attention to the electric cables running overhead, Warburg sees "Uncle Sam" not only as the conqueror of the Indian but also as the one responsible for the death of lightning—"the conqueror of the serpent cult and the fear of lightning." Having "wrested lightning from nature... imprisoned [it] in wire—captured electricity," Uncle Sam produced a world that had no use for the serpent cult or the serpent that beseeched the lightning. Slayer of these gods, he makes way for the apotheosis of electricity and thereby brings to light a very different world where a very different sort of man dwells.[9]

Warburg's Jewish parents, always thinking he would become a rabbi, strongly objected to his entering academic life, especially the discipline of art history, because they believed it would violate the Mosaic prescription against trafficking with images. A nonpracticing Jew who, against his father's will, married a member of the Evangelical-Lutheran Church in Germany, Warburg would go on to "expose the ruptures at the heart of Christian sacred art."[10] He wrote famously about the occult and alchemical fascinations of major figures in the Christian art of the Renaissance and about the astrological interest of major Christian leaders of the Reformation. Ancient pagan tendencies, he claimed, were only repressed, not destroyed, by Christianity, and they survived, lived on, or enjoyed an afterlife in the religious art and thought of the West, as well as in the modern humanistic tradition that dawned with the Renaissance. Sensitive to this still-living past present in the images of nascent modern Western art, Warburg sometimes thought of himself as trying "to diagnose the schizophrenia of Western civilization from its images." He would be "the first to perceive this ambiguity [at the core of Western civilization's supposedly highest moment, the Renaissance] in an epoch in which the Renaissance still appeared as an age of enlightenment in contrast to the darkness of the middle ages."[11]

This work of diagnosing "the schizophrenia of Western civilization," Warburg continues, arose "in an autobiographical reflex." Jewish, urbane, a cultivated scholar of the Renaissance, and a member of one of the wealthiest families in Europe, Warburg does not seem like a natural or easy fit in the wilds of the American southwest. It is not hard to see the absurdity of it (fig. 11). Warburg admits to seeing himself "placed along the dividing lines between different cultural atmospheres and systems. Placed by birth in the middle, between Orient and Occident," as he put it, his life and work, somewhat like that of the Pueblo child's picture of the lightning, would straddle the European humanism he inherited from the Christian Renaissance and the pagan primitivism he inherited from prehistoric times (fig. 12).[12]

Warburg grew disenchanted with the history, traditions, and culture of the Europe he seemed by birth to exemplify, and then disheartened by that of the east coast in America, so he turned to the south and the west. "The emptiness of the civilization of the east coast of America," he writes, "was so repellant to me that, somewhat on a whim, I undertook to flee toward natural objects and science," a flight that would take him to the Pueblo land of New Mexico. He associated the humanistic culture in Europe and the east coast with what he called "the sterile trafficking

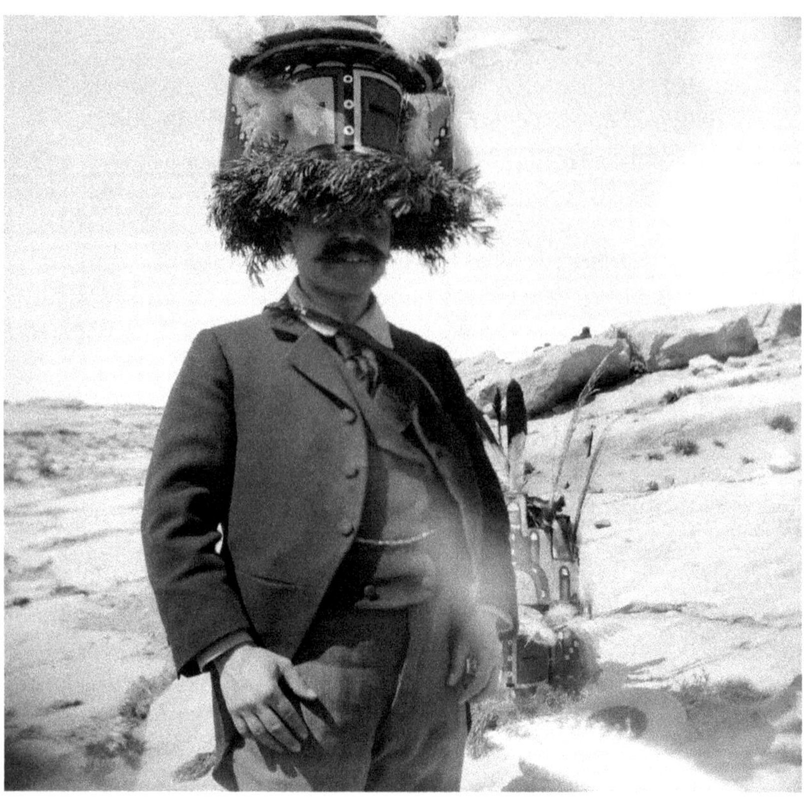

FIGURE 11. Anon., Aby Warburg in a headdress (n.d.). Courtesy of The Warburg Institute, London.

in words" of "aestheticizing art history." All the things that came to light thanks to the illumination cast by his sophisticated academic colleagues skilled in "the formal contemplation of images" made for him only a great emptiness.[13] Their judgments of taste and their specialized knowledge of great figures and great works brought things to light at the same time as it carried them away with the knowledge of the objects they constituted.

Dreaming instead of a flight "toward natural objects and science," Warburg walked the "story of civilization in reverse. Each step ahead toward the country of the Pueblo in Arizona and New Mexico corresponds with a step back."[14] From culture and the overdeveloped fields of sophisticated experts, he dreamed of taking a step back, into nature and its own directions. From "the sterile trafficking in words" of "aestheticizing art history," he dreamed of taking a step back, to things and the sciences that would, he believed, lead him to these things. Knowledge and science, it seemed, would be enchanting and could be put to the service of discovering the mysterious charm of things whose nature had been thought away

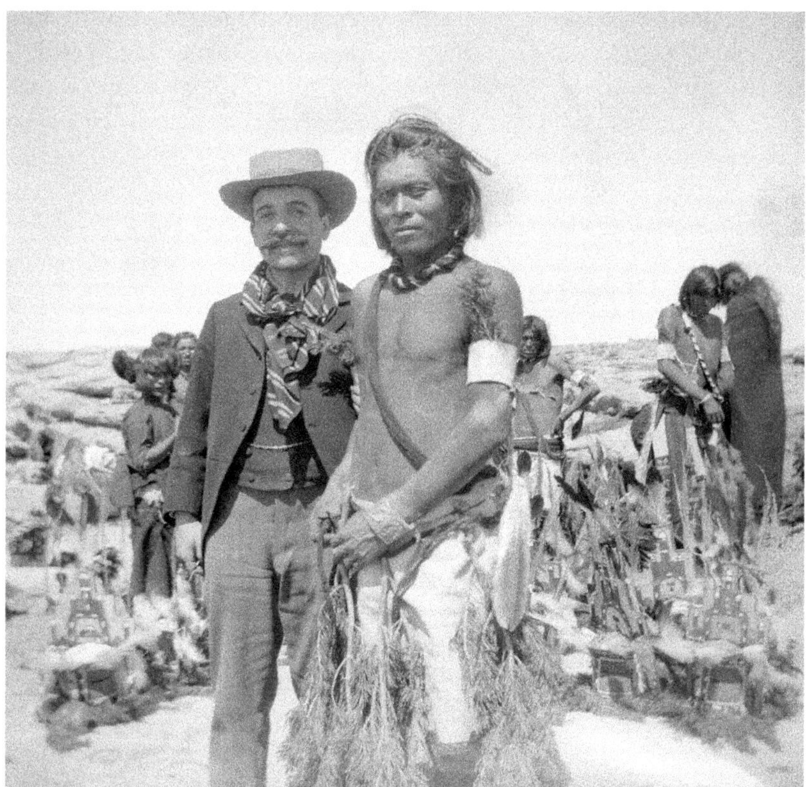

FIGURE 12. Anon., Aby Warburg and a friend (n.d.). Courtesy of The Warburg Institute, London.

by the sun of art history and its enlightening rays. Ernst Gombrich, in an important biography of Warburg, alludes to this, somewhat disdainfully, as Warburg's "uncanny gift for extracting a personal meaning from historical material," a gift that does not always serve well those who seek to make careers in the sophisticated institutions of academic science and its specialties.[15]

The difficulty of placing Warburg's lecture clearly and distinctly within the disciplines that make up the landscape of the modern academy has been noted by Sigrid Weigel. While Warburg's name invokes the authority of art history, "this authority is immediately called into question by the subtitle, 'A Travel Account,' calling literary scholars and perhaps historians as well to action." Its situation grows more confused: as a second title page bears the title *Images from the Region of the Pueblo Indians of North America*. This suggests the book should be handed over to the ethnologists. But they "will be hardly thrilled—especially after a second glance when they turn over yet another page and find a different subtitle on the third title page, which identifies the publication as a text written in a mental hospital: Lecture given at the Bellevue Hospital in Kreuzlingen on April 21, 1923." Let the psychoanalysts deal with this one! Inside, one finds nearly as many pictures as pages, leaving us unsure whether the expert in textual or in visual criticism might be best equipped to tell us what is going on. What is more, the provenance of these pictures is confused: some come from ethnographic science; some appear to be personal photos; and some seem to come from the annals of medieval history and classical antiquity. Just what period is at issue here, what geographical location?[16]

The book's inability to be claimed by any one of the specialized disciplines does not make it, however, an example of "interdisciplinary research." For it does not really shine the light of different scientific expertise in the hopes of gaining a more fulfilling knowledge of the matter at hand. Seeing from different angles and different perspectives afforded by different specialties would not yield information that could be synthesized into a better, more objective picture of what Warburg was intending to present. His lecture instead performs a way of thinking that falls through disciplinary boundaries—a nondisciplinary or undisciplined thinking that lays no claim to expertise precisely because it does not have a specialty, field, or object (chronological, geographical, textual) to master. While the experts might know more and more thanks to the methodical division of knowledge into fields and disciplines, Warburg's lecture seems to aim at some nameless thing beyond them—something that might be called, in its nameless nonobjectivity, human being.

This makes it what the philosopher Giorgio Agamben has called a "nameless science." Lacking a definite name, it takes on many names. Warburg variously referred to his project as "a psychology of human expression," "a diagnosis of the schizophrenia of Western culture," and "an iconology of the interval," that is, the interval between culture and nature, modern and primitive, human and nonhuman.[17] Summarizing all of these, Agamben speaks of it as "a general science of the human" that belongs to a "future 'anthropology of Western culture.'" In this science, the image stands "at the center of the human,"[18] providing invaluable testimony to this anthropology of Western man in his tragic, schizophrenic position, ever between enlightenment and paganism, cultivated humanism and primitive nature.

A knowledge such as this has become unfashionable in late twentieth- and early twenty-first-century studies of culture. As Agamben acknowledges, "By the end of the 1970's, anthropology had entered into a period of disenchantment that in itself probably rendered this project obsolete."[19] While following Warburg in his avoidance of the study of great men and works, the cultural studies of recent anthropology prefer the culturally and historically specific account of local culture and particular human being to Warburg's general anthropology. To this discipline's eyes, Warburg's idea of studying humanity—in fact, the very idea of "humanity"—is obsolete because culturally unspecific, historically unlocated, and very often politically laden, with roots in projects aimed at excluding others from the supposedly universal category of "human." Cross-cultural comparisons of, for instance, Pueblo Indian and Renaissance symbols and artifacts often, the argument goes, rely on or aim to produce ahistorical notions like *humanity*. They produce a text that, far worse than nameless, cannot claim the name science. Essentially lacking in objectivity and specialization, Warburg's "science" produces not knowledge but a myth, and this myth must, like all dreams, vanish at daybreak, when the light dawns and the myths are demythologized, the mysteries demystified, and the world disenchanted.

And yet, Agamben contends when reconsidering his essay on Warburg in 1983, "the project of a general science of the human . . . strikes [me] as one that is still valid, but cannot be pursued in the same terms."[20] There might be something to that.

## HUMAN EMERGENCE IN "THE ANTIQUITY OF AMERICA"

One of Warburg's chief contributions to art history is found in his studies of the influence of antiquity on Renaissance art, which contributed to a "profound revolution in Renaissance studies." Whereas the Enlightenment took the Renaissance recovery of antiquity as a means to promote what its leading figure, Winckelman, called "the noble simplicity and quiet grandeur . . . of a great and composed soul," Warburg claimed that antiquity gave the Renaissance an "emphasis on phenomena of transition over the treatment of bodies at rest . . . and on becoming over motionless form." What Warburg saw the Renaissance taking from antiquity was not the motionless, balanced, static ideal of beauty (an ideal drawn chiefly from consideration of antique architecture and its geometry) but the image of the human being "caught up in a play of overwhelming forces." What was classic about classical antiquity, according to Warburg, was not the ideal of a human triumphant (like a work of architecture) over the tensions and instabilities that, tragically and schizophrenically, rend it. Rather, what makes a classic classic is the image of man caught up in the contortions and writhing of a pathos that charges, energizes, and animates it.[21]

Strangely, it was in the desert darkling of New Mexico, while living among "the primitives," that Warburg would be struck by this vision of classical antiquity, this vision that would revise and revitalize the vision of Western culture and humanism exemplified by the European Renaissance: "After my return [from New Mexico], I turned to the Florentine culture of the Quattrocento in order to examine—on an entirely new basis, much larger, the psychic structure of Renaissance man." What light dawned on Warburg in these deserts? What bolt from the blue struck him here? Warburg admits to having discovered what he called "the antiquity of America,"[22] as if he found ancient culture in the New World, the antique roots of Western enlightenment in the dark of America's Wild West—and as if America, often deemed insensitive to history and so future-oriented as to have no past of its own, did in fact have an antiquity, one, moreover, represented by the Indians it exterminated in order to secure its future.

There is much disagreement as to just what relation Warburg's general science of the human posited between the Indians found in "the antiquity of America" and the modern, enlightened mind that dawned with the Renaissance and reached full bloom with *lucem post nubila reddit* and the apotheosis of electricity. Ernst Gombrich represents one position: "A convinced evolutionist, [Warburg] saw in the Indians of New Mexico a stage of civilization which corresponded to the phase of paganism ancient Greece left behind with the dawn of rationalism."[23] On this reading, modern disenchantment would progress beyond the primitive Indian and leave the antiquity of America in a past that is forever past. The other position, voiced, if not adopted, by Michael Steinberg, takes Warburg's general science of the human as expressing "sympathy for an auratic, mythical past as opposed to the disenchantment of rationalized modernity."[24] On this reading, supposed progress is in fact decline that can be reversed by returning to the ways and minds of the past, before the world was clearly illuminated.

My own sense is that neither position says well what bolt from the blue struck Warburg in the dark desert of the land of enchantment. As he journeyed from the cultivated fields of the enlightened academy and the east coast drawing room to the barren vastness of the unilluminated west, Warburg would discover something like the emergence of culture and also its culmination in the Renaissance and Enlightenment; this is after all what antiquity, even if "the antiquity of America," signified for him, as for all the other art historians. It would not be too far amiss to say that in this emergence of culture Warburg would even find the tentative emergence of our humanity and the opening of a human world. Gombrich might be right, then, to say that Warburg found the dawn of enlightenment in New Mexico. But controverting the evolutionism Gombrich ascribes to Warburg, the general science of the human need not see this moment of emergence of the human world and culture (this "antiquity" or "enlightenment") as something that happened once and for all in the past. What Warburg learned from the Pueblo in the darkling of New Mexico was that the achievement of humanity and culture was not a definitive accomplishment, having happened in the past and now being handed over to succeeding generations who will improve upon it. Rather, Warburg saw this moment of emergence as something that is accomplished again and again, at each moment of history. What he saw in "the land of enchantment," he would find again eternally returning in the history of man, a history that makes no progress.

In his general science of the human, Warburg would call this moment of emergence "the eternally constant Indianness within the helpless human soul" or the "indestructibility of primitive man, who remains the same throughout all time."[25] These are phrases that many today will find troubling because they smack of an ahistorical, acultural, or perennial philosophy common to all men at all times. What is more, they might locate this perennial, timeless wisdom in a particular people (the Pueblo Indian) who are then denied a history and the possibility of growth or change. No doubt, there are difficulties. But, what remains interesting to me is that Warburg's account of human being does not refer to an accomplished essence of man, as the critics might suppose, but rather to humanity as it emerges or comes to be—perhaps each time differently. The "eternally constant Indianness within the helpless human soul" is not some thing, but a possibility or potentiality of being.

What Warburg saw being played out in the antiquity of America was not some thing, essence, or unchanging nature of man, but rather an event—the struggle of "the helpless human soul" to emerge so that, once in the position of the helpless human exposed to the vicissitudes of time and the contingencies of nature, it might then struggle for help. The "helpless human soul," our "eternally constant Indianness," rests, and rocks, on the cusp between nature and culture, wild cause and technological rule, dark and light, at each moment threatening to fall into one or the other. The object of a "general science of the human" is this fragile moment in which we are always on the verge... and all that is done to maintain it, full of promise and potential.

The drama of history, then, is not man's struggle for mastery and control over nature, but rather the struggle for human birth or emergence—which involves, inevitably, exposure or vulnerability and, more precisely, exposure to the helplessness that is the human soul. The drama of history, which Warburg saw performed in living color, as it were, in "the antiquity of America," is the emergence of humanity from the protective shelter of its roots, its earthiness, or the grasp or hold that nature exercises over it. Becoming human means exceeding nature and, in this distance from a niche in nature, being exposed—so that human being might take in hand the means to deal with its fluctuating situation. The important question is not what is the essence or nature of man, but in what contexts or events humanity emerges, again and again, flashing into existence.

## GETTING A HAND ON THE LIGHTNING

Warburg found such an event of opening the human world performed and reperformed in the raindance, which is, it bears repeating, in fact a lightning dance, since in the mythologies of the New Mexican Indian, it is the lightning that causes, somehow, the fields to be fertile, the corn to grow, and therefore the human world to be maintained.[26] In the raindance, Warburg saw the helpless, miserable human soul ("the misery of the Indian who struggles for his life in the arid steppe") exposed to the flickering yet tremendous power that causes fertility (the lightning) and, from this position of exposure and helplessness, try to assert itself. This effort at self-assertion takes the form of a ritual dance with serpents, where the snake is the lightning that the Indian summons. "A snakelike form, enigmatic movements, which have no clearly determinable beginning or end, and danger: these are what lightning shares with the snake, which presents a maximum of movement and a minimum of graspable surfaces." One has to add to this list the obvious: sudden strikes and surprising occurrences.

What Warburg saw happening in the raindance was the self-assertive Indian trying, from his miserable and helpless position, to get his hands on the slippery cause of his misery, famine or drought. "When one holds a snake in one's hand in its most dangerous form—namely, the rattlesnake—as the Indians in fact do . . . , human force tries to comprehend [*begreifen*] through a sheer grasping with the hands, something that in reality eludes manipulation."[27] The raindance tries to get a handle on the lightning that causes the rain so that this lightning might be manipulated and our misery lifted. But, Warburg observes, lightning, like the serpent, "eludes manipulation," even by those who hold it in their hands.

In fact, the climactic moment of the dance is not the grasping and holding of the serpents, even if this is the most dramatic, but the moment of their release, when they, no longer under control of their handler, are rendered to the lightning they are meant to summon. "Released alive, as lightning bolts, [the snakes become] messengers for the storms and rain."[28] The Indian hopes that this message will arrive and be effective, but since he has released the snakes, the eventual success or failure of what Warburg called this "danced causality" is now out of his hands; he has rendered the snakes to the darkness and wild, where the capricious cause of rain, the lightning, hides. In this dance between the causality we release into the world and its uncertain effect lies human being. The Indian, eternal in us, is a helpless, miserable handler and manipulator of snakes. We pray they will do our bidding, but often they go their own way. We hope it works.

The essence of the hand that manipulates—its function, if you will, or the meaning of manipulation—is therefore other than what most of us might think. The hand is not essentially about grasping, but about letting go. In most of the accounts of the lightning dance that Warburg consulted, the serpent chief grabs and holds the serpents using his mouth. He becomes like a handless, nonhuman animal who consumes what it grabs. When the Indian transfers the snake to his hands, it is most often in order to release it from his toothy grasp. In beseeching the lightning, the Indian is brought back to the verge of becoming human. Unlike the mouth, Warburg claims, the hand "renounces any right to possess the object other than by palpably following its outer contour. It therefore does not completely renounce touching the object, but it does renounce taking possession through comprehension."[29] In touching without grasping, the hand caresses and lets go. For all his supposed savagery, the Indian evidences a loving touch to the world in which he seeks to assert himself when he handles the serpents that might bring rain.

The dance entails a tragic moment, one that Warburg saw as integral to the essential schizophrenia of human being:

> I see man as *an animal that handles and manipulates* and whose activity consists in putting together and taking apart. That is how he loses his organic ego-feeling, specifically because the hand allows him to take hold of material things that have no nerve apparatus, since they are inorganic, but that, despite this, extend his ego inorganically. That is the tragic aspect of man, who, in handling and manipulating things, steps beyond his organic bonds.

The tragedy of humanization, what makes "all humanity . . . eternally and at all times schizophrenic" or split,[30] is that in the laying on of hands by which we self-assertively manipulate the world, we grasp what is not us and thereby lose any dreamed-of autonomy or integrity. The very event that asserts our humanity also puts us beyond the limits of any distinctly defined being: having laid hands on the serpents, the human animal does not know exactly where his limits are. While a serpent might still be organic and have a nerve apparatus, the tool that stands in its place for most of us moderns is not. The birth of humanity becomes a tragedy, according to Warburg, in that it gives birth to a schizoid being, one who becomes what he is by including what he is not.

While in the west, Warburg also saw that the humanizing event was being threatened. "The conqueror of the serpent cult and of the fear of lightning... is captured in a photograph I took on a street in San Francisco." "Uncle Sam in a stovepipe hat," Warburg called him, and we might see here the "apotheosis of electricity" in flesh and blood (see fig. 10).

Warburg notes that "above his hat runs an electric wire. In this copper serpent of Edison's, he has wrested lightning from nature.... The American of today is no longer afraid of the rattlesnake. He kills it; in any case, he does not worship it. It now faces extermination. The lightning imprisoned in wire—captured electricity—has produced a culture with no use for paganism." The apotheosis of electricity has dissipated the fear of serpents and of lightning by stealing fire from heaven (as d'Alembert said when Ben Franklin sent his kite into the heavens become sky and brought down the lightning). The American heir to the apotheosis of electricity kills the rattlesnake; he does not need to hold it in his hands because the cause that he seeks to manipulate, the lightning, has been wrested from the darkness and the clouds where it flashes wildly and capriciously—now here, now there—and imprisoned it in wires that contain it and channel it. The Indian had his tool in hand (the serpent) yet could not be certain that his danced causality would result in the desired effect; his tool only helped him move into that humanizing gap between cause and automatic effect. With the apotheosis of electricity, we have nothing in hand yet are all the more in control. "Our own technological age has no need of the serpent in order to understand and control lightning. Lightning no longer terrifies the city dweller, who no longer craves a benign storm as the only source of water. He has his water supply, and the lightning serpent is diverted straight to the ground by a lightning conductor.... We know that the serpent is an animal that must succumb if humanity wills it to."[31] Far from helpless and miserable, Uncle Sam, the apotheosis of electricity personified, is confident that any effect can be achieved: "everything 'is made' and 'can be made' if we only muster the will for it."[32] No slippery serpent or lost cause will slip through the iron cage of our law-governed and regular world. We can rest secure, knowing that we can count on the countable, calculate the calculable, unlike the Indian, whose humanity entails that he, miserably and tragically, count on the uncountable, calculate the incalculable.

Warburg will speak of this extermination of the serpent or forgetting of the lost cause in terms of overcoming distance. "The modern Prometheus [Ben Franklin]," Warburg concluded, and "the modern Icarus [the Wright Brothers], are precisely those ominous destroyers of the sense of distance." The distance, implicit in the serpent ritual, between cause and effect, the serpent handled and the lightning beseeched, is "undone by the instantaneous electric connection."[33] The danced causality of the helpless human soul leaps into the gap. Uncle Sam's wave of the hand or flick of the switch entails no such leap; it is an all but stationary gesture. Who is more the magician?

Contrary to many interpretations of modernity as the age of human manipulation of nature, what the apotheosis of electricity seems to have meant for Warburg was the end of manipulation and the disappearance of a human touch to the world. The hands that manipulated or touched serpents become unnecessary to the production and control of lightning, now imprisoned in the "copper serpent." The apotheosis of electricity seems to hold out the promise of securing our autonomy, integrity, and identity as we no longer need to bond with serpents to summon the rain. We can neglect the serpents, abandon the religion and "danced causality" that ties us to these impossible-to-grasp causes. We have ready reservoirs of water, and access fire from heaven—"lightning imprisoned in wire"—with a wave of the hand. The empty hand "has produced a culture with no more use for paganism." Thus we resolve culture's schizophrenia and become fully modern enlightened men.

But while the apotheosis of electricity might resolve the "tragedy of manipulation," that same flick of the switch does away with the event of humanization. Warburg's observations seem to suggest that a man with empty hands is hardly human. In abandoning the helpless, miserable Indian, exterminating the rattlesnake, and capturing the lightning, Warburg wonders, has Uncle Sam ("the apotheosis of electricity") lost touch with the events that perform the emergence of humanity? Has "a culture with no use for paganism" lost touch with the miserable and "helpless human soul" and in this way let fall into oblivion the place or the "darkling" where humanity dwells?

* * *

Somewhere near the Indian villages where Warburg's lightning dance was practiced, I thought that I, in the bright days of my recent life, might find a darkling where the lightning flash still illuminates "the helpless human soul."

## Being Almost There

*The Lightning Field* is located in a place that can't easily be placed or found. Official information from the Dia Foundation, which owns and manages the site, lists its location as "Southwestern New Mexico," but this does not really help us find the place. What we need is a map or aerial view.

But seeing *The Lightning Field* clearly, from outside and above, the prospect in Wolff's *Lucem post nubila reddit*, you lose it. (Check Google Maps.) As De Maria states, "Because the sky-ground relationship is central to the work, viewing *The Lightning Field* from the air is of no value." This frustrates the ascension stories of a disenchanted modernity for which, "the takeoff, far from directing the gaze toward the superior world [as was the case for the medievals], has no other effect than to allow the earth to be seen from higher up."[34] *The Lightning Field* stands somewhere between a modernity that seeks to look *from on high* and a premodernity that seeks to look *to the heights*. Disenchanted modernity ascends in order to look down and see this world more clearly, while premodernity ascends in order to look up and see the otherworld more closely. But, *The Lightning Field* promises no ascent. Instead, it brings us to stand on the earth under the sky: it makes us earthlings and leads us to the ground, but a ground that does not exist without the extraterrestrial, the sky overhead. The work disappears when seen by Warburg's "modern Icarus," who flies thanks to mechanical extensions that replace hands with wings, or by angels, who, winged by nature, never touch their feet on the earth. Likewise, it disappears if you try to see it from inside the on-site log cabin, where, however much on the earth, you do not have the sky over your head. As the instructions included in a folder at the site remind you, "The cabin and porch are nice, but the experience is on the *Field*."

My own search for this obscure darkling took me first by plane to the arid city of Albuquerque. From there, I traveled eighty miles west on I-40 through the desert to a gas station and gift shop at exit 89, where I turned south on Route 117. The view is vast, its limit unattainable. The distance confounds your sense of measure: no matter how far away something is, it always remains in sight and never seems any closer—until it is upon you, suddenly and surprisingly, even if not unexpectedly. Quemado, the town from which the Dia Foundation runs a van that takes you to the site, is another eighty miles. *The Lightning Field* is farther still, another hour or so drive of untold distance into the desert. Like Warburg, I was going south and west, from the built into the cleared, taking a step back into the darkling. While Albuquerque is anything but the overcrowded, dense urban metropolis of America's east coast, the contrast was nevertheless striking. In the city, where everything and the crowd crowds around you, there is little distance. There is lots to see, but the close-up view means no distance adds depth to your vision. As the car and highway propelled me into the great desert vastness, I began to look into the distance, where less and less at first appeared to be seen as more and more distance opened up whatever I did see. Things are shallow, I learned by contrast with the desert darkling, when they don't fade away into the depth opened up by distance.

The road from Albequerque to Quemado passes by land reserved for the Acoma and Laguna, both Pueblo peoples whom Warburg visited, and it takes you over the edge of the Navajo world, beyond the southern boundary of their old country. This edge is marked by one of the sacred mountains, Mount Taylor, or in a literal translation of the Navajo name, "Mountain Tongue" or "Turquoise Mountain,"[35] formed at the time of the Emergence or "cosmic ordering process" when the ancestors emerged from the ground and became earthlings walking under the sky, not just chthonic beings buried in the earth. For a while, the road follows or nearly parallels a trail used by Zuni and Acoma traders. Sandstone cliffs form an insurmountable rock wall on the eastern side, and for almost twenty miles, the road follows the edge of the El Malpais lava beds, a flow that erupted long ago, its inexorable rush seeming to come to a stand here, now, still, nature's own inefficient version of the concrete poured to make the road on which I was driving. The Pueblo and Navajo peoples use the flows as pathways to medicinal herbs they still gather in the lava fields today, as they have done for many generations, and they still perform rituals to renew their ties to this land, a land whose hardness would seem to admit no hold for any tie I could lay. In more than one version of the Navajo emergence story, the lava is the coagulated blood of Yé'iitsoh, chief of the enemy gods, a monster who in aboriginal times, before the beginning, made his home on Mount Taylor and was killed by the Twin War Gods, Monster Slayer and Child Born of Water. The legend holds that should the lava flows that are currently held apart by the San Jose River grow together, Yé'iitsoh will return and wreak destruction on the land and the people. Significantly, the weapons used by the twin gods who defeated him are Lightning that Strikes Crooked and Lightning that Flashes Straight.[36] Their numerous battles left behind traces that give shape to the landscape we see today: rivers were made to spill forth from the earth, and mountains were split open by lightning strikes.

Once in Quemado, travelers are met by a guide who drives them another forty minutes' distance into the desert, where they are left at a rustic but well-provided cabin on the site of *The Lightning Field*. Abandoning their own automobiles and pursuing a path known only to their guide, travelers give up any hope of returning on their own by their own movements or machinations. You are helpless, a shipwreck, marooned amid the flowing sands of a desert you cannot backtrack or cross again.

Interestingly, the Navajo may have seen another side of Quemado than that known to the disenchanted modern. The town was given the name

Rito Quemado, "Burned Creek," in 1880 by Jose Antonio Padilla. "The Spanish name referred either to burned rabbit bush on either side of the creek, or to the scorched appearance of the volcanic soil. . . . The name later became simply Quemado [*Burned*]."[37] To my enlightened eyes, such a name initially seemed well-deserved, as the constant light of an unbroken sun has burned up all there might be to see. The Navajo, by contrast, called the place Tó Háálí, a name that translates as "Flowing Spring" or "Water Flows Up Out."[38] What seemed to me like the apocalyptic outcome, end result, or final resting place to a history of enlightenment was for them a spring, source, or place of emergence, where all things flowed and continue to flow.

## YES, IT FLOWS

At first glance, I was tempted to take this landscape as a strange twist on Wolff's *Lucem post nubila reddit*, the apotheosis of electricity realized here where nothing can escape the unrelenting light. The still desert landscape, a frozen lava flow, the distinct line of a wall of solid rock, all appearing in omnipresent light. It was an image of unchanging reality or timeless eternity, each thing fixed in place, resting before me on solid and stable ground. It reminded me, strangely, not only of Wolff's *Lucem post nubila reddit*, but of an epiphany Michel Serres once had when he saw "the quiet presence of things in their exact place" as he gazed upon a pastoral landscape in his natal land: "Transparent and large, space seems to have swallowed time."[39] No future, no past. A strange twist on the "best of all possible worlds" to find it here in the desert. And perhaps even a strange twist on an apocalyptic revelation, a final unveiling of all things now exposed in the light of unchanging eternity. Was this the vision that drove so many of the religious into the desert?

I also recalled the artist Robert Smithson reciting words from Samuel Beckett's *The Unnameable* while the camera pans across desert scenes in the film version of Smithson's *Spiral Jetty*: "Nothing has ever changed since I have been here. But I dare not infer from this that nothing ever will change. Let us try and see where these considerations lead."[40] In the case of Beckett's disembodied voice of modern disenchantment, they lead to a dead end, as the voice proves unable to escape the perspective of the tenuous I. Riveted to its own deathly existence or its own living death, it lives only an unchanging and unending present, an eternity in which no day dawns or night falls. Even if it cautions against inferring from past permanence a future persistence, it remains unable to hope for a future in which something might indeed change.

Might there be another way to look at things, such that the things might not be burned away by the unrelenting sun? Michel Serres proposes that of the natural sciences: "I invite into astrophysics or biochemistry [and geology, I would add] whoever proclaims that the sciences disenchant the world; the sky and life itself will quickly appear to him full of wonderful miracles."[41]

Like Warburg when he "undertook to flee toward natural objects and science," I accept Serres's invitation into the sciences. Seeing from their perspective, my measure of time is altered: from my own human life (in which indeed little or nothing has changed here, certainly not since I have been driving on this road) to the more vast time scale known by the geologists, paleontologists, and even astronomers for whom the rocks and fossils around me are like so many books, brain cells, or other recording devices, bearing the memories of a past that is different from this present into a still different future. The geologist, for instance, knows well that something has changed here and indeed will change again. What I see as the fixed features of a landscape against an eternal background of solid cliffs under an unchanging sun, he puts into motion. The solid and stable presence of all things, each in its place under the sun (as in Wolff's image), is animated and begins to flow—the sandstone cliffs and lava fields on either side of the highway being a good example. I see them as rock, solid and stable. If I even think of them as flowing, it is through an erosion that befalls them from outside themselves, a force alien to their objective presence as stable and secure identities. But this is not so—as Serres learned from the geologist: "water flows, but so too does the cliff; it flows . . . like water and the history of men, in as many and still more stages or levels."[42] The erosion is always happening to the stone such that it entirely misses the thing if you conceive the cliff ever not eroding, ever not flowing beyond the edges of the place it occupies, ever not subject to outside forces. Isn't its flowing therefore crucial to an objective account of the cliff, its exposure to others that change it and make it other crucial to its identity—like my own inevitable aging and eventual return to dust that will blow away if not held and buried in a box that retains it?

What I see now, when I look with the eyes of such a scientist, is hardly a world of objects fixed in place, but a world of things that happen and, happening, flow in time. The solid and stable world becomes one that flows and erodes. Looking again at the timeless eternal presence of the desert or of *Lucem post nubila reddit*, both seeming to depict landscapes fixed in place by the light of an unchanging sun, I hear Serres call to me: "I invite you to see them, not immobile but slow. Copying Galileo, I would gladly say: 'And yet, all these red cliffs flow' . . . I can no longer contemplate sun, stars, and landscapes without their time carrying away, with its formidable sweep, my eyes and my body. Yes, indeed, science nourishes and reverses vision." Fed by this science, when I look at *Lucem post nubila reddit*, I can see "millions of fountains, gushing or of infinite slowness before the country house."[43] And here, in the "land of enchantment," science tells me, the lava fields still flow! The Navajo are right to fear that they may eventually come together. Things happen, always.

The more one comes to know about this place the more mysterious it becomes, as the seemingly empty desert, totally present under the blazing sun, betrays fabulous stories and histories. There are things whose beginnings I (or someone like me who resides here) can remember: roadside stands, passing cars, a few houses. Then there are things whose beginnings I can remember through the work of historians: Pueblo villages and burial grounds, the Spanish artifacts found nearby. And then there are the things whose beginnings exceed both me and the historian and call for natural science or myth: a Douglas fir that has lived 1,274 years and still lives on; lava fields, some as old as 115,000 years, others only 3,000; sandstone cliffs over 200 million years old, formed when the desert was under the sea. So many relics of so many pasts, archaic as well as historical, ancient as well as modern. All of these are gathered together in this place and are flowing away, each at its own pace. A monstrous combination of old and new, slow and fast.

Looking differently, then, with my eyes opened to flowing wonders by this enchanting science, I see space here crossed by many paces: the slow-moving time of the Native American peoples whose stories still remain present for those who listen, the even slower-moving time of the rock and sand, and the swiftly passing time of my car—which threatens, if I do not take care, to take it all up and lose it in the oblivion induced by its onrushing sweep. The only time that is absent here, I think, is the unchanging, entirely present non-time of *Lucem post nubila reddit*, a reality that is bathed in a single light and can be grasped together in a space that dissolves all time.

## The disenchantment of the weather

On the day that I visited *The Lightning Field*, a fellow traveler told me that he had "done a little raindance" before leaving. I did not doubt him, and I expect he was not the only one. How surprising it was to find so many of the disenchanted culture mavens and lovers of contemporary art beseeching meteorological phenomena! How surprising that we should be praying for the darkness and clouds to return: "*Nubila post lucem reddat*, O that he might bring back the clouds!" Weren't we disenchanted moderns supposed to be the ones who said, "Not for us the raindance of the Zuni," a Pueblo people who still live not far from here in a village that Warburg visited at the end of the nineteenth century.[44]

## NUBILA POST LUCEM REDDAT

Our talk about the weather that day was much more than the idle chatter about "how it is out there" with which we usually fill the empty spaces of our days. Commenting on what I would call the disenchantment of our talk about the weather, the anthropologist Michael Taussig has observed that "the cliché concerning the cliché of weather talk is that we talk about the weather as a way of avoiding talking about anything else."[45] For disenchanted moderns, the idleness and incessancy with which we talk about the weather is a symptom of our boredom, and this boredom grows with the increasing control we exercise. The world is more and more devoid of eventfulness as all is so well managed and we manage so well. When reality has rendered itself in the light of reason and is, therefore, at least in principle, calculable, then "nothing bores the ordinary man more than the cosmos. Hence for him the deepest connection between weather and boredom. . . . Nothing is more characteristic than that precisely this most intimate and mysterious affair, the working of the weather on humans, should have become the theme of their emptiest chatter."[46] When the not-so-boring forms of weather do return, they return precisely as chatter about others with which we fill and overfill the boredom of our boring days.

In what Taussig calls "our ever-more impoverished weather talk,"[47] we speak of numbers: heat as so many degrees, hurricane winds as category 1, 2, 3, 4, or 5, rainfall measured in inches. The weather has become truly calculable. Represented in these numbers, it is available to us, objectively, in the knowledge reported by the ongoing activity of institutions such as *U.S.A. Today*, the Weather Channel, and the latter's website, weather.com. The gathering and dissemination of data never stops. The purpose of these institutions is, as Andrew Ross puts it, "to make news out of the weather. . . . [The Weather Channel's] continuing success is driven by what its managers describe as its 'continuing goal of becoming the nation's primary source of weather information.' Programming consists of a ceaseless flow of different narrative segments and features strung together in a highly organized schedule." Tuning in to the pictures, images, and numbers produced by these media and the sciences they employ provides us with so much information, all the knowledge we need to predict and manage our own exposure to the weather in advance of any encounter with the cosmos. This is what the weather is today. Thanks to these media, all of us, all across the world, can, it seems, know all about the weather of all the others. We have each become what Ross calls a "weather tourist,"[48] endlessly fascinated with seeing the sights presented to us in the numbers and pictures on our screen, like so many informational brochures. We read our way through the world become information and know what we see, instead of seeing it. Idle entertainment to entertain the idle?

How could talk of the weather not be boring when we access it by tuning in to the media, not by attunement to the cosmos? It is the perfect thing with which disenchanted modernity can fill the increasingly idle, boring life of administrators in and to the calculable world picture. "The climate never influences our work anymore. How do we keep ourselves busy? With numerical data, equations, dossiers, legal texts, news bulletins hot off the press or the wire: in short, language. True language for science, normative language for administrators, sensational language for the media." Preoccupied by our occupations, we are traffickers in symbols, busy with language, be it words or numbers, rarely given over to things that happen and that might render us subject to their caprice and the effects they might cause. These symbols are moved practically at will, by a minimum of effort only mental, never taken in hand like the oar or shovel, which are manipulated by human beings, mostly peasants and sailors, whose work is shaped by "the state of the sky and the seasons."[49]

But like the Indians at their "raindance," those of us at *The Lightning Field* were not bored, and our talk about the weather was anything but idle chatter. Like them, we wanted the lightning to come. Seriously interested in the weather, we spoke of the lightning in tones of sometimes anxious, sometimes patient hope and profundity. I remembered that, in the so-called primitive religions as well as in classical mythology, when one spoke of the storm or the sun, one spoke of a god—not always or only that a god controlled the storm but that the storm was a theophany, the manifestation of a god in person.

## WHAT BEFALLS YOU

Pueblo (Zuni and Hopi) mythology holds that lightning fertilized the maize and therefore bore original responsibility for the generosity of nature.[50] Arrow points or spear stones, generally held as talismans bringing good luck or protection from evil, are also associated with lightning, being found frequently near trees that have been lightning struck. The Hopi (in whom Warburg took a great interest) hold that these stones "have dropped from the fingers of Lightning himself and, when discovered, should be picked up by Lightning's representative, the Flute Society chief."[51] This is the chief who also leads the raindance ceremony in which lightning is summoned to fertilize the fields.

The Pueblo are not the only people to collect these talismans. They exert a profound charm on many moderns too, who know them as fulgurites or petrified lightning. Hollow tubes of glass formed when lightning melts and vaporizes quartz-rich sand or soil, fulgurites have been exhibited in museums of art and science, fashioned into jewelry, and incorporated into other decorative objects, such as wind chimes. In the fulgurite, lightning proves creative, nature an artist. These natural artworks are rare and fragile, unstable things of opalescent beauty, placed here without rhyme or reason. They are like documents recording the occasions of chance, occasions accessible to us only after the fact through this record of its mysterious gesture.

Medieval Christians too knew of something like fulgurites, or stones that dropped from the fingers of Lightning. They called them "ceraunites," from the Greek word for lightning. These were stones whose nature, origin, and function were unknown but that were believed to have fallen from the skies during terrible storms. Marbodius, bishop of Rennes from 1096 to 1123, writes of such stones in his *Liber de lapidibus*, a compendium describing the peculiar powers and charms of precious stones and gems: "When the turbulent air heats up beneath the raging winds, when it thunders terribly and the fiery ether unleashes the lightning bolt, when the clouds smack together, then there falls from the sky a stone whose name among the Greeks comes from that of the lightning. It is only in those places that were visibly struck by lightning that one can find this stone. This is why it is called, following the Greek, *ceraunite*, for what we call *lightning*, the Greeks called *ceraunos*." These stones fallen from the sky assured their possessor that when he "travels by boat on a river or on the sea, he will not drown in the storm or be struck by lightning."[52] Not all that befalls one unawares need be unfortunate, it seems.

However much good fortune the lightning might bring the Pueblo who find these stones, this good also threatens to spread pollution; its effects must be carefully contained and managed by rituals of purification lest the lightning-struck field become a polluted swamp, the clearing a miasmic haze. The Hopi embody this overdetermination of lightning in the figure of Sho'tokününgwa, who is "Lightning shooting arrow points from his fingers" and so a bringer of good fortune and fertility, but who is also a starry war god who initiated the practice of scalping.[53] The need to contain lightning, to keep it in place lest it spread contagiously, is seen in the practice of separating people struck by lightning from the rest of the community. Treatments vary but often include a four-day fast during which the patient drinks only a potion of rainwater from the storm that produced the lightning mixed with black beetle and suet and is then made to vomit each day. Should the treatment fail, the patient will "dry up" and die. During treatment, only the previously lightning-shocked, forming a society of doctors or shamans, are allowed contact with the recently shocked victim, thereby containing the lightning with the lightning.[54] Navajo culture, too, evinces an ambivalence toward lightning. It is sometimes depicted ritually in sand painting because its charge is said to have curative effects, but there are again numerous taboos designed to quarantine the lightning-struck: one should not use wood from a partially burned tree because it might have been lightning struck; one should not eat the flesh of an already burned animal because it might have been killed by lightning. Particular animals, such as the nighthawk, and particular trees, such as the aspen, should not be killed or chopped down because they are associated with lightning and will cause it to strike you if you use it.

## SECULARIZATION OF THE LIGHTNING

The anthropologist Elsie Clews Parsons, a noted expert of Pueblo religion, classifies lightning in the highest category of spirits, above even the sun, the moon, the stars, and the winds. Like the *wakan* or *maya* of the Indians about whom Emile Durkheim writes in *The Elementary Forms of the Religious Life*, lightning, Parsons suggests, represents a divine force prior to its determination as this or that, before its being located here or there—prior, that is, to its being contained in a single, easily grasped concept or place. Parsons's observations regarding the supremacy of lightning over the solar gods connect with some more general observations made by Mircea Eliade, one of the most influential figures in the modern academic study of religion. In *Patterns in Comparative Religion*, Eliade observes that in many mythologies, the sun gods were not creative; the sky gods, best manifested in the lightning that was their chief attribute, were.[55] The sun could continue the work of creation, but it did not have the divine spark—sunlight, thus, can make the maize grow, but it is the lightning strike that fertilizes the field and clears, in a flash, an opening for everything then to come to light.

Eliade's research in the history of religion leads him to propose a hypothesis in which the history that begins with the lightning flash falls into oblivion and is replaced by one that begins with the sun. As mankind comes to dominate his environment, a project that Eliade claims begins with agriculture, sky divinities such as the lightning are gradually replaced at the summit of the divine pantheon by sun gods "well-disposed toward mankind." These solar deities might appear amid the parting clouds with a smiling face, whereas the sky gods are more remote, more transcendent—and more capricious, of less determinate visage, like the lightning. The sun, "although always in motion . . . always remains unchangeable" and so reveals a cosmos that is the forerunner to that which always renders its reason when *lucem post nubila reddit*.

It is no mistake, then, that one sees the sun in Wolff's classic figuring of enlightenment. It is the solar god whose desacralization drives the emergence of modern disenchantment; one still sees this sun, even if desacralized and secularized, in Wolff's frontispiece. "In the end," Eliade concludes, "*sun* and *intelligence* will be assimilated to such a degree that the solar and syncretistic theologies of the end of antiquity become rationalistic philosophies; the sun is proclaimed to be the intelligence of the world . . . solar hierophanies give place to *ideas*. . . . This desacralization of solar hierophanies" will not alter the structure of illumination in so-called more enlightened times.[56] Eliade's theory is consonant with what my students, as reported in the introduction to this book, sense, vaguely and inchoately, when they voice a continuity, structural similarity, or indiscernability between the enlightenment and their modern religion, between reasonable thoughts and God as the light of the world, the light in which "all things in general" might come to light. What has changed, both Eliade and my class suggest, is the referent for the sun, but the sun is maintained as the light in which all that is comes to light, the same light and so the same objects.

The solar god is thus allied to the reason that enlightens, together in the disenchantment of the world, together oblivious to the immemorial lightning flash and the "helpless human soul" in its "eternally constant Indianness." What would a world look like in the light of this lightning and its hierophany, rather than that of the sun? What would a modernity look like that is founded on the desacralization of lightning? Is this even imaginable?

## WEATHER, OR NOT

Our talk about the weather that day at *The Lightning Field* aimed to avoid empty generalities and idle speculation about other people's weather. Far more interested in what was happening here and now, at this place, in this locale, we cared about the "unique" or the "unusual," the singular, capricious event of a lightning flash—now here, now there, but always now, in this place, wherever it might be. However rare and intermittent lightning might be, we did not let that stop us from hoping and praying that our wishes might cause it to come here and now: *nubila post lucem reddat*. Michel Serres says that "scientists can predict the hour of an eclipse, but they do not know how to predict whether or not they will be able to see it."[57] The knowledge of these savants, a knowledge based on calculations applying physical laws to observations made in a systematic way over time and in many places, was, however accurate a predictor of the motions of heavenly bodies like the sun and the moon, no concern of ours. What we wanted, what we longed for, was to know where and when we should render our own appearance so that that we might be there to see a rare and unusual event.

The sort of event we sought fell at one time under the heading of *meteors*. According to the historian Vladimir Janković, "the first meteorological facts were unusual meteors, not numerical observations. Unusual meteors were found in public spaces, not in barometric tubes. . . . Meteorological facts were events: observations were narratives about unusual meteorological activity. Outside the intervals in which activity took place, meteors did not occur and could not be observed. The meteoric tradition was in this respect a 'chronicle' of individual . . . *meteora*." What Janković calls "meteoric reportage" took as its subject the "fleeting, uncommon, and unstable character of phenomena" such as lightning, fireballs, the northern lights, and water dragons.[58] These were rare occurrences, singular and therefore various, but also intermittent flashes that came to light suddenly. These "events" lacked a history since they emerged as if from out of the dark, appearing suddenly out of "intervals" during which they could not be observed, were not in the picture, and were not supposed to exist. Faced with such uncommon, intermittent events, meteoric reportage took the form of what Janković called a "chronicle," a catalog of individual events, rather than a history of occurrences connected over time, or the measurement of recurrent and reliable patterns, or a science of organized facts related by laws in a coherent system. Citing the entry "Meteorology" from the 1798 *Encyclopaedia Britannica*, Janković claims that neither methodological advances nor better measurements seemed to offer any hope that a "person can pretend to reduce [meteors] to any kind of rule [since] some causes in their own nature [make them] *irregular*; that is capable of such endless variety, that no assignable space of time is sufficient to exhaust it."[59] Irregular and nonrepeating, each time only themselves, meteors came to light and vanished in a flash. They could not be contained in any measurable period or span of time that would hold them present before an observer.

These meteoric events and the gaze that contemplated them fell into oblivion—banished like the clouds of *Lucem post nubila reddit* and the lightning imprisoned in copper wire—when the rise of a new science introduced to our eyes the generality, continuum, and global system of something now called the weather:

> Meteorology explained *meteora*, not the weather; events, not processes. . . . The new science [the science of weather] concentrated on recurring, predictable, and long-lasting changes in the atmosphere. However, rather than discovering the causes of these changes, its champions searched for those rules, correlations, and patterns [that governed movements in the atmosphere]. The emphasis changed from the experimental philosophy of the air to the rationalization of prognostic signs, from theoretical knowledge to prediction, from causal explanation to forecasting rules, and more generally, from the science of meteors to the science of weather and seasons.

Concerned with "identifying long-term changes, recurrent patterns, and, if possible, the methods of forecasting," weather science directs our attention away from the sudden and singular emergence of the intermittent meteoric event and toward "the regular, cyclical, and wholesome processes embodied in the predictability of unfolding seasons."[60] This weather science, and the objects it constitutes, have been deemed "a sharply modern science" by the historian Katherine Anderson, who goes on to claim that, in keeping with "other kinds of physical knowledge" shaped by the currents of modern disenchantment, "the weather would become mathematical and certain."[61]

While study of the weather might not be new or entirely modern—indeed, predictions about events in the sky are very old—several characteristics distinguish the modern science of weather from meteoric reportage.

First, *a new object,* indeed an object instead of a miscellany of singular events. This object was the weather, a global system of the atmosphere, what John Herschel would later term the "ideal 'unity' of the weather." Whereas the meteoric tradition "was about extraordinary phenomena" or extravagances, weather science looked for patterns and recurrent phenomena in a coherent, lawfully bound system. Its object was global and therefore depended on "the removal of meteorological practices from places of life to places on the map," where they were coordinated with other observations in a picture of the world as a whole.[62]

This new object, the weather system as a unity, appeared in what is one of the greatest of modern world pictures: the weather map. The weather came to be in the map that represents it as a whole. The geographer Mark Monmonier claims that "maps that could warn of storms and cold waves were a triumphant collaboration of science, technology, bureaucracy, and cartography."[63] Working together, these could synchronize vast reaches of space, bringing distant places into relation with one another in a single, unified present pictured in the map. The first weather map, Monmonier writes, was invented in 1816. For some thirty years prior to that, data regarding weather events had been collected locally, in the tradition of meteoric reportage, but these givens had never been synchronized or plotted in such a way as to produce knowledge of what we call "the weather." "Bare diaries of [events] in particular spots" do not contribute to knowledge of the weather, and knowledge of "local events [is] useless if collected for its own sake," insofar as it does not contribute to the prediction of future occurrences or the assertion of one's own intentions in the face of such occurrences.[64] The first publicly printed weather map, Monmonier continues, appeared in 1848 in a newspaper in England. It was coordinated by data conveyed by railway travelers and designed with the express intention of providing travelers with knowledge they could use to make predictions that would let them manage their trips.

Maps representing the weather required that data be gathered from scattered locations and synchronized by a central authority. This means, as Anderson puts it, that "the science of weather was also modern in another sense. It called attention to the new scale of scientific activities, which required coordination and centralization that put the work beyond any one individual's abilities and resources."[65] The infrastructure for this was provided by military offices as well as newly emergent national corporations such as Western Union, whose telegraph operators were asked to replace the previous "OK" with which they signaled the opening of the office each morning with a message of either *clear, cloudy, rain,* or *sun.* The company then sent these messages to a national weather service in Washington that could plot them on a single unified picture, representing the very earliest form of the weather. Obviously, new and faster technologies of communication were crucial to the success of this picture, as the speedy transmission of data was necessary for distant locales to be gathered in the single present pictured on the map. For such maps to be useful in predicting what was to come, "weather data [had to] travel faster than the winds themselves" so that information could arrive in advance of the things that happen.[66] And bureaucratic management was crucial as one needed to manage "dispersed networks of volunteer weather observers" if one was to collect data simultaneously and communicate it synchronously.[67]

This leads to a second factor crucial to the banishment of *meteora*. The representation of the weather-object requires *the ongoing activity of regu-*

*lar, eventually constant, observation and collection of data*. Whereas meteoric events were ephemeral and existed only intermittently, separated by long intervals of absence or nonexistence, the weather was a constantly observed object, remaining permanently present before us in the maps that represent it. The science of the weather, in contrast to the chronicle-like quality of meteoric reportage, involves observation carried out over a period of time, sometimes longer even than an individual human lifetime but nonetheless determinate or bounded, and therefore recurring. If in the case of meteors nothing could be observed when they were not happening, in the case of the weather constant observation always produces something to see—the maps, pictures, and representations with which we are so familiar and which exercise so profound an influence over our daily plans and practices.

Initially provided by military scouts, railroad station agents, and Western Union telegraphers, the ongoing activity of observation and data collection would eventually be assumed by increasingly sophisticated technological devices. When these devices take over, what is observed also changes. Machines measure the weight of air masses, the velocity of the wind, levels of humidity and of temperature, and much more. These measurements produce the numbers that inform the calculations that represent the weather in the maps placed before us in endlessly streaming media. As the meteoric tradition fades into oblivion, as "numerical observations" made by machines replace "bare diaries" reporting sensations of how it is out there, the nature of the data collected is denatured.

The invention and representation of the weather therefore entails that the cause and nature of things fall into oblivion as we look instead for *mathematical laws and formulae* that let us compute and predict appearances. This constitutes a third distinction from the meteoric tradition. To be sure, weather science provides a model of what causes the rain, but by contrast with the Pueblo, the capricious, occult causes of extravagant effects (lightning/serpents) have been banished from its world picture, replaced by law-abiding, calculable ones (atmospheric conditions). To state the matter more precisely, the maps that represent the weather for us tell us when conditions are right for such and such an event to occur, but they do not tell us when and where it will happen; we do not know what causes a given singular event. Janković therefore observes that no participant in the nascent science of weather "would have conflated the certainty of the 'a-causal' wisdom with the uncertainty of the causal" conjectures of intermittent meteoric reportage.[68]

As mathematical laws replace causal observation, a fourth distinctive characteristic of modern weather science is *the integration of the local into the global*. For modern weather science, the passage from one to the other is reversible: what is happening "here and now" is of interest to weather science because it manifests a global pattern whose unity can be known from it, while, inversely, the global pattern lets us know what will happen in this locale, which is part of that unity. With the rise of weather science, "scrutiny of local weather, whether in the form of rules of prediction or series of observations, mattered only to the extent to which atmospheric 'unity' manifested itself in a locale. Rather than seeking meteorological attention to place, observers began to monitor the atmospheric vagrancy displayed in the motions that now had a global significance."[69] Nothing could disturb "the 'ideal unity' of the weather," a closed system that admits no caprice and nothing extravagant. This law-governed but uneventful object is the atmosphere that constitutes our weather. The modern weather-object, then, is not so much events that happen here and now, as it is a certainty about what happens in a reasonable world (this, the best of all possible worlds) and therefore a prediction about what will happen in a time and place with neither here nor now.

## IN LOVE WITH THE LIGHTNING

I suppose, then, that that day in the darkling of *The Lightning Field*, we didn't really care about the weather. We were driven by stories and by a picture (that fabulous image), more so than by our knowledge of the weather, whatever certainties it might predict. We didn't care if what we observed was or could be integrated into a body of other observations collected by other observers in other places and at other times. The description of a single lightning strike, however purposeless and lacking in predictive power, was immensely important to us. What we desired was one, only one, and you can't count on that.

Very much like being in love. We were waiting for the lightning strike that the French call *un coup de foudre*, a lightning strike that the language uses idiomatically in the English sense of "love at first sight."

It was plain to me that our search was for an event to which no method could guarantee access. No path could bring us all the way through to a vision of this eventful strike. The rule or law of the weather and atmospheric science remained in place; the forecasts and predictions were accurate and provided a certainty on which we could count. But we gained no assurance from their certainties, in love as we were with an event that exceeded the very rule that predicted it. Yes, of course, we know, even if you or I do not, the circumstances that occasion a flash of lightning: electrical charges of such and such disposition in the atmosphere, humidity and moisture at certain levels, a darkening of the skies, and so on. But the knowledge that conditions might be suitable could not assure us that our desire would that night be satisfied. We were in love with an occult cause, the cause of events that was occluded in the still law-governed world.

* * *

For us to have any hope that our love might show up, we have to wait on it. We must tarry here for a while, linger in this place, while away the time, patiently but not without yearning (our time here is short, after all). Moving yet all the while remaining in place, a tingling runs through me.

## Tools and techniques that expose us to waiting on . . . and on . . .

If the Pueblo solicited lightning through the serpent rituals, the vision sought by modern visitors to *The Lightning Field* is solicited by the lightning poles. Strong conductors of electrical current, steel rods provide a path of least resistance through which a surplus of negatively charged electrons in the storm clouds overhead might discharge themselves to an area of excess positive charge. This discharge can result in momentary flashes here on earth of temperatures hotter than the surface of the sun. When positive and negative connect, lightning flashes, joining heaven and earth, sky and ground, in an instant that is revealed as quickly as it disappears. "Sky fuses with earth as the end of the world is proclaimed," wrote José de Caldas, one of Colombia's most famous scientists, while watching a lightning storm.[70]

### THE END OF TIME AND SEASONS

The connection between lightning and the end of the world in a final unveiling of heavenly truth is not foreign to the Christian scriptures. A lightning flash marks the moment when the skies tear open and the firmament is rolled back like a curtain in a final apocalyptic unveiling of celestial truth that does away with the difference between heaven and earth, uniting them in a single reality. The book of Luke says, "The time is coming when you will long to see one of the days of the Son of Man, but you will not see it. Men will tell you, 'There he is!' or 'Here he is!' Do not go running off after them. For the Son of Man will be in his day like the lightning, which flashes and lights up the sky from one end to the other" (17:22–24). Lightning is also associated with the gleaming face of Jesus as seen by the disciples at the transfiguration on Mount Tabor and with that of the risen Christ seen by the women and the disciples. The

Gospel of Matthew tells that after Christ returns, "as the lightning comes from the east and flashes to the west, . . . the stars will fall from heaven" (24:27–29), as if the difference between earth and sky is no more. If the lightning of apocalypse means the stars and heavenly bodies fall from heaven, it brings with it the end of the recurrent periods that make up the weather. Time having stopped, there is no weather in heaven: "The 'lights in the firmament' that demarcate the seasons in Genesis disappear in Revelation. 'And the city had no need of the sun, neither of the moon, to shine in it: for the glory of God did lighten it, and the Lamb is the light thereof' (21:23). . . . The cycles of growth and decay regulated by the seasons are erased. In the city of Revelation the tree of life 'yielded her fruit every month' (22:2)."[71] Subsequent theologians would also see this lightning flash that joins earth and sky as further evidence of the apocalypse and end of time. Rémi Brague reports that "in the Christian realm, the distinction between sky and earth is only temporary. At the Resurrection, 'sky and earth will be joined, and there will only be the sky remaining.' Alain of Lille develops this idea. . . . Once perfect man has won a victory over the vices, the earth no longer has anything to envy the sky."[72]

But human beings do not dwell in this indifference of sky and earth, this earth lit as clearly as a clear sky. *The Lightning Field* reminds me of this: it makes us earthlings by putting us on the earth under the sky. "The experience of being on a planet is powerful and immediate at *The Lightning Field*, but not wholly exhilarating," Kenneth Baker writes. "Defined by a plain below, *The Lightning Field* opens a plain above."[73] By stretching out its poles, *The Lightning Field* opens the difference it tries to bridge between sky and earth and puts us there in that middle, as if trying to take the measure of a dimension we cannot hope to cover. A glorious work: the poles stand there, forlorn and somewhat despairing, in the grandeur and glory of an effort to reach out and up into a distance that exceeds their reach.

## ANGELIC VISIONS

In other times and cultures, the vision of lightning or fire from heaven was not repressed but taken as the vision of angels and angelic redemption. In the *Chaldean Oracles*, fragmentary texts from the second century AD that were influential in Neoplatonic thought, and perhaps through the Neoplatonists in certain, mystical forms of Christianity,

> the divine principle, being itself a fire, could penetrate the strata of the cosmos with fiery light and thereby enliven them. Thus, for example, fragment 34 of the *Oracles* says:

From [the Source of Sources] leaps forth the genesis of complex matter.
From there a lightning bolt, sweeping along, becomes less distinct as
It leaps into the cosmic wombs. For from there, all things
Begin to stretch forth wondrous beams towards the place below.[74]

Linked with the manifestation of the cosmos from the source of sources, penetration to earth by fire from the heavens (lightning) also served to rouse the earth to return to the heavens. Theurgic rituals were designed with the express intention of provoking the heavenly forces, the angels, to bring down the light that would lift up the enlightened. Within an explicitly Christian context, one finds a similar connection of lightning and angelic vision in the authoritative angelology of the sixth-century father of Christian mysticism Pseudo-Dionysius—for whom the seraphic angels, being closest of all creatures to the divine Light, burn most brilliantly in the ardor of their love. "Seraph," coming from the word for "fire," is literally "fire from heaven." The illumination of the seraphic angels, and through them of the remaining angelic orders, Dionysius claims, will "purify by means of the lightning flash and the flame" the remaining cosmic orders below.[75]

Like the mystics and ascetics of the Dionysian universe, then, disenchanted moderns go to the desert in search of the angelic light, whose illumination will purify and thereby stimulate the ascent to the heavens. Just because modernity is, as some say, the age without angels does not mean that these moderns do not beseech their light.

Four hundred stainless-steel supplications summon it: "Come!"

·
·
·

But the lightning rarely comes, and we remain still dwelling in-between, in time and the changing seasons, held in suspense, between earth and sky, with the silent poles, gloriously forlorn, forlorn in their glory, chasing after fugitive angels.

Despite the elaborate techniques devoted to beseeching the lightning, despite the methodical research that went into knowing the most auspicious place to summon it, most of the time nothing flashes and we wait—abandoned, shipwrecked on a sea of shifting desert sands blown by an empty wind. We wait for a light that cannot be turned on and off by our own doing, a light that, when it comes, if it comes, threatens our very destruction. Will it come?

What is one to do with this disappointment? How does one respond to this frustration of desire? For some, it grows painful and they flee their frustration by asking experts or common opinion to fill the void with easy-to-consume meanings. Despair, of course, is also always an option. One could try to leave these provinces, this desert darkling, and return to the safety of the solid and stable things on the secure, poured-concrete ground of our sprawling urbanity. One could stay in one's room, in one's house, where the light always comes, summoned by the mere wave of a hand and flick of a switch.

Or one could wait . . . and wait . . . and wait . . . , with the patience of a lover waiting on his or her beloved, lingering a while in this place alongside the bare, slender, almost negligible, almost invisible, mute poles, the tools through which we patiently and lovingly beseech the skies to send a flash of light.

Waiting long enough with these minimal works of minimalism, one learns that the lightning is indeed a false climax, a fantasized consummation to a more prosaic, endless courtship in which "the light is as important as the lightning."[76] One comes to learn that not all of our existence is absorbed in having experiences, not all of life heads toward some end that would fulfill it, that most of life is lived without the crisis provoked by a sudden flash or brilliant revelation.

Much remains to be seen even when the Light will not reveal itself in a flash of lightning. Though the Light itself might remain invisible, the object absent, light is everywhere. Drawn by the lightning field's stated promise that "*The invisible is real*,"[77] those who have the patience to "bear the stillness of hidden growth and awaiting"[78] might see what they cannot make appear—as invisible, sourceless light materializes in the poles burning white-hot, aflame with their own love of the setting sun. As the sunlight shrinks away, the light grows on you, slowly, without your even noticing its arising or fading away, an event that has begun to happen before you know it and even without you.

One of the best descriptions of the light I saw materializing in the poles is offered by Erin Hogan, who recounts her own venture from the sprawling urbanity of Chicago and its bright lights to the desert darklings of the American west, where she visited the sites of monumental land art:

> The sun was sinking, and the relentless heat of the afternoon was starting to abate. . . . No longer were the poles static, dully lit rods effaced by the sun high above. They had come alive, reflecting every movement of the setting sun. They blazed with color that stirred, as the sun went down, in a slow wave across the entire field. Every moment was different; the shadow of every cloud created a new view; the poles were illuminated, shifting, pulsing. . . . Earlier the bright sun had rendered the poles mute. . . . But now, in the early evening light, the poles were singing. It was a chorus of soft hues. . . . Every single one of those four hundred

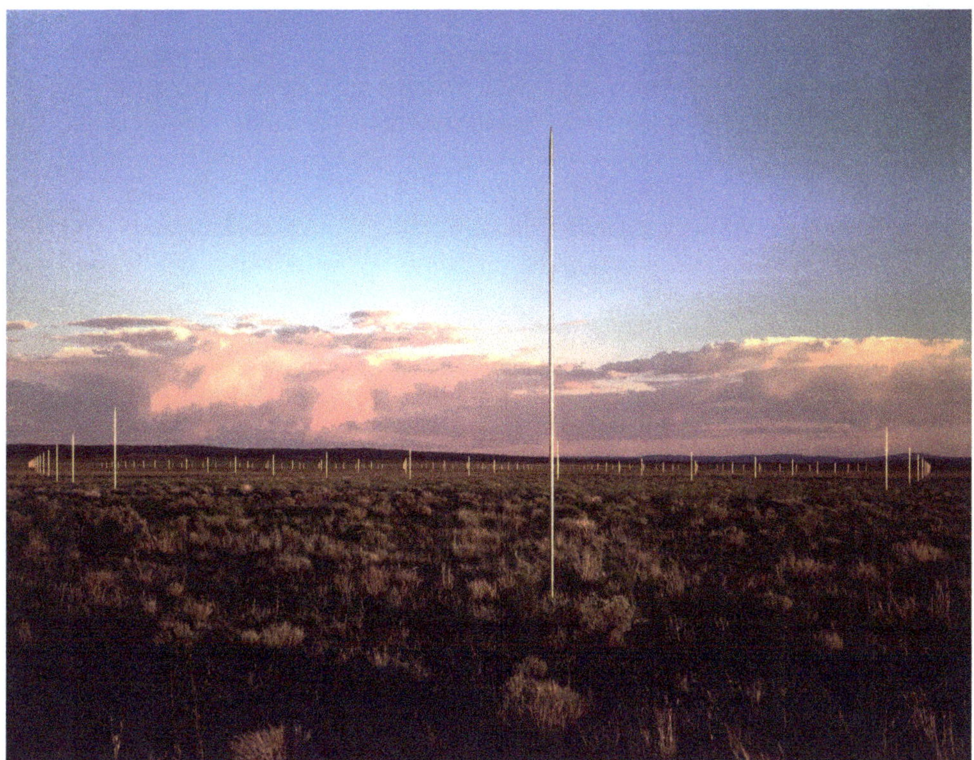

FIGURE 13. Walter De Maria, *The Lightning Field*, 1977. Photograph by John Cliett. © Dia Art Foundation, New York.

> poles was *doing something*; together they shimmered and undulated, like a cornfield stirred by a strong wind.[79]

Clouds and shadows, winds and waves, undulations and pulsations: an eventful scene, as the poles begin to happen when the sun falls, its dying light held for a faint moment in the poles, which come alive with its passing and then pass on themselves, alive in the wave of a light that passes through them like a shudder or like desert sands (fig. 13).

The poles, she says, brought her to the verge of sentimentality and clichéd inspiration; they "made me write sentences like these, think grand thoughts in an inarticulate whir, be grateful and humble." When Hogan saw the poles come alive and happen, when they were "*doing something*," it was, she admits, "a revelation," but not one in which the clouds parted and a smiling face appeared. It was the revelation of a clearing in which everything that becomes visible is not held in place before our gaze but comes alive and does something, "shimmering" and "undulating" like flowing water, desert sand, or a serpent. "To live always in the heightened state must be nightmarish, overwhelming, but I imagine that most people, including me, could benefit from more of those moments in which the atmosphere itself, the air and the light, becomes so powerful that one cannot experience anything else, if only for a few seconds at a time."[80]

The revelatory vision is communicated even, or perhaps especially, in the absence of the source of the light the poles manifest. The clearing opens inseparably from what it makes visible; in other words, "the radiant poles turn from solid objects into beams of dazzling light that pierce the air like tones. They lend themselves to light, which makes its appearance by intensifying theirs."[81] Those who can't believe this will find that they share the fate of the enlightened critic John Beardsley, who did not see the light or hear the poles sing. Observing that the elaborate staging of the event conspires to "insure that one will fully expect to see God" at *The Lightning Field*, Beardsley goes on to complain, "needless to say, He doesn't appear. No artwork could live up to this hype, least of all one that involves the dematerializing effects of sunlight and the subtle interrelationship of sculpture and landscape."[82] Beardsley seems to have missed the point quite precisely. He assumes that God cannot appear because the work that gathers him into presence before us is made of dematerializing sunlight, not the breakthrough of a bolt of lightning or a solid and stable object. But what if the light itself is divine, not the Light, its source? What if the light appears only in what it makes visible? What if *The Lightning Field* is a clearing opened from without a definite position or a locatable source? What if the clearing is not illuminated from a position outside it? Then we might see divinity in the dematerializing light that materializes everywhere in the poles. Then we might hear the poles sing. "It's not about the lightning; it's about the light."

Working in and through the poles, *The Lightning Field* makes light manifest by means similar to those whereby

> ancient sages . . . sought to secure the presence of divine beings by the erection of shrines and statues; they perceived that, though [it] is everywhere tractable, its presence will be secured all the more readily when an appropriate receptacle is elaborated, a place especially capable of receiving some portion or phase of it, something reproducing and serving like a mirror to catch an image of it.[83]

While the modern man who inhabits the electrified city might dream of securing the divine presence in a lightbulb or in the "copper serpents" that convey electricity more or less as he wills it, *The Lightning Field* does not work whenever one wants it to. Like prayer, the Indian's serpent dance, and many other religious technologies, *The Lightning Field* beseeches something shifting, pulsing, alive, something that *does something.*

The mystery of this something that is only as it does means that the technologies, the prayers, and the rituals are not guaranteed success. The technology represented by the poles, like the serpents that the Indian releases into the world, is inefficient: it cannot produce any effect or revelation on its own, seeing as it wants something other, and its causal power is not governed entirely by a law or rule that would make it an efficient aid, something on which you can count in your pursuit of the light. The poles state nothing and make nothing; they are the barest minimum of human gesture, only on the verge of meaning. Very nearly insignificant, they make nothing secure, and nothing is sure to happen on account of them. Instead they "indicate only an intention to enter into relation, a kind of offering, 'indicating' in this way a kind of otherness they do not present to themselves or to us. . . . Perhaps the evocation of the sacred comes from the fact that they face the sky and offer themselves to light."[84] We make an offering or sacrifice to the light with these poles. Stating nothing, they seem to say only "Here I am!" to an endlessly deep blue sky as they stand there in this godforsaken place. This offering or sacrifice by which a relation is indicated and sustained (as we say "hello" or "here I am" to those whom we do not know as a way to open a conversation in which we might then say something, this or that, and get to know them) is the very opening of a world; it makes sacred in the etymological sense of *sacri-fice*.

As offerings or intentions, saying "Here I am," the technology of the poles does not secure and shelter us but first exposes us in the making of an offering that opens us to something other. The poles keep open the distance in which things might come to befall us. What these poles do is hold us out into the open, keeping us dangling, there where we take the risk of meeting something capricious and slippery like the light, which they let go of even as they grab it from the sky. Even if modernity is the end of the age of angelic orders, this "does not mean the end of all encounters with the Angel—it means that every encounter will now have to begin by putting ourselves at risk."[85] These poles render us vulnerable to that risky open clearing where we invoke, by giving to, what we hope will give itself. Nothing much themselves, they are technologies that work on us as much as if not more than they serve our work on the world.

Like Jacob wrestling with the angel, the invocation made by these poles struggles with a presence that is not so easily pinned or pinned down. The occasions when the technology of the poles works are those most difficult to seize because those most swiftly passing—as witnessed by the difficulty of photographing *The Lightning Field* or capturing it in an image. In the half-light of dawn and twilight, when light is not overhead but rising or falling most quickly, invisible light is visible in the transformation of the steel poles into burning light. But there is very little to see when the light illuminates all, fully and totally; the noonday sun, blindingly visible, casts no shadow. "During the mid-portion of the day 70 to 90 percent of the poles become virtually invisible due to the high angle of the sun."[86] *The Lightning Field* thus manifests a light that is not secured and stored in a usable reserve, but seen only in passing, as it passes away or ascends to the point where it disappears. What the work does when it works best is not to establish secure and lasting effects permanently present before you, but to make you, to make you over so that you can see the passing.

# 2 : Diller + Scofidio, *Blur*

THE CLOUD THAT DOES NOT PART WHEN WE SEE THE LIGHT

## From cloudy to clear and back again

Consider once again the two images that opened this book, two images of cosmic light and a dawning universal transparency. Clouds part, and a light is revealed, one that illuminates "all things in general" by pushing away the clouds. The parting of the clouds is the central drama in the story depicted, and the clearing made by this parting is the visual focus of each picture.

What these images of modern disenchantment also show us is that this light works (this illumination produces a cosmic clarity in which solid objects appear) when the light is patterned or structured in a particular way—as a cone of rays emanating from a point, a source that causes or controls the light it shines. One can easily see the cone and its point source in each of the two pictures. The cone model produces a clearing for solid objects to appear; when the sun is in the sky or God in the heavens, "all things in general" show themselves distinctly in the clearing effected by this difference between the lit space and the source of light. They are securely founded in their foundation, grounded in their ground, when led back to this ground or foundation by the light that is rendered for them by this elevated external source. They do not fade into the clouds, float about in the background of the tidal sea, or drift away in the running river, but stand secure, established in a seeming permanence on solid and stable ground.

Whether the summit of the cone is God or reason, the position remains the same and the function equivalent. What is required for the picture of the solid and stable world to emerge clearly and distinctly is that the difference between the source of the light, rays of the illuminating light, and the things to be led to the ground by this illumination be maintained. These images, insofar as they culminate in the apotheosis of electricity, suggest that this difference between ground and grounded, this clearing, is made and held open by technology. As Martin Heidegger has suggested, technology is thus, before being a means to an end or an instrument to produce actualities, a mode of revealing, a clearing in which things can come to light as what they will be.[1] As realized in the second image, with its celestial electric factory, we dream that these technologies are under our control, that we direct this light in which all things appear, that technology is an instrument for realizing human ends and arranging the world according to our plans. The man of modern disenchantment is devoted to these technologies, be they church and prayer (assuming the sun to be God) or factory and bulldozer, and dutifully believes they will afford control of the clearing where he can live with solid and stable objects that appear clearly and distinctly in place.

## REVEALING CLOUD

Now compare those images with three discussed by Hubert Damisch in his book *A Theory of /Cloud/: Toward a History of Painting.*[2] Two are frescoes painted by Antonio Allegri da Correggio sometime around 1520 on the interior of the cupola at the Benedictine church in Parma: *The Assumption of the Virgin* (fig. 14) and *The Vision of St. John on Patmos* (fig. 15). The third, attributed to Giotto and believed to have been done sometime around 1290, is *St. Francis in Ecstasy*, a fresco at the church of Assisi (fig.16).

In the Giotto painting, St. Francis does not stand in a clearing. At its center is not an event in which clouds break or part but rather the cloud itself: it serves as the place in which St. Francis receives his heavenly vision, from a figure itself cloaked in a cloud. In Correggio's *Assumption of the Virgin*, Mary is in blue, ascending, carried on a cloud held aloft by angels. She rises to join the divine company, floating in the glorious glow that crowns the clouds. As much as the clouds do part to admit Mary, one hardly has the sense that they are about to disappear. The upward thrust of the surrounding figures, their outstretched arms and legs, as well as the shape of the clouds, which seem to tend upward, lead one to suppose that these clouds are in fact in the picture in order to close behind Mary, to complete the picture by hiding her, engulfing her in the nebulous place where she will live in divine company. Here the "apotheosis" (more exactly, the assumption of Mary into celestial glory), unlike that of electricity, is completed not in a final clearing of clouds, but in their becoming the place where she dwells. Not even then is the light seen clearly and distinctly; it appears rather as a splendid blur coming from an indistinct source, itself dissolved into clouds.

Correggio's *Vision of St. John the Evangelist* might be thought to depict the inverse movement. When one recalls that St. John's vision was basis for the apocalyptic book of Revelation, one supposes that the clouds are opening so that we might see Christ clearly in a final lifting of all the veils that obscure the heavens. This apocalyptic expectation of parting clouds and clear vision would appear to ally the *Vision of St. John* to Wolff's *Lucem post nubila reddit* and "The Apotheosis of Electricity."

But this apparent alliance ends when one notices several distinguishing features. First of all, the clouds in Correggio's *Vision of St. John* are hardly dynamic clouds in motion. They seem static, more a frame or barrier than a curtain about to part. If anything, they might even be about to close behind the figure who is falling from above. In either case, the clouds are in the picture not in order to vanish as the veil between heaven and earth is torn or the firmament dividing earth and sky is rent asunder, but to block or hide the fullness of the glorious light above, a light that can only be glimpsed in the clouds. Damisch makes this point by contrasting Correggio's cupolas with examples from his contemporaries. "Whereas Correggio's contemporaries, for instance Bramante, deliberately aimed for the effect of an opening, by piercing their cupolas by oculi and lighting them through a lantern, the Parma cupolas [of Correggio] are more or less blind. . . . The solid-looking clouds with which the cupolas are filled . . . obscure most of the splendor and light that reign beyond them."[3] Precisely there and then, when we see the light (the apocalyptic vision on Patmos), Coreggio gives us clouds and lets us see the light only in the cover they provide.

All three images frustrate the model of light as a source emitting a cone of rays, separate from itself, so as to clear a space in which one can see clearly and distinctly. In Giotto's fresco, the haloed figure in the beclouded sky does not come to light for St. Francis in a previously opened clearing—St. Francis remains in a cloud while he sees this shining figure who appears to him in a cloud. The figure in the cloudy sky shines of itself, the radiant aura of its halo finding no resistance in the cloud, which therefore need not part. In Correggio's *Assumption*, the source of light dissolves into the light of the clouds, which rise up toward and even into it. In his *Vision of St. John*, we do not see a source directly or face-to-face but only in the glow of its withdrawal behind the advance of the falling figure. Not structured as a cone, the light in Correggio's pictures, as in that of Giotto, does not clear a place in which to see solid and stable objects. None of the figures are grounded by the light that illuminates the picture. None of them stay on the ground.

In each of the three images, clouds abide; they remain in the picture as something with which we must abide—indeed, something in which we seek to abide, insofar as they become, at least in *The Assumption* and *St. Francis in Ecstasy*, if not also in *The Vision of St. John*, the place of divinity. As bearers of revelation or illumination, the clouds are something like

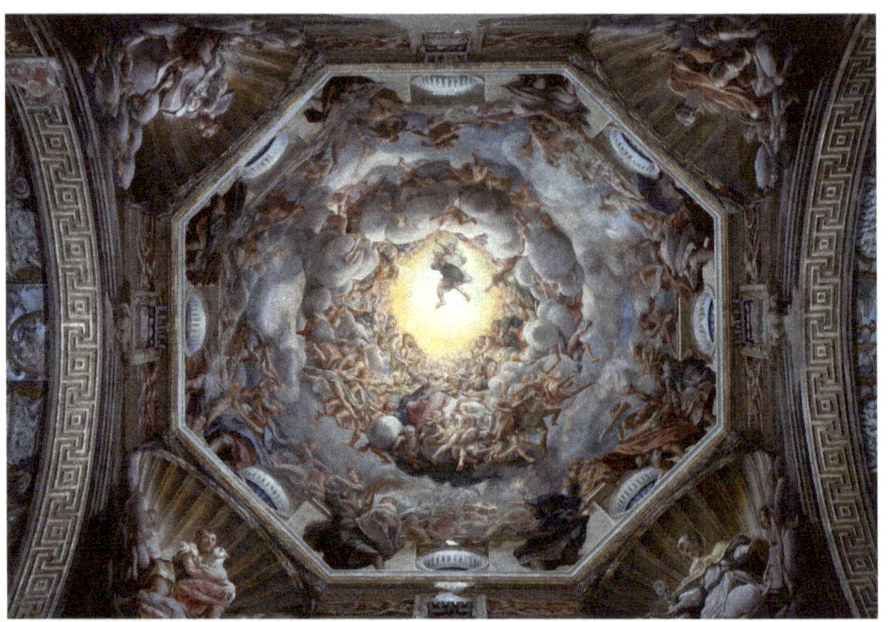

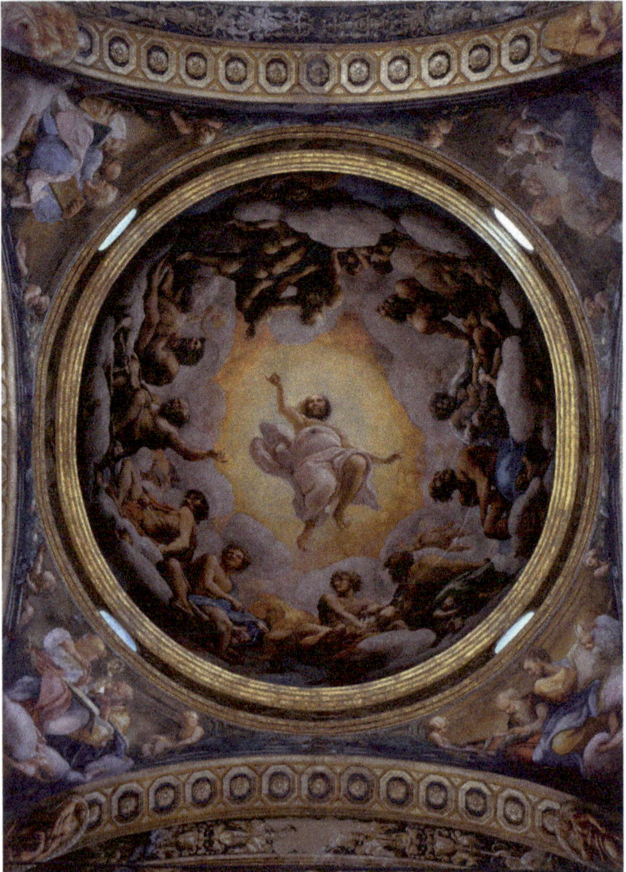

FIGURE 14. Antonio Allegri Correggio, *The Assumption of the Virgin* (ca. 1524–1530). Photograph: Scala/Art Resource, New York.

FIGURE 15. Antonio Allegri Correggio, *The Vision of St. John the Evangelist* (ca. 1520–1521). Photograph: Scala/Art Resource, New York.

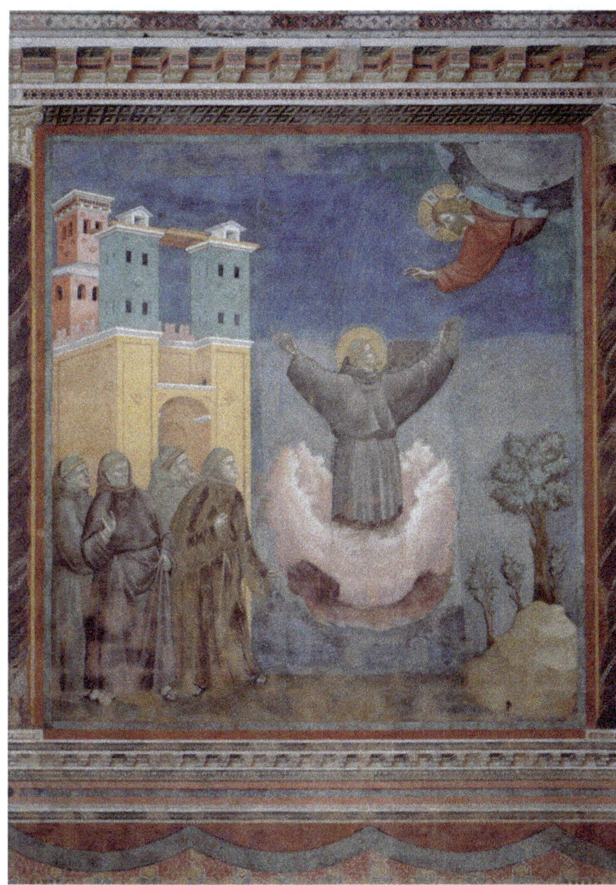

FIGURE 16. School of Giotto di Bondone, *St. Francis in Ecstasy* (ca. 1298). Photograph: Scala/Art Resource, New York.

the element, atmosphere, or even the light in which we catch sight of the divine life.

## CONCEALING CLOUD

When Wolff's *Lucem post nubila reddit* and "The Apotheosis of Electricity" are considered within this religious history of pictures of clouds, one sees again that the clouds that in Giotto's and Correggio's paintings provide the light and place inhabited by divine figures are here in these pictures of the disenchanted world, only in order to disappear in the clearing made by the smiling sun. The banner unfurled by the smiling sun (a task assumed from the angels!) says as much in two short words, *post nubila*, "after the clouds"; this is when the light returns and all can be gathered together in the unity of the clearing it makes. One will now, in the framework set up by modern disenchantment, see most divinely when one sees clearly—that is, when one sees in the light of a light whose illumination clears the clouds.

## INTO THE CLOUD: DILLER + SCOFIDIO'S *BLUR*

The world of modern disenchantment is founded on the exclusion of clouds, fog, mist—anything that, by resisting the clarity afforded by light, would result in blurred edges and hazy borders, indistinct places and insubstantial things. Seen in the clearing made by such light, the world of modern disenchantment includes only objects of a particular character. More specifically, objects seen in the clear light will be distinct and well-defined such that they appear solid and stable. Read together, *Lucem post nubila reddit* and "The Apotheosis of Electricity" reflect this dream of clear and distinct vision and that vision's correlate: the solid and stable world, one you can grasp, not one that floats away, gets lost in the clouds, or is surrendered to the tumultuous sea and its waves.

Who then are the people in this picture (fig. 17)? Down what road do

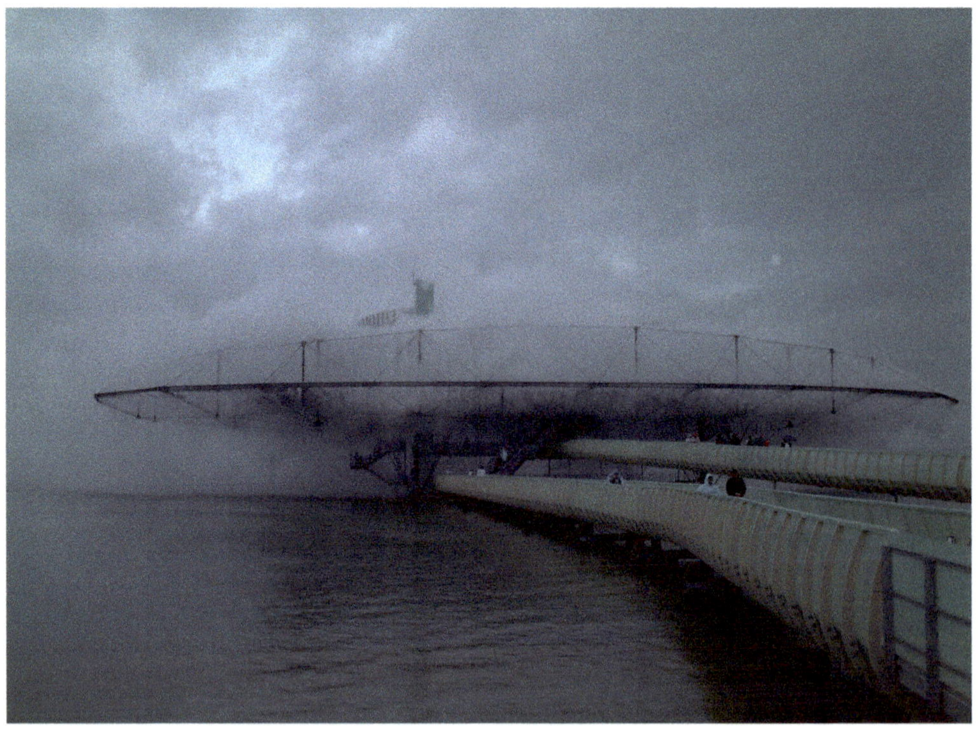

FIGURE 17. Diller + Scofidio, *Blur* (2002). Photograph: Norbert Aepli.

they walk? Is there solid ground ahead, or are they walking into a cloud? Who in the world, in the wake of modern disenchantment, would ever build such an insubstantial, impermanent, and nebulous thing or approach such a shady, doubtful place?

This is *Blur*, a contribution to SwissExpo 2002 by the New York-based architectural team Diller + Scofidio. It is documented in a book entitled, aptly enough, *Blur: The Making of Nothing*, and its project was put forward programmatically in a short quasi-manifesto, "Blur/Babble," by Elizabeth Diller.[4] Acknowledging, then confounding, the picture of the disenchanted world as we see it in *Lucem post nubila reddit* and "The Apotheosis of Electricity," Diller claims that the project aims to think blur positively. "To 'blur' is to make indistinct, to dim, to shroud, to cloud, to make vague, to obfuscate. Blur is equated with the dubious. . . . For our visually obsessed, high-resolution, high-definition culture that measures satisfaction in pixels per inch, blur is understood as a loss. Yet blur can also be thought positively."[5] As architects charged with building the world in which we dwell, Diller + Scofidio aim to make blur habitable, hardly a dream associated with those who want to dwell in a light that banishes clouds. With *Blur*, they proposed that we can live creatively without banishing the indistinct and the unclear, the ephemeral and the unstable.

Throughout the 1980s and 1990s, the years preceding the *Blur* project, Diller and her partner, Ricardo Scofidio, were best known for multimedia, performance-based pieces and site-specific installation work that often led to their being classified as designers or conceptual artists rather than architects. This began to change with *Blur* and, more significantly, with their commission to build a home for the Institute of Contemporary Art in Boston, a commission received in 2001, shortly after their proposal for *Blur* won the contest to develop one of the SwissExpo sites. (The ICA, their first freestanding building in the United States, would open in 2004.) The firm has since received several other high-profile commissions. In 2003 they were hired to redesign the public spaces of Lincoln Center, a commission that quickly grew to include an addition within the School of the American Ballet, an extension of the Julliard School, a renovation of Alice Tully Hall, and a new restaurant in front of the Beaumont Theater. They have also received a significant commission to direct the redesign of the High Line district along the Hudson River in Chelsea, parts of which opened to the public in 2009.[6]

For *Blur*, Diller + Scofidio worked collaboratively with an international team to design and build a cloud, a mist or fog off the shore of Lake Neuchatel in Yverdon, Switzerland, in which visitors would become enveloped travelers, advancing without hope of seeing things in clear light from a privileged, transcendent position outside the picture. Visitors were drawn into the cloud along a four-hundred-foot ramp, which methodically directed them toward and into the incredible vision of *Blur*. They were thus invited to inhabit the crisis of clear and distinct vision. *Blur* was undoubtedly "a spectacle," Diller admits, but a spectacle in which all there is to see dissolves in the omnipresent light of an unimaginable fog: "as the visitor nears the fog mass, visual and acoustical references are slowly erased . . . ; what remains is only an optical 'whiteout' and the 'white noise' of pulsing fog nozzles."[7] She often refers to it as "a spectacle that nevertheless offers little to see." Whether one sees nothing for seeing too much or sees it all when seeing nothing is a distinction that grows increasingly difficult to make clearly as one enters or draws near the cloud.

As they were assumed into the cloud, millions of visitors found "the cloud has enchanted the country," as one journalist wrote. With vision saturated and overexposed, visitors found they had entered a beautiful realm of admiration and wonder and could hardly find words adequate to the beauty to which they had been exposed. Christening it the "wonder-cloud," this same journalist commented excitedly on its excessive beauty: "We don't need the cloud either. It doesn't water our fields nor does it regulate our climate. It is just simply beautiful. . . . The cloud is enchanting visitors right off the bat. What a crazy idiosyncratic thing! How deliciously without purpose! Miracles are possible."[8]

The miracle of this useless wonder-cloud was effected by tech-savvy architects and engineers, who designed and created a complex system of pipes (nearly twenty-four kilometers) and pumps that pushed lake water through atomizers (with some 31,500 nozzles), yielding what the designers frequently called "a habitable medium" in the absence of a solid building or stable form. The computer-driven fog-making technology yielded a formless "building," or rather a building whose form would transform with every gust of wind. On a good day, it measured three hundred feet wide by two hundred feet deep and floated seventy-five feet above the lake, but its dimensions were never certain or stable. Sensitive to fluctuations in the wind and atmosphere, it was always in flux, dissipating as it grew and growing as it dissipated, such that it was always very difficult to know exactly where to draw the line and measure it. Limits grew hard to define as the clarity that would let them appear distinctly was replaced by the hazy light of the cloud.

In an important sense, nothing had been made, for what has been made and on what was it made (where is the ground and where is the grounded), when the thing in question is made from the very water on which it appears, with no permanent standing on solid ground? Indeed, a quixotic "resolve to build on water" was crucial to the concept of the project,[9] and it would take a great amount of re-solve to solve again and again, ever anew, the questions raised by building on rocking, waving depths without surface. Forever dissipating into the lake from which it was made, only to rise again, the cloud was continually being made and unmade, never achieving perfection or permanence, the solidity of objects that count as things in the world pictured by *lucem post nubila reddit* or the apotheosis of electricity. Hardly a heroic vision of the architect as one who builds timeless monuments and establishes permanent places. And hardly a vision of technology guiding ships safely to shore or to some permanent harbor. Visitors in fact followed the inverse path as they were assumed into the cloud and lost the secure grounding of the shore.

## Descartes's clouds: "We no longer have occasion to admire . . ."

The cloud of *Blur* would appear as anything but a "wonder-cloud" to a vision that aims to see a solid and stable world. If the cloud were admitted as "enchanting" or a "wonder," the admission would be made only in order to put us on guard against admiring it. Listen to René Descartes—whom many scholars take to be an, if not *the*, inaugural figure of the modern European Enlightenment—speak about a cloud in the opening pages of his treatise *Les météores*:

> We naturally have greater admiration for things above us than for those which are at the same level or beneath us. Although the clouds hardly exceed the summits of some mountains, and one sees them, often indeed, lower than the tops of our bell towers, all the same, because we must turn our eyes up toward the sky in order to see them, we imagine them so lofty that even the poets and the painters depict them as the throne of God and show him there using his own hands to open and close the doors of the wind, to pour the rain on the flowers and to throw lightning on the rocks. This makes me hope that if I explain their nature, in such a way that we no longer have occasion to admire anything that we see there or that falls from there, one will easily believe that it is possible in the same way to find the causes of everything most wonderful on Earth.[10]

Descartes thus makes it his project to triumph over the wonderful clouds by bringing them down to earth. If this could be done, they might be illuminated by the same cone of light that illuminates "all things in general," and we would have little or no occasion to admire them.

*Les météores* is little read today; it is not even included in one of the most widely used editions of Descartes in the English-speaking world, *The Philosophical Writings of Descartes*, published by Cambridge University Press. Perhaps this is because the program it launched was so effective in putting an end to its subject matter (meteoric weather events, such as clouds) and the gaze that might see it (admiration and wonder). Originally appearing together with *La dioptrique* (concerning optics and vision) and *La géométrie* (concerning geometry), *Les météores* was part of something like an appendix to an essay that is still widely read today, *Discours de la méthode* (*Discourse on the Method*). This mode of publication positions the treatise on meteorology as an outworking or realization of the method whose operation Descartes narrates in the *Discourse*.

## A METHOD FOR CERTAINTY, BEYOND THE SHADOW OF DOUBT

In *Discourse on the Method*, Descartes sought a way to secure for himself the certainty that all his knowledge was true. It was not enough that something simply appear to him and that he know this appearance as truth. Descartes wanted to be certain, certain of these appearances and certain that the knowledge he held was true indubitably. As criteria of this certainty, he proposed that we become more certain of things when they are seen by the mind clearly and distinctly. This implies that what is seen clearly and distinctly appears in a truth that is beyond the shadow of doubt. The problem then becomes knowing in what light things appear clearly and distinctly. In response, Descartes proposes a way to secure clear and distinct vision, a way to shine the proper light, as it were: adopt a procedure for seeking it that adheres to the proper method. "The method which instructs us to follow the correct order, and to enumerate exactly all the relevant factors, contains everything that gives certainty. . . . As I practiced my method I felt my mind gradually become accustomed to conceiving its object more clearly and distinctly."[11]

In stating these concerns, Descartes expresses a grave and serious anxiety that arises with modern disenchantment. If one loses confidence that things might present themselves in their own light or that the light of truth is self-revealing, then one must ask what way leads to them. From the perspective of a disenchanted modernity, it was a delusion of the ancients to trust in a natural luminosity of truth, and the medievals, while they did not believe in a *natural* illumination, were ignorant and superstitious in believing that a *supernatural* light would be given graciously from beyond and allow us to see truly. Both the ancient and medieval position evidenced a naïve trust in what seems to show itself as truth. Mature, enlightened men, by contrast, see the world more as it is shown in "The Apotheosis of Electricity": nature is dark and the heavens concealed by stormy clouds; we cannot count on a self-revealing light of nature or wait for a transcendent light to bring things out of their hiding places; rather, we must be self-assertive and shine a light of our own doing or making.

Whence the eventual apotheosis of electricity—and, anticipating that, Descartes's own effort to shine the light of the mind on all things.

As the world must be illuminated in a light that is not a given, the man of modern disenchantment expresses deep concern about having the light at his disposal. The focus on method is his way to address this concern. The light of truth "is [for modern man] dubious [*zwielichtig* = shady], as long as it lacks a well-ordered origin in *method*. . . . In the idea of 'method,' which originates with Bacon and Descartes, 'light' is thought of as being at man's disposal."[12] Anxious to ensure that the light will indeed be under his control, the first question, preliminary and necessary to all uncovering, revelation, or disclosure of what is, becomes, for modern man, what procedures will ensure the correct operation of this light. If I want to produce the clearing or illumination in which truth will appear beyond a shadow of doubt, what I need to know is *how* to use the light. This means I must follow the proper method. I could, after all, shine a dim, flickering, or diffuse light in which things would not stand still but appear momentarily, would not be shown clearly but in a haze, and would not present themselves distinctly but remain shadowed or shady.

Following Descartes's methodical approach to illuminating the world guarantees that I proceed in such a way as to shine a light in which things will appear clearly and distinctly. Seeing things this way, "we could," he concludes, "know the power and action of fire, water, air, the stars, the heavens and all the other bodies in our environment . . . and we could use this knowledge—as the artisans use theirs—for all the purposes for which it is appropriate, and thus make ourselves, as it were, lords and masters of nature [*maîtres et possesseurs de la nature*]."[13] When the light we shine produces clarity and distinctness, the world that appears in it is at our disposition, ready for our mastery. This light clears a place for a world of reliable objects, ones that render themselves serviceable to the self-assertive project of mastering nature and building a secure world.

## BRINGING THE CLOUDS DOWN TO EARTH

*Les météores*, appended to the *Discourse on the Method*, is one of the treatises in which Descartes will follow the method and "show quite clearly what I can, and what I cannot, achieve in the science" produced in the light cast by adhering to it.[14] In other words, *Les météores* is a realization of the self-assertive human project proposed to the proper devotee of the method. Banishing or killing clouds proves to be one of the first of these achievements, for they induce the admiration that stands paralyzed in wonder, as one looks at what cannot be seen or comprehended clearly or distinctly. How could one so transfixed by beauty, mouth open and head in the clouds, rise to meet the challenge of assuming the self-assertive position of master and possessor, of lighting a darkened nature?

The very first sentences of *Les météores* state the project of neutralizing or leveling the clouds as the necessary prologue to realizing the aim of mastering the earth. After they have been reduced to the measure of the earth, the world that remains will be one in which we will, Descartes concludes, "no longer have occasion to admire anything that we see there... [and can] find the causes of everything most wonderful on Earth." Recall the text:

> We naturally have greater admiration for things above us than for those which are at the same level or beneath us. Although the clouds hardly exceed the summits of some mountains, and one sees them, often indeed, lower than the tops of our bell towers, all the same, because we must turn our eyes up toward the sky in order to see them, we imagine them so lofty that even the poets and the painters depict them as the throne of God and show him there using his own hands to open and close the doors of the wind, to pour the rain on the flowers and to throw lightning on the rocks. This makes me hope that if I explain their nature, in such a way that we no longer have occasion to admire anything that we see there or that falls from there, one will easily believe that it is possible in the same way to find the causes of everything most wonderful on Earth.[15]

Descartes here speaks of his desire to remove occasion for men "to admire" the clouds, chiefly by bringing them down to our level or at least by reminding us that they are not so high as the invisible heavens in which we often suppose them to reside. No god sits enthroned on them if they belong, not to the sky of the heavens, but to the earth and its skies, he implies. Leveling the clouds brings them down to earth so that if they appear they will appear for one whose interest has been redirected from contemplation of the sky to curious investigation of the earth. In other words, Descartes's method reduces the wonderful clouds and all that falls surprisingly from them (*ceraunies*, lightning, rain, Correggio's Christ) to obedient citizens subject to the laws of the mundane earth. With all the turbulence of motion through cloudy skies removed, nothing that happens will befall us—fall upon us accidentally or unexpectedly from obscure heavens or skies clouded over by hidden causes. If ordinarily we must look up to the clouds, Descartes proposes instead that, lest we grow dizzy with our heads thrown back in admiration, we should look out—look *out* for what is coming by looking out, not *up*, as if into a lit room. Descartes's leveling of the clouds exorcises the world of its mystery by putting an end to the horizon that is part of the picture when earth meets sky, assuming a sky to be there for the earth to meet. With no horizon, the visible world does not include within it any intimation of an invisible beyond.

## FROM "CAUSE TO WONDER" TO "CAUSE THAT EXPLAINS"

In removing "occasion to admire" the clouds, Descartes hopes to "find the causes of everything most wonderful on Earth." When clouds have been banished from disenchanted skies, one can hope that the causes of everything will appear clearly and distinctly. Here Descartes's methodical approach to clouds partakes of a major turn by which wonder was detached from admiration or awe and paired with the curiosity that seeks, methodically, a cause that explains. The wonder of the clouds is not denied; they are indeed among the things "most admirable on the earth." Descartes's Latin translator calls them *mirabilia*. What Descartes rejects is the attitude of the man who will stand rapt in contemplation or admiration before such wonders, leaving them unexplained and their causes shadowy.

This can be understood in relation to two responses to the wonder of the world: the curiosity of the nascent sciences of modern disenchantment, on one hand, and, on the other, the admiration of the medievals. The historian Lorraine Daston writes, "According to much of early modern psychology, wonder and admiration were the fuses which ignited curiosity. . . . This coupling of wonder and curiosity contrasts sharply with Augustine's pairing of wonder and reverent awe. For Augustine, the astronomers' proud curiosity was due to *lack* of wonder; for Descartes, curiosity was the *effect* of wonder. Without wonder there would be no curiosity, without curiosity, no science."[16] For Augustine and the medieval Christianity he represents, Daston argues, Descartes's curious investigation into causes that will explain "everything most wonderful on Earth" (first of all the clouds) would evidence a lack of true wonder; true wonder would lead to awe and admiration, not the methodical pursuit of an explanation.

It is important to note, too, that when wonder is made part of the methodical pursuit of certain knowledge, cause is understood differently. "Explaining their nature," Descartes believes, will remove occasion for admiring the clouds. With our eyes opened wide by an explanation, the wonder of the earth will be reduced to its causal explanation. The sequence is worth noting. The removal of the occasion to admire happens when we offer an explanation, and this explanation gives access to the cause of all the wonders on the earth. Significantly, the causes that come to light when the light is shined by Descartes's methodical procedure do not serve the same purpose as do the causes to which most medievals hoped to lead our mind. In much of medieval theology, running from certain strands of Augustine to the nominalist theologians of the late Middle Ages, pursuit of cause heightened our ignorance or led us deeper into the mystery of the world. Augustine, for example, referring to the astronomers' all too earthly knowledge of the skies, will object that their curiosity leads them away from the cause of all and therefore distracts the mind from reverential admiration: the knowledge the astronomers (whom we might call astrologers) gain of the law-governed movements of the stars informs them of the future, not of the secret origin of the heavenly bodies in hidden causes, and ultimately the mysterious cause of all. Rather than seeking this ultimate cause and thereby highlighting the mysterious depths out of which the world might have come, steps that lead to awe and reverence, the astronomers seek a law or explanation that makes the future available, brings it out from beyond the (eliminated) horizon, and lets them predict what is coming.

The causes that come to light by following Descartes's method, disenchanting the skies, are, in contrast to Augustine, causes that also explain. As Daston puts it, for Descartes, "ignorance of causes was a prime component of wonder, and a stimulant to scientific curiosity. . . . This brand of wonder had been decoupled from its originally religious context, in which the wonder of ignorance had been the hallmark of the marvelous and the miraculous."[17] For Augustine, one feels wonder before the hidden and secret. This sense of hiddenness was enhanced by pursuing cause because the cause was ultimately hidden in the divine mystery. Pursuit of cause was therefore a means to inspire awe and reverence, not curiosity; the more the world became an effect, the more its made or contingent character was highlighted, the more awe-inspiring it was, and the more one stood reverently.

Descartes, by contrast, seeks causes as part of a project aiming at an explanation that will remove occasion for admiration and serve the self-assertive project of becoming master and possessor of nature. These must be causes that afford a knowledge that allows one to reproduce or make the effect—namely, mechanical causes, obedient to laws and predictable or regular in such a way that one can rely on their operation, as on a machine. This triumph over the wonder-inducing cause eliminates what might befall us contingently or out of a cloud, like the rainstorm or singular lightning. All that happens has a reason when nothing befalls us contingently, from the hand of a God who manipulates the world or by virtue of a "danced causality" of uncertain effect or from out of cloud-covered skies.

## Blurring technologies

If the fog or cloud of *Blur* offered an experience of a vaporized, massless or light world, it provided the perfect setting, Scofidio claims, for the experience of "another all-pervading, yet massless medium"[18] of light and flickering messages: the Internet.

### LONGING TO SEE THE FACE OF OTHERS

The *Blur* project proposed to include a media installation, called *Babble*, a central core in which vertical LED columns would serve as glowing signboards, displaying messages that would appear inside the cloud, resolve themselves in the cleared space, and then disappear again in the fog. "Messages sent out to the Net by participants climb up the field of LED columns; responses rain down,"[19] in a storm of information brought on by the luminous cloud of fiber optic cable and electromagnetic waves encircling our globe and making up our telecommunications networks. The flickering lights of the tower of *Babble* would record and display communications exchanged by anonymous, international visitors on shore, but for all intents and purposes these lights would come from nowhere, an unattainable beyond, an unseen and incomprehensible source of flickering signs glimpsed in the cloud but never fully deciphered. Those inside the cloud would never know but always have to believe that the signs glimpsed in this torrential downpour did in fact come from somewhere and someone—and that they meant something.

Whether or not anything in this flow of messages was intended for me, inside the cloud, was something of which I would never be certain, but I would still, as any user of the Internet has experienced, feel an intense, addictive connection with these others whose face I longed to see. This connection was maintained even as I remained in foggy incomprehension of whom I might be connected to—and of whether the messages were meant for me or, for that matter, for anyone. Cyberspace is populated by those longing for connection in the heart of a cloud where one cannot see clearly or distinctly the face of those others to whom one is nevertheless connected.

To enact this, Diller + Scofidio planned to design what they called a "braincoat," which users would don upon entering the cloud. The braincoats were to be programmed on shore with profiles created by users through their responses to a simple set of questions. The information in each user's profile would be broadcast electronically into the cloud, such that the cloud itself would be not just a cloud of vapor but also a cloud of information communicated anonymously by all the users who participated in it. Braincoats would not only transmit information; they would also receive it and respond to it. When two information profiles connected, the braincoat would respond positively or negatively, blushing red or lighting up green, for instance. Braincoats could also interact with web users through the central LED tower. Notably, these connections would be made in the absence of a certain awareness of what exactly it was that one might have in common with the other, whose face and identifying features remained lost in the cloud.

The babbling stream of signs in *Babble*'s central LED tower would make for a place saturated with meaning and message, ever rambling on but never brought to a stand where it could be grasped clearly. Anything significant that did appear would be seen like lightning flashes—a message pulled from the noise, momentarily and often discontinuously, only at pains connected with what preceded and followed. The cloud in this way, Scofidio claimed, would make "palpable the ineffable and scaleless space and time of global communications" in an interconnected world whose complexity exceeds what any individual can see clearly or distinctly, but in which we nevertheless participate.[20]

Like the biblical tower of Babel, however, *Babble* was never completed and the braincoats never produced. This part of the project could not be funded owing to the seizing up of liquidity in financial markets built on the cloud of expectation surrounding the vague promise of profiting from the Internet. One of the participants in the design team, Ben Rubin, would, however, go on to be principal in a project that realized a version of *Babble*, though without the cloud as setting. Created in collaboration with Mark Hansen, the project, called *Listening Post*, can be explored online.[21]

## TECHNOLOGICALLY INDUCED GLOBAL BLUR

In connecting one of the most significant emblems of modern technology (the Internet and Worldwide Web) with a cloud, Diller + Scofidio are a far cry from "The Apotheosis of Electricity," where technology is supposed to make a solid and stable world by clearing or banishing clouds. In *Blur*, technology produces a cloud in which we dwell with things, people, and messages of which we have only dim awareness yet a clear feeling of connection. The prescience of building a cloud as the place to inhabit the world of today's telecommunication networks is evident in that one of the prevalent models for computing in 2009 and beyond has been "cloud computing"—a model in which users connect with applications and others that exist virtually, in no particular place but spread across the network, acting together only when activated by a remote user.

Dwelling in what the designers and builders of this technological

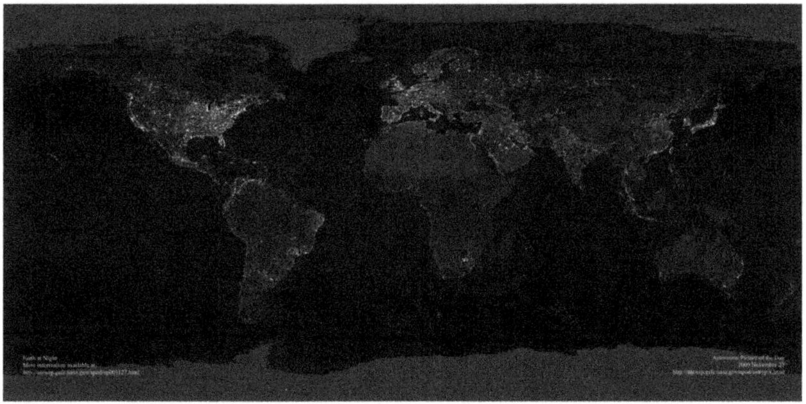

FIGURE 18. Satellite photograph of earth at night (n.d.). Photograph: C. Mayhew and R. Simmon (NASA/GSFC), NOAA/ NGDC, DMSP Digital Archive.

infrastructure call "the cloud" has had profound consequences for our relations and connections with others and the world. As the cloud more and more becomes the place of these connections and relations, and the temporal and spatial difference supposed by communication are overcome by nearly instantaneous and omnipresent transmission, we more and more *interact*, moving together as a faceless mass in one extended present, rather than *communicate*.[22] What communication still remains increasingly involves transmissions between faceless senders and receivers of messages who long to draw near to one another in and through the medium of "the cloud," but find the sought-after face-to-face meeting constantly deferred by that very medium. How much easier it is to stay in touch thanks to the cloud of telecommunications, but how far away we find ourselves from the faces of those with whom we remain in contact.

The technological cloud where we meet one another today spells the end of the model of light as a cone of rays caused by a point or source separate from it. The light in which our world appears is the light cast by the luminous web of fiber-optic cables and electromagnetic waves that encircle the globe like what Paul Virilio has called "a second sun that illuminates the expanse of our territories." Witness the satellite photographs of an increasingly urbanized world, fast becoming a single, global city (fig. 18). Where has the sun gone, and who needs it anyway? Today, the earth, on Virilio's reading, illuminates itself by the light of transmitting signals. When the sun is not needed to bring the earth to light, one sees the evaporation of the founding distinction between the sun in the sky and the earth it illuminates, the light and the lighted, the ground and the grounded. The technologies of light and illumination that were supposed to render the world clear and distinct have outdone themselves and produced a global blur—a cloud of light.

One might be tempted to despair of the indistinct blur of this all-encompassing light. Claiming that "we are faced with an apocalyptic time," Virilio himself despairs that "the planet is becoming uninhabitable."[23] Others might despair of despairing and instead seek, desperately, clear and distinct places in which to dwell with solid and stable objects, maintaining a knowledge of who they are and where they are going by securing hard and fast lines, definite borders to delineate the place where they belong. Sometimes this desperate search shows itself in the certainties of a religion confident it has access to a divine perspective that illuminates the place of everything. Sometimes it shows itself in the confidence of a techno-science certain that knowledge and technique afford control over the light in which everything else comes to light. *Lucem post nubila reddit* is, in short, as likely to be adopted by the scientific devotee of a truth shown with certainty in the light of reason as it is by the devout religious believer who knows exactly a truth he believes that only a god with a smiling face brings. Both remain faithful, and desperate, believers in the myth of technological control—the myth that methodically operated technologies (prayer, righteousness, the bulldozer, the lighthouse) afford mastery and control.

A myth of desperation.

Rather than despair or flee, Diller + Scofidio propose that we try to live creatively in this supersaturated world-cloud where erasing the distinction between founding and founded, light and lighted, means the absence of the space of the clear and distinct. *Blur/Babble* is that endeavor, a creative affirmation of the cloud that figures the conditions in which life is lived by today's technological humanity.

## What is so divine about life in a cloud?

Amid the flickering lights of the all-encompassing cloud, what would travelers who dwell in *Blur* "experience"? One saw less and less; there were fewer and fewer images or things to see amid the "optical 'whiteout' and the 'white noise' of pulsing fog nozzles."[24] As one advanced, distinctive characteristics of the objects we experience clearly and distinctly were removed, and one became a resident of what Diller + Scofidio called the "featureless, depthless, scaleless, spaceless, massless, surfaceless" world of the cloud. And yet, though one saw less and less, light was everywhere, and one saw more and more, even if nothing clear and distinct. There was indeed a lot to see, so much that one could not take it all in and found oneself with a vision saturated, overexposed, and blurred by the surfeit given to see. As Tom Keenan, an eloquent member of the design team, noted, “If we are talking about blurs, it is hard to say that there is ever just one.”[25] Visions multiply and vision is multiple; one loses the clear and distinct vision of stable reality. Things are far from certain but grow doubtful—in a literal sense if we accept one of the proposed etymologies of “to doubt”: *duo-habere*, to hold or consider more than one.

As Keenan goes on to observe, light inside a cloud is everywhere equally because it comes from nowhere in particular: any identifiable, external source is lost in the light it sheds. The model of light as a cone, so crucial to modern disenchantment's picture of the world, is broken as the summit proves invisible and ungraspable, the cause (source of light) missing from the effect (light that illuminates), which nevertheless remains in effect. This light that is everywhere affords no clarity, as it is not withdrawn from the space it illuminates but saturates and overexposes all that appears in it. Features and surfaces, scale and depth, the distinction of center and margin, all that would make for a solid and stable world, is dissolved when space is not empty but full of such a light. Despite this loss of center or origin, Keenan points out, in a cloud, “strangely things are not bleak but bright.”[26]

In seeing a bright spot in the clouds themselves, a light in the cloud that blurs clear and distinct vision, Keenan bespeaks an optimism of uncertain grounds. He shows a willingness to abandon the model of light that clears a place for dwelling with the solid and stable to dwell creatively within the cloud of our global blur.

## SEEING DIVINELY: IN A CLOUD OF LIGHT OR IN LIGHT OF A CLOUD

The question of dwelling creatively is in some basic sense the question of building and architecture, but I have been trained as a theologian and know that the task of making our global blur habitable—indeed of making any world habitable—is also in some ways a question for religion. But what could possibly be divine about life in inside a cloud? Is there a model of religion that sees a revelation of the divine life not when the clouds part, as in *Lucem post nubila reddit,* but in the cloud itself?

The answer can be Yes, if we get our model of religion from mystical theologies, for an important motif within them is what came to be called the “cloud of unknowing.”[27] According to such theological visions, the encounter with the divine happens in a cloud. This is put most directly by the anonymous author of the medieval classic *The Cloud of Unknowing*: “This darkness and cloud is always between you and your God, no matter what you do, and it prevents you from seeing him clearly by the light of understanding.... If you are to experience him or to see him at all..., it must always be in this cloud and in this darkness."[28]

Urging the seeker of the divine life to put behind himself every "clear picture," since such a picture can only be of "something beneath God," the anonymous author of *The Cloud of Unknowing* exhorts his reader, "lift up your love to that cloud"—as if the lover of clouds was not a stranger to be banished but a true devotee of the divine life.[29] Indeed, the entire treatise is something like a manual or guide in the proper method or technique of directing one's love into the cloud—a sharp contrast from Descartes's method for rightly conducting one's reason into the clarity where one could be certain of where one is and what appeared in truth. The author describes his work on the cloud as an exercise ("I call this exercise a darkness or a cloud") and claims that its intent is to show us "how that hidden love, raised up in purity of spirit upon this dark cloud of unknowing, delicately and perfectly contains in itself perfect virtue."[30] It would appear, then, that for this theological tradition, staying in the cloud, without wanting to clear things up, is the virtuosic approach of the divine life. Things appear in truth in light of a cloud or in a cloud of light.

"The cloud of unknowing" has roots in a long tradition of mystical theology, going back at least to the mysterious Christian author Dionysius, and through him to biblical precedents, chiefly in the life of Moses and the experience of the lover in the Song of Songs. Dionysius's own identity remains nebulous. Long thought to be the Athenian named Dionysius, whose conversion by Paul on the Areopagus hill is recorded in Acts 17:34, this identification was refuted in the nineteenth century, though suspicions had arisen much earlier, especially among the Renaissance humanists and the Reformers. His identity demystified by the scientific studies of modern scholars, Dionysius became known as Pseudo-Dionysius, with scholars in the know pushing his life ahead several centuries, from contemporaneousness with Paul to somewhere around 500 CE. His place of work is agreed to have been present-day Syria. Dionysius's importance to medieval theology and to the history of mysticism is widely recognized—and has been asserted by the authority Bernard McGinn: "This still-unidentified figure not only created the term 'mystical theology,' but also gave systematic expression to a dialectical view of the relation of God and the world that was the fountainhead of speculative mystical systems for at least a thousand years."[31]

The phrase "cloud of unknowing" has conceptual roots and historical parentage in a passage from Dionysius's short but pregnant text known as "The Mystical Theology." The passage concerns Moses and the biblical account of his ascent of Mount Sinai into a cloud where he received a passing vision of the glory of God. In fact, the text in Dionysius speaks not of a cloud but of darkness: "he [Moses] plunges into the truly mysterious darkness of unknowing."[32] Indeed, the author of *The Cloud of Unknowing* renders the phrase as "the darkness of unknowing" in his own translation of Dionysius's Greek text, a rendering that he claims "clarifies [the difficulties of the literal text by] following the interpretation of the Abbot of St. Victor."[33] The near synonymy of darkness and cloud appears, too, in the text of *The Cloud of Unknowing* itself, when the author juxtaposes the terms: "If you are to experience him or to see him at all . . . , it must always be in this cloud and in this darkness."[34]

A similar confusion of darkness and cloud appears in another important mystical text, the treatise known as *The Life of Moses* by the Cappadocian father Gregory of Nyssa, written around 390 CE. Gregory observes that, according to biblical accounts, Moses led the people up from Egypt guided by a cloud: "By divine power a cloud led the people. . . . Moses himself watched the cloud, and he taught the people to keep it in sight. . . . They always rested from their march wherever the cloud indicated by stopping, and they departed again whenever the cloud led the way on. . . ." The cloud is also for Gregory the place where Moses will encounter the glory of God, the scene or setting for the revelation atop Mount Sinai. "Then the clear light of the atmosphere was darkened so that the mountain became invisible, wrapped in a dark cloud." But Gregory's account will also tend to use the language of darkness precisely in those place where the narrative would seem to suggest he speak of a cloud: "he [Moses] boldly approached the very darkness itself and entered the invisible things"; "After he was instructed in these and other such things by the ineffable teaching of God while he was surrounded by that invisible darkness, and having surpassed himself by the aid of the mystical doctrines, he emerged again out of the darkness."[35]

One could take this confusion of darkness and cloud to mean that mystical theology equates clouds with darkness and wants us to live simply in the dark. This reading, I believe, would reflect a coding of cloud governed by the framework of modern disenchantment. That is to say, if light can arrive only after clouds have been banished (*lucem post nubila reddit*), then of course clouds will be equated with darkness, and revelation will be complete only when clouds vanish and we see all things clearly in the light of the smiling face of the sun.

But I do not think that this is how the mystical theologians of the cloud of unknowing see matters. However dark the cloud might be, it remains for them the place of revelation, the place where Moses goes to see and sees the light or glory of God. As Gregory reminds us, "when Moses grew in knowledge, he declared that he had seen God in the darkness . . . for the text says that *Moses approached the dark cloud where God was*."[36] The cloud, as the place where Moses sees God, is therefore not understood as darkness pure and simple, opposed to clear light and in which nothing can be seen at all. Rather the cloud is what Gregory calls "the luminous darkness"; there Moses lives in the divine presence, as one might dwell in a cloud where the luminosity that shines from everywhere but nowhere in particular saturates vision, overexposes it, and leaves you in the dark, seeing all. Tom Keenan's hypothesis regarding *Blur* and the uncertain world it calls us to inhabit ("in a cloud strangely things are not bleak but bright") seems divine when read in terms of the mystical theology.

In an important predecessor to the author of *The Cloud of Unknowing*, Richard of St. Victor (d. 1173), we find another text conveying the sense that a cloud, however bleak, is bright, a "luminous darkness" in which we might have divine visions in a light that does not clarify.[37] On Richard's reading, what is to be disclosed to Moses—what will come to light when he ascends the mountain—is the ark. Moses does indeed receive this vision of the ark, yet the light in which he sees is not the light of a clearing but of a cloud: "In order that Moses might be able to see the ark . . . , he ascended the mountain and entered into the cloud. . . . Moses enters into the middle of the cloud when the human spirit, overtaken by the boundlessness of the divine light, is put into a state of sleep with supreme forgetfulness of self. . . . You ought justly to marvel, how the cloud harmonizes with the fire [i.e., a source of light], and the fire with the cloud."[38] For Richard, then, cloud is not opposed to light (i.e., fire) but "harmonizes" with it. Here the cloud is made by the overabundance of radiance or brilliance of a light source that, shining boundlessly, exceeds Moses's capacity to receive it. What comes into the picture with such a cloud of light, or what gets into the picture in the light of such a cloud, is the mystical ark—the highest, most divine, vision of all there is.

A lovely phrase from Thomas Gallus (d. 1246), whose contribution to the Dionysian renaissance of the later Middle Ages is widely recognized, helps formulate what I have alluded to as a cloud of light or the light of a cloud. Commenting on the line "I am black but beautiful," found in the Song of Songs, Gallus connects blackness not simply with darkness or the privation, removal, or negation of all distinguishing features (colors), but with a cloud that is, he says, "superlucent." He writes, "'I am black,' that is, enveloped in the superlucent cloud of divine incomprehensibility."[39] Here the black or darkness of the cloud is not simply the absence of light or the opposite of light; it is instead a result of superlucence, that is to say, of a light above or beyond light.

What Gallus's "superlucent cloud" suggests is that "cloud" need not be taken as a negative term, like "darkness," but can be read instead as a term belonging to that very special mode of theological language known as eminent predication or sur-eminence. These terms were meant to address the loftiest mysteries of the divine life itself. Formed by adding the prefix "hyper-" (in Greek) or "super-" (in Latin) or "beyond" or "transcendent" (in English renderings) to attributes or qualities we predicate of something, these terms are positive in form but negative in content. That is to say, while they have the form appropriate to what is most high, lofty, or transcendent in divinity, they contain no affirmation and make no assertion of what we might know or see clearly and distinctly regarding that transcendence of divinity. In saying that a cloud is superlucent (beyond bright), we confess our own ignorance and inability to see distinctly how bright it is or even to say it is bright at all; it is a way of saying that we do not know its measure or comprehend its totality. And yet the incomprehension and ignorance, the lack of a clear and distinct vision, confessed when the theologian calls a cloud superlucent is not the same as equating it with a negative term like darkness or night. This equation would simply affirm a negative or assert that cloud is indeed dark, as if that negative were something we saw clearly and distinctly to be true of the object in question. On the contrary, calling the cloud superlucent says that it is brighter than bright, more light than light, in such a way that it is not opposed to light and therefore need not disappear for the light to come.

Theologically speaking, then, cloud is not dark; indeed, the darkness that negates light must itself be negated or overcome. The superlucent cloud is the negation of this darkness, itself a negation of light, but the superlucent cloud negates darkness without returning simply to the light in which things are seen clearly and distinctly. Superlucent is not the same as lucent or light; superlucence passes beyond the light just as it passes beyond the darkness that negates the light—passing beyond, transcending, into clouds that now lie at (or better, beyond) the summit of a mountain or cone that one must ascend as one makes progress toward revelation or enlightenment. One sees most divinely in light of a cloud, albeit not clearly or distinctly.

## THE LIGHT LOST IN THE LIGHT: CLOUDS, ANGELS, AND THE FACE OF GOD

When Dionysius recounts the ascent of Moses, he notes that as Moses "pushes ahead to the summit of the divine ascents . . . , he sees the many lights, pure and with rays streaming abundantly." But though he might see the light and rays shining in great abundance, Moses does not see God himself. The source of the rays remains lost or invisible, as if the summit had been detached from the mountain, the peak cut off from the cone of light. "He [Moses] does not meet God himself, but contemplates, not him who is invisible, but rather where he dwells."[40] This divine dwelling place is not a clearing but a superlucent cloud of light, in which Moses does indeed see divinely, seeing God in the invisible source of the luminous rays of a light that is everywhere and so without distinct place for its source.

Dionysius's theological account of Moses's ascent thus frustrates those like Jonathan Crary who would speak of a point-to-point model of light and observe "how deeply theological was the notion that light was radiant (composed of rays)."[41] While this model might pertain to theologies fitting the framework set up by modern disenchantment (Wolff's *Lucem post nubila reddit* clearly fits Crary's model), it does not pertain to the mystical theologians for whom the source is lost amid the light it shines. When the source is lost in this way, it does not occupy a position as available to or as easily manipulated by "the apotheosis of electricity" and other such technologies. Dionysius will liken this nonconic theological account of light and its rays to fire: "The Word of God seems to honor the depiction of fire above all others.... Visible fire is, after all, so to speak, in everything. It passes undiluted through everything and yet continues to be completely beyond them. It lights up everything and remains hidden at the same time."[42] The all-embracing light in which everything appears remains hidden amid the light it shines. Universal light and the enlightened universe thereby testify to the divine ubiquity *and* to the absence of the divine in this very omnipresence—as if divinity were a cloud.

This is witnessed by the angels. Dionysius claims that the angels are the divine radiance, the first revelation or shining of the dark hidden divine light as it bursts forth into the universe. They therefore have "the first and most diverse participation in the divine, and they, in turn, provide the first and most diverse revelations of the divine hiddenness. That is why they have the title angel or messenger." But just as in a cloud the source of light is lost or dark amid the brightness of light, so too in the angelic orders is the divine light hidden amid the light it shines in and as these angelic communications. Hence, Dionysius observes, "the word of God represents [the angels] also as clouds," and he goes on to give the following explanation of a cloud: "This is to show that the holy and intelligent beings are filled in a transcendent way with hidden light." Overfilled by a superlucent light, the angels make up a divine cloud, which Dionysius calls, when speaking again of the angels, "the divine place of the Godhead's rest."[43] Those who seek to live as intimately or as closely connected with divinity as possible endeavor to follow this angelic paradigm and, as Gregory of Nyssa tells us, "seek God hidden in the cloud" (fig. 19).

A beautiful text from Nicholas of Cusa (d. 1464) conveys the sense in which the pursuit of the divine life means learning to live in a cloud. The

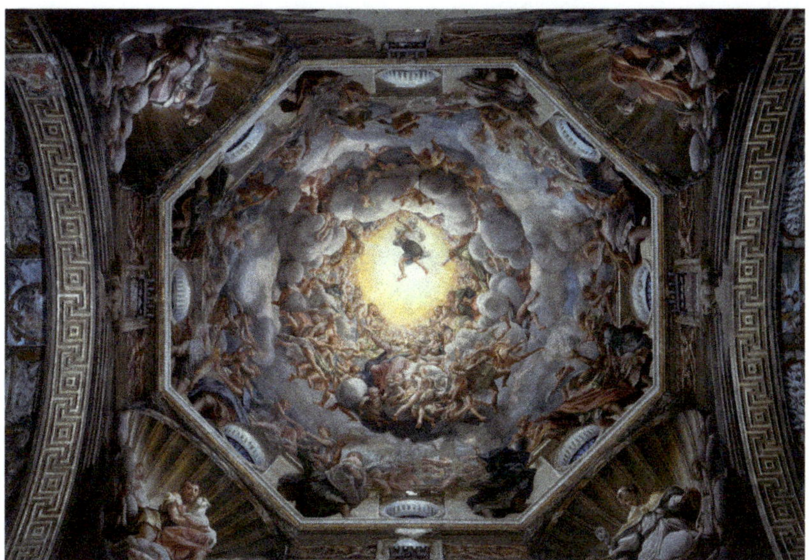

FIGURE 19. Antonio Allegri Correggio, *The Assumption of the Virgin* (ca. 1524–1530). Photograph: Scala/Art Resource, New York.

cloud proves revelatory, according to the mystical logic of superlucence, and is the very place where one meets the clouded face of divinity:

> This cloud, mist, darkness, or ignorance into which whoever seeks your face enters when one leaps beyond every knowledge and concept is such that below it your face cannot be found except veiled. But *this very cloud reveals your face* to be there beyond all veils, just as when our eye seeks to view the light of the sun, which is the sun's face, it first sees it veiled in the stars and in the colors and in all the things which participate its light. But when the eye strives to gaze at the light unveiled, it looks beyond all visible light . . . it knows that so long as it sees anything, what it sees is not what it is seeking. Therefore it must leap beyond every visible light . . . and thus is darkness to the eye. And while one is in that darkness, which is a cloud, if one then knows one is in a cloud, one knows that one has come near the face of the sun. For that cloud in one's eye originates from the exceeding brightness of the light of the sun. The denser, therefore, one knows the cloud to be the more one truly attains the visible light in the cloud.[44]

Those seeking to connect with the face of God look for him not in the parting of the clouds, but in the cloud where "one knows that one has come near the face of the sun." As one draws nearer to the inaccessible divine light of this face, one's world becomes darker and denser: the very abundance of light shining from the face has dazzled and overexposed the vision of the one who sees it, leaving him to see all the less clearly the more he sees the light. The face of the sun shining, Nicholas says, makes not a clearing but a cloud. This is a cloud into which (not through which) one must look and venture, in order to dwell close to the face that has no distinct place but is lost in it. Entering the cloud in pursuit of the divine life means leaving behind the world of solid and stable objects seen clearly and placed distinctly to run after the elusive and mysterious, the face that is seen less and less clearly the more truly one attains sight of it.

## "Love and other technologies" for abiding (in) the cloud[45]

Mystical theology teaches that those who want to follow the angels and live in approximation of the divine life must heed the invitation of the author of *The Cloud of Unknowing* to "come to this cloud, and live and work in it, as I bid you to do,"[46] just as those seeking connection with the face of others on Lake Neuchatel in 2002 learned to dwell in a technologically induced cloud or blur. Making progress on such a search requires skills or practices, methods and techniques, that, far from clearing up matters, maintain one in this cloud or cloudy place. What are they?

### THE INEFFICIENT TECHNOLOGIES OF *BLUR*

If the clearing in which what comes to light might come to light is made by technology, then a consideration of the technologies used by Diller + Scofidio might help at this point. Opposite "The Apotheosis of Electricity," their technologies move us away from clarity and distinctness, introducing us into the clouds and bringing us to inhabit the blur of a world without clear and distinct, high-definition or high-resolution images.

Having renounced the dream of technological mastery as a means of progress toward a more enlightened future, *Blur* can be understood as an example of "*inefficient* technologies."[47] They are inefficient in two senses: first, in that they do not have definite effects or make (effect) anything solid and stable like an object that could be set before me and secured in permanence, and second, in that their technologies do not offer ultimate security, certainty, or control; the things generated out of their operation are hardly part of the calculable world made by "the apotheosis of electricity." Instead, these technologies bring to light things that appear when we abandon the myth that technology should be something man masters and controls as part of a project of becoming "master and possessor" of the world.

The blur brought into being by such inefficient technologies is, Diller says, “going to be very naughty,” much like our children and all that comes to be in the love we have for them.[48] Just as raising a child is less about practicing self-assertive techniques of control over a calculable object and more about cultivating patient, indeed loving, techniques of constantly renegotiating a changing relationship with what grows on and with you, so too did Diller take delight in her relationship with a naughty project that would not always work in predicted ways. One might even say she loved it.

The technologies of *Blur* engaged in a constant change and adaptation to an environment they also created. They did not so much produce or make an object as they let loose a cloud that grew with and beyond it so that it might give back to its maker and have an effect on its cause. The cause does not remain the same after the effect has been produced, just as a parent cannot remain him or herself when the child is born, cared for, and looked after. Ashley Schafer describes this coadaptive system, made up of the cloud and the technologies that brought it to be:

> The system combined software with data from weather sensors that continually monitored temperature, humidity, and wind speed. Every eight minutes, the system compared current conditions with saved scenarios, adjusting the output of the eighty-eight high pressure pumps to maintain an “acceptable quality of fog.” The ever-changing form’s dimensions and configuration remained indeterminate and unpredictable for the duration of the Expo, to the periodic dismay of adjacent café and bar owners—especially on cool days, when the “building” came ashore. The constant fluctuation in *Blur’s* shape, size, density, and location emerged as a result of technology “out of control.”[49]

With “technology ‘out of control,’” the future of our relation with *Blur* becomes open and indefinite. Indeed, *Blur* has a future precisely because, its makers having renounced technological control in order to maintain a relation with this “naughty” cloud, it will never be the same in response to its partner.

The *Blur* project had a highly sophisticated, scientifically designed “climate control system” that could detect fluctuations in wind speed or variations in atmospheric temperature and pressure and adjust the pumping system accordingly to produce more or less cloud on this side or that. In this sense, the cloud is, Diller claims, “always unstable, always trying to correct itself.” “The project,” she continues, “is always out of control, while the system is thinking to get into control in some way.”[50] You might say that the cloud is always being born again in each moment owing to the never-ending effect that is produced on it by the environment it has shaped. Thanks to a sophisticated but inefficient technology, *Blur* was a never comprehended and forever incomplete mystery. As Schafer noted, “Blur’s irregular cloud in constant flux is an example of uncontrolled and uncontrollable excess,” as it involves techniques that overreach the grasp of their supposed masters.[51] Here technology “made” (perhaps “enacted” or “performed” are better words) not a solid, stable object but a cloud—an uncontainable, unmappable fog of vapor swarming in unending flux or turbulence that was ever again unmaking and making itself.

One of the crucial ingredients of the indeterminacy and unpredictability of the building was the way in which the inefficient technologies of *Blur* embraced a temporal lag or delay rather than seeking to erase it in the immediacy and simultaneity of a total present. There was an eight-minute interval between the weather monitors’ detection of a change in atmospheric conditions and the system’s response. Out of this interval, unexpected effects emerged and the communication of singular events became possible. “This lag time made for adjusting to lone gusts of wind impossible, and even gradual weather changes were accommodated slightly after the fact, producing a constant variation in the density, shape, and limits of the fog. This instability affected the form of the fog,” making it never quite fit in with the conditions or situation in which it emerged and permitting effects to emerge that could not be sufficiently accounted for by their causes.[52] That “lone gust of wind,” little more than a breath of air blowing for only a moment, would communicate itself in an inefficient system whose technology was designed not so much to absorb or repress this singular gust as to register it. Just as we delight in our children’s singular initiative and incalculable responses, Diller seems wonderfully pleased that this cloud should prove so indeterminate, unpredictable, and “naughty.”

But can we too look forward to dwelling in the world opened by such technologies? Can we say “yes,” joyfully, to the hazy and unpredictable things, seen only indefinitely, that might come to light in this cloudy clearing? Does abiding (in) such a cloud offer any charms? Is it appealing in any way? In short, is there any way for us to love such a cloud?

## LOVING WITHOUT ANY CLEAR IDEA

In fact, *The Cloud of Unknowing* is itself very much a treatise on love, and mystical theology might therefore provide some guidance as to how we might come to see a cloud as worthy of love, indeed how we might come to see love as the method to abide (in) such a cloud. If the author refers to the work as an “exercise” and calls “this exercise a darkness or a cloud,” the exercise to which he refers is love: “I write as I do [to show] you the worthiness of this spiritual exercise... how that hidden love, raised up in purity of spirit upon this dark cloud of unknowing between you and your God, delicately and perfectly contains in itself the perfect virtue of humility, without any particular or clearly defined sight of anything under God."[53] The book can be read, I believe, as a technical manual in the exercise of love—the "method" for maintaining yourself in the cloud, which is the divine place.

The *Cloud* author is not alone in teaching love as this affirmation of seeing in a cloud of light. For many mystical theologians, it is precisely love that stays inside the cloud without wanting to clear things up—or, seen the other way, to love one must find life in the cloud divine.

Consider Gregory of Nyssa. His commentary on the great biblical love poem, the Song of Songs, intended to teach "lovers of transcendent beauty" where and how they might live in the presence of their beloved. Ventriloquizing the bride, he exclaims, "I seek him hidden in the cloud. Then did I love my desired one, even though He escaped my thoughts.... I called him by name as far as was in my power to find him who lacks a name, yet the meaning of a name would not help me attain him whom I sought." Crying out with love, the bride asks the angels where her lover might be seen, but they too keep silent, testimony to his being lost in the clouds. Undaunted, the lover continues to run after him, hidden though he might be in the cloud. Love, the model of the bride testifies, can stay there in the cloud, where thought, comprehension, and certain knowledge cannot, because love does not need to see with objective certainty, clearly and distinctly, in order to love. Love is a connection with one whom we call on by name precisely because we lack words to state definitively or objectively, clearly or distinctly, what we have secured by our knowledge of it. The names we have let us cry out, calling on or addressing the other whose face remains hidden and unknown, but they do not say anything about that faceless face—whether it smiles or grimaces, shines or pours rain. The certainty that comes with objective knowledge, seeing clearly, and having a concept that states a solid object might bring mastery and control; one might come to rest securely with this, but it brings no relation. Love is a relation, precisely because we do not grasp fully what we love—the bride "cries out" beyond what she has hold of in cries that are those of love. "She realizes that her sought-after love is known only in her impossibility to comprehend his essence, and every sign becomes a hinderance [*sic*] to those who seek him."[54]

The author of *The Cloud of Unknowing* recognizes well the instability and uncertainty of the cloud into which love leads as one seeks to dwell in the divine presence. "If ever you come to this cloud..., [it will] seem to you, perhaps, that you are very far from him, because this cloud of unknowing is between you and your God." In this distance, it is tempting, the author observes, to turn to more solid and stable objects and focus on things seen clearly and distinctly. Ideas of certainty and distinct images rise up and press themselves upon you; they promise "clear sight here in this life." But, for this reason, they interpose themselves between you and the divine cloud. Clarifying thoughts, seen with certainty in the light of the mind, "must always be put down," the author advises, because they allow for the mind to be occupied "not with this darkness but with a clear picture of something beneath God."[55] When the mind is filled with objects seen in the clear opening, it is closed to the cloud—the place of the divine life. "Every sign becomes a hinderance [*sic*]," the bride realizes.

The temptation of clear pictures, obvious signs, and solid objects is all the more compelling when the thing at issue is God himself—pictured with a smiling face, for instance. "Though it is good at times to think of the kindness and worthiness of God in particular, and though this is a light and a part of contemplation, nevertheless in this exercise, it must be cast down and covered over with a cloud of forgetting."[56] One who seeks the divine life is tempted by pictures and thoughts that bring to mind all sorts of wonderful ideas about who God is, his greatness, and how much he has done for one. Such thoughts let the face of God come into the picture clearly; they offer a clear and distinct picture of the beloved, God, and render him an accessible object, whose smiling face is seen clearly, known certainly both to be worthy of one's supposed love and to love one back.

Such a picture might not be wrong in what it depicts; the author even admits that such a picture of God as smiling and kind is indeed "good and holy." But this is not what or how one sees when one dwells in the divine place. One is advised instead to "put down such clear pictures, no matter how holy or how pleasant they may be," for they are seen only in a light that falls short of the superluminous cloud of light wherein the divine life is lived.[57]

How then to keep down the objects that come to light clearly and distinctly, especially if one such tempting object should be God himself? The *Cloud* author advises the seeker of the place of the divine life as follows: "Tread them down quickly with an impulse of love, even though it seems to you to be very holy, even though it seems that it could help you to seek him." "You are to step above [these clear pictures] stalwartly but lovingly, and with a devout, pleasing, impulsive love . . . you are to smite upon that thick cloud of unknowing with a sharp dart of longing love."[58] Love is indeed the answer, it appears. Like the movement of transcendence uttered in hyper- terms such as "superluminous," love is a movement beyond what is seen clearly and distinctly in the light, but a movement that does not dwell simply in the opposite, the darkness of seeing nothing at all. Love beats down (or negates) the clear picture of objects so as to remain in the cloud which alone offers a place for the incomprehensible and invisible divine face to give itself to be seen (in a cloud of light).

If it is indeed by technology that we make and sustain a clearing in which what comes to light might come to light, love is one such technology, but it makes and sustains an opening better understood as a cloud than a clearing—perhaps a cloudy clearing. The mystical theologians, like Diller + Scofidio, surely love the clouds that Descartes methodically leveled.

# 3 : James Turrell, Works with Light

## SEEING THE LIGHT THAT DOES NOT ILLUMINATE

*Light is not so much something that reveals as it is itself the revelation.*
JAMES TURRELL[1]

### Light—Clearing? Illuminating?

I think again of the two images that obsess me: *Lucem post nubila reddit* and "The Apotheosis of Electricity." Two images of cosmic light and a dawning universal transparency. The clearing in which men dwell safely and securely. The technology that makes this clearing. Read together they reflect a dream of enlightenment and clear and distinct vision. The correlate of this vision, what it aims at or intends, is the solid and stable world, one you can grasp. "God, the world, the human soul, and all things in general"—objects taken hold of.

As Michel Serres points out, the world of solid and stable objects requires well defined borders and limits to distinguish each object. A solid object occupies a distinct place—here, not there—and this place is defined by sharp borders that contain it. Whence, according to Serres, the "association of the distinct with the clear, the language of light with the language of borders."[2] For the edges and borders that define distinct objects appear sharply only in a light (be it from the sun or the electric factory) that is bright enough to clear the fog or empty the air that would blur them.

The secure borders and definite limits of solid objects, Serres emphasizes, "efface the bifurcation" or "destroy the double" that would shadow or blur the solid object and thereby cast doubt onto the world and our position with respect to it. Doubt, or *dubitare*, "is only the frequentative of *duo habere*, to consider as two, and, much later, to oscillate between two positions."[3] How can one proceed methodically on one's way with certainty when one is faced with shadowy, hazy things—double images? The opening of a world in which objects appear distinctly, then, becomes the correlative of a way of human being that can advance with certainty.

The uncertainty or shadow of doubt of seeing double can be eliminated, modern disenchantment proposes, if you adopt the proper technique or method of seeing—that is, if you shine the right light on matters. You can be as solid and stable as the world of distinct objects if you focus on them and only them, and you can be sure to focus on distinct objects if you see in the clarity made by a light that illuminates or clears a space for clear vision. Distinction, according to this logic, is the means to efface or eliminate the shadow or double that appears in doubt and renders our path through life uncertain, wavering, and tentative. Clear vision focused on distinct objects proposes to save you from the uncertainty and confusion, the blur and lack of focus, of a *duo habere* in which, at every turn of life, your "path becomes a crossroads," and you must always, again and again, decide which way to go, which turn to take, because more than one appears.[4] Unfocused vision, ever in doubt, brings with it incessant and irrepressible anxiety aroused by the multiplication of possibilities and the continual need to decide, as one stands at the crossroads of two (or more) paths—uncertain and not knowing which way to turn, which thing to attend to, what to care for. What do I love? What does my beloved want of me? Is there a path that will take me there? These, the lover's questions that cloud the mind more than any others, can be avoided if one follows a method of seeing clearly that presents distinct objects.

*Lucem post nubila reddit* and "The Apotheosis of Electricity" show such a light: Light clarifies. It makes a clearing, and it clears a space in which objects can appear distinctly, but it can do this only if, at the same time, it withdraws, disappears, or remains invisible, nothing itself. Our world grows full of solid and stable objects seen clearly and distinctly, then, to the degree that we let invisible light fall into oblivion, consumed by the void it itself creates. Inversely, we forget the invisible light by which we see, let it fall into oblivion, and neglect it most perfectly when we see objects most distinctly in the void. Our forgetting earns us a certain and secure sense of ourselves and our position in a solid and stable world. We live beyond a shadow of doubt. In some ways, this forgetting is the forgetting of a necessary absence, the oblivion of a necessary void, neglect of what will not be bound. But, as the philosopher and theologian Søren Kierkegaard reminds us, there is forgetting and then there is forgetting about forgetting.

* * *

What in the world is this then (fig. 20), if indeed it is of the world? Does it belong to the clearing made by the advance of a light that withdraws? Does this light clarify—make a clearing or clear a space? It seems so otherworldly.

And this (fig, 21), where in the world does it lead? Does it beckon you to enter or hold you fast where you are? Is it a doorway or a flat wall, an opening or a surface? Does the light grant you prospect into a clearing or does it stop you from seeing? If you enter the light, if you can enter the light, will you ever leave? Is there a way that will take you through with certainty of reaching the other side?

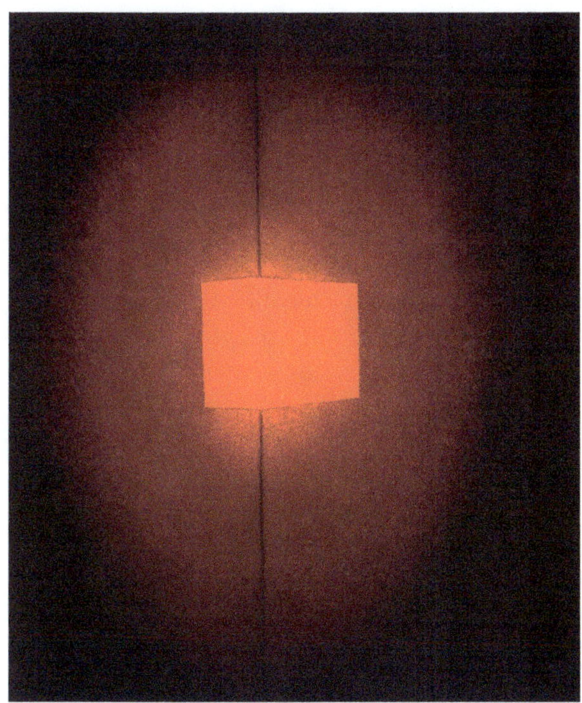

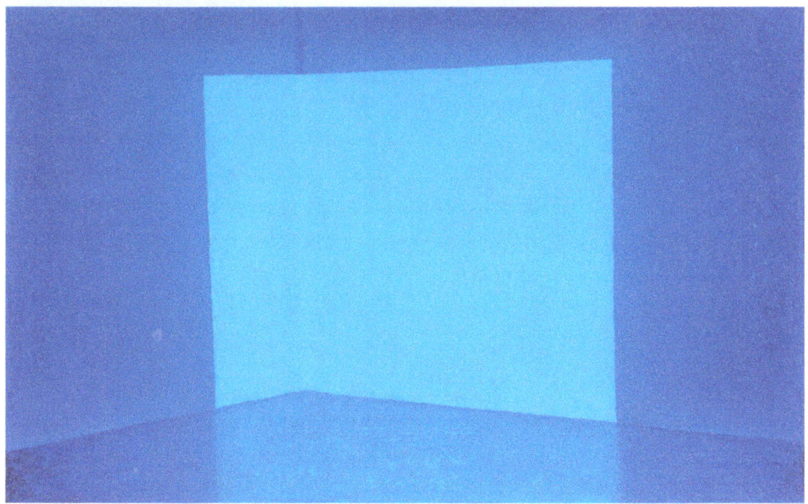

FIGURE 20. Cynthia Hooper, *Red Cube of Light*, oil on board (2011). Photograph: Cynthia Hooper.

FIGURE 21. Cynthia Hooper, *Blue Wall or Doorway*, oil on board (2011). Photograph: Cynthia Hooper.

* * *

These are works of art, things made by a contemporary artist. In fact, they are paintings made by Cynthia Hooper to illustrate the elusive experience of the artwork of James Turrell. Many critics and art lovers agree that Turrell is one of the most exciting artists working in the late twentieth and early twenty first centuries. But, however much contemporary art is a standard bearer of modernity, the things Turrell makes, as we see in Hooper's illustrations, do not belong to the disenchanted world that opens with the clearing shown in *Lucem post nubila reddit* or "The Apotheosis of Electricity."

Invisible light becomes visible before your very eyes; you see the immaterial materialize.

Turrell's light defies the purposes of disenchantment. It does not make a clear space in which we might see distinct objects. Instead, Turrell creates viewing chambers where we are brought to see the light we most often forget in our everyday fascination with the objects it makes visible. "In my work," he says, "light is not so much something that reveals as it is itself the revelation."[5] These viewing chambers become contemplative spaces where we encounter a mysterious, nonobjective presence: we see the light, but no object in the light. "There is no object in my work," Turrell claims. "There never was. There is no image within it." And yet, even in the absence of object and image, we see something, as illustrated by Hooper. These revelations of (not in) light are not themselves objects or images, nor do they present objects or images in the sense in which modern disenchantment deals with them. They cannot be grasped clearly and distinctly, either by hand or by eye. This is another light besides the light that illuminates a clearing where disenchanted objects appear distinctly on solid ground.

## Encounters with the revelation of light

The Mattress Factory (Pittsburgh, Pennsylvania, September 24, 2005)
*Pleiades* by James Turrell

*You wait in the darkling. How long, you cannot tell, for you cannot see anything, so nothing passes; it seems like eternity. It is so dark that close your eyes or open your eyes, what you see is the same. Like a cave. You gaze intently, but see at first only the flickering afterimages generated by your own retina continuing to fire as a lingering effect of the light from the world you just left. It's a delightful show, to be sure. The information disseminated by the museum offers an apt description:* "Fervent staring conjures a milky galaxy, which might not be there, but is the bright image generated by the viewer's neural networks." *Pressure exerted on the nerves in your eye can also produce some of the flashes you see in the dark. This pressure might come from your own blood pulsing through arteries and veins or from your breathing. Your own life flashes before your eyes.*

"Twenty minutes later the galaxy may glow blue; a peripheral glance might turn its edges red." *If you dwell patiently in this dark, deserted place, waiting long enough for the physical and sensory activity inside you to switch off or fall quiet, the retinal afterimages fade away. Then, a light or a shadow might rise or fall in the darkness, a slowly dawning or fading cloud of color pulsing dimly on the edge of existence, hardly anything at all. When your eyes have been opened by the darkness, the slow rising of a dim light begins to grow on you—a light that is even dimmer than the residue left inside you by the bright world whose past you carried. In your inactive calm, even without the support of a curious hand or mind that grasps what you see, you suspect that maybe, just maybe, there might be something out there... out there? Is there an out there?*

*"Let there be light."*

*The barest minimum of photons detectable by the human eye. Is it really there? What is it? Where is it? You are unsure if this barely existing color begins in you or comes from the outside. How to know what it is? Is there anything out there? Will it stay? Will it grow? What are you to do with it and for it, abandoned as you are to this darkness, with little guidance from others and nothing more complicated to do in the dark than open your eyes and see the light? What could be more simple, and therefore more difficult to achieve?*

*You hesitate to say what you see. Even several days after you leave, you remain uncertain of what you saw. Art historians and critics might draw on the scientific literature in order to explain how the effect is achieved. Journalists might, in interviewing Turrell, unveil all the secrets, expose the inner workings and mechanisms, and render the reason for what has been produced, allowing it to be produced again and again. The museum, too, might try to help eliminate your uncertainty by offering you information about the work, the artist's intent, the experience of others, and the relation of this work to others in the history of art. They all might, in short, turn on the lights. But none of this puts to rest the question. Did you see what there is to see? Was there anything there to see? What did others see? The artist himself says of his work,* "It's not about my seeing; it's about yours." *He claims not to be showing me something that he saw, but delivering me over to a situation where I might see the light, or not. It all comes down to me.*

*Far from empowering, for those with eyes opened by the dark this can be totally disarming. You are almost embarrassed to speak about it for fear of having seen wrong or of being unable to make others see the same thing, like a cloud-watcher who struggles to make his friend see what he sees in the nebulous atmosphere. Even when your friend says, "I see. I see it," you remain unsure. Have you communicated what you intended? Has your vision been shared? Is your friend only trying to make you feel better or to stop you from badgering him? It is better, you are told, to stick with the objective accounts of the scientists, critics, and journalists, who at least know what they are talking about and talk only about what they can be sure really does happen that way. Then you can be certain that the message has arrived, that your friend really does see what you have tried to communicate. Better to avoid communication that revolves in and about clouds, or revelations of light—to stick with the things seen in the light.*

*You know that if this barely existing thing, the dimmest revelation of the faintest light that you might have seen, is to consist in anything at all, it depends on you, in the unique singularity of your being struck by its beauty. It consists in your own embrace of the unproven, uncertain experience of this beautiful almost nothing. And you know, too, the delight of communicating it, speaking without knowing or even caring whether the message has arrived. It is the communication of lovers, who take delight in speaking to and hearing from others, even in the mistakes and ruses and failures of exchange.*

*You do not look* at *this light, seeing it with the measuring gaze of a disengaged onlooker; if anything, you look* into *it—as Turrell himself claims. I wonder, though, if it might be more about looking* over*—in the sense not of overlooking but of watching over, looking over things that are easily overlooked, especially easily overlooked because they do not benefit from the solidity that comes from a shared reality. Watching over is not looking at. Watching over takes care, but here it takes care in the dark, like a vigil for the dead beloved, whom you must love all the more to watch over so vigilantly, since he, dead, will not return what you give him. I must watch over these fragile, delicate next to nothings, dim revelations of a faint light, like the dead, if they are to consist in anything at all.*

*The philosopher Bernard Stiegler calls the situation in which such things are met* "le plan des consistances." *What does not have its own solid and stable, objective existence, he claims, "consists in my existence," in the same way that my wife, whom I love, does not exist objectively in the psychologists' and sociologists' illuminations and explanations of my love; rather, she con-sists, together with me, so long as I care enough and love—even if no reason can be rendered and no light will let her appear in the common light. As Stiegler claims,* "because these consistances do not exist, we must take the greatest care of them."[6]

*The unsettling experience of this dark viewing chamber consists in being delivered over to the free and open (which you experience in the darkness of a clearing, the clarity of a darkling) where you are not supposed to see anything but what you see—you alone in the dark with the thing you see in a void of reference, iconographic content, or any other information that might shine a light on it. Turrell has likened this to an encounter with a lover.* "I take seeing down to the light level where the iris opens. The eyes feel, like touch, when you look into the eyes of a lover and experience that intensity of touch with the eyes. The intimacy of being invaded with that kind of look can be frightening."[7] *Love is made in the dark. The vision that keeps things at arm's length by seeing in the light that illuminates yields in the darkling of Turrell's work to the more intimate vision touched by the dim lights of a beloved whose revelation it cannot see clearly and distinctly in the dark.*

*So accustomed to the direct lighting and focused rays of modern illumination have we become that this freedom of vision, this intensification of you in the intimate presence of almost nothing at all, can be the hardest thing to achieve. So comfortable are we with the solid and stable objects appearing in the clarifying light of a world that this summons to a nighttime vigilance and caring or watching over what barely exists in the world can be one of the calls most difficult to hear. So secure are we with the objectivity that comes to light in our enlightened times that the love that must be made in the dark is difficult to sustain. Are there many spaces left for such seeing under the spotlights of this stage that all the world has become?*

## The Mattress Factory (Pittsburgh, Pennsylvania, September 24, 2005) *Catso Red* and *Danae* by James Turrell

*Before you: a colored wall (fig. 22)—what Georges Didi Huberman describes in the best book I know about Turrell's work as* "an absolutely frontal rectangle,

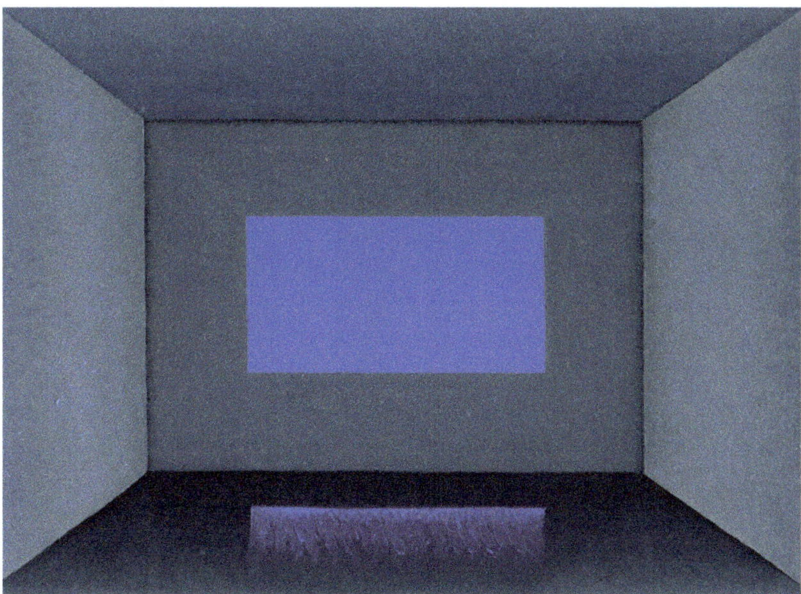

FIGURE 22. Cynthia Hooper, *Blue Volume of Light at a Window*, oil on board (2011). Photograph: Cynthia Hooper.

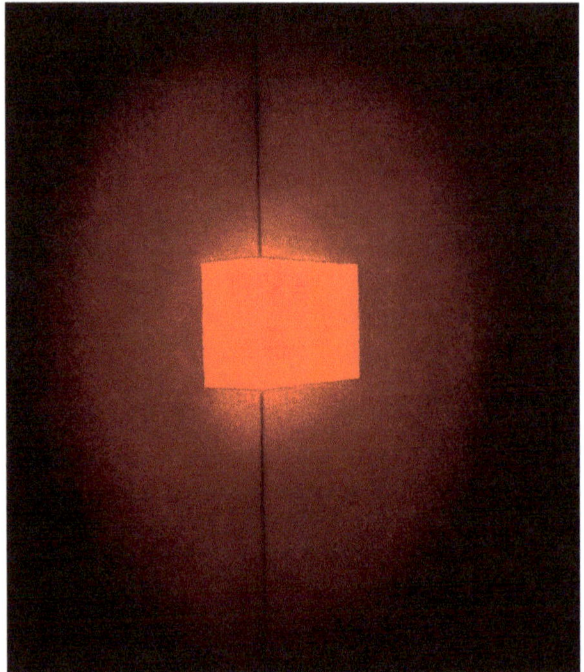

FIGURE 23. Cynthia Hooper, *Red Cube of Light*, oil on board (2011). Photograph: Cynthia Hooper.

a colored mass, without shadow, without nuance"[8]—*and a colored box (fig. 23)—glowing, shining radiantly. A glowing rectangle and a shining cube (again illustrated by Cynthia Hooper). Pure and perfect geometry: the most evident of all, the clearest and most distinct of all that is possible, requiring little or no intuition other than what the mind can intuit even in the absence of any thing. Isn't that what "mathematical" means? There they are before you, these voids of things that nonetheless set the standard for evidence today.*

*What are they made of? How did they come to be set here before me? What mechanism or force keeps them balanced in the air, hovering like clouds in seeming defiance of weight and gravity? I remember what Didi Huberman said of his own experience:* "Let us say that it floats massively."[9] *Massive floating: Can this really be? It must be either an illusion or a special effect produced by technologies that remain hidden but nevertheless secure for this mass its floating.*

*In order to ascertain what this is, you might try moving around to gain a better perspective or to see other aspects of the unknown thing. But changing perspective does not change what you see. There is no better position from which to see this thing, no position that would let you see it more correctly than you already do. What is more, there is no more information to be gained by seeing it from different angles, no more information to be added to what you already see in order to constitute an adequate mental image of the object. This thing has emerged suddenly and all at once. In its pure frontality, its seeming superficiality, it is like the Byzantine icon that you saw the day before at another museum in another city. The flatness hides nothing but confronts you face on, demanding that you stand observantly before it. A revelation of light, without prior light to illuminate it.*

*However much it is unchanging, with nothing hidden in reserve, it is hardly a solid and stable object. Solid and stable objects appear in the clarity of a light that illuminates, and illumination from such a light leaves traces on the surface of the object. The play of light and shadow, and its changing over time, give us information about the shape, the limits, and the position of objects in space. As the light rises or falls, advances or withdraws, or moves across the sky like the sun, the object appears differently and different aspects of it are revealed. The summing up or assembly of these aspects by the knowing mind constitutes the object we see clearly and distinctly. But this thing before you does not vary. Could it be that no light illuminates it, that it does not appear in the clarity of a light that illuminates? Yet there it is, fully revealed, totally present, before you. Obstinate. Unmoving.*

*Again I recall Didi Huberman, who suggests that when your eyes fail to grasp what they see, you try your hands.*[10] *But if, here, you reach out your hand and try to grasp the colored light, seeking some anchor in reality, some reassuring connection by way of which you might position yourself, you find there is no distinct edge or border, nothing solid—and yet something is there to see. Your hand searches in the light forever without finding a limit at which it can come to rest. Unable to touch its edges, you cannot measure it, put it on the balance and weigh it, or explain where its colored surface comes from since it appears in no light, neither that of nature nor one you control.*

*The immeasurable, ungraspable, or nonobjective thing that faces you in a viewing chamber is not an illusion, Turrell insists, rejecting any suggestion that his work be conceived as trompe l'oeil.*[11] *An illusion vanishes, or is at least explained, when you find the right place from which to see it or get behind or beneath the surface of things. In Turrell's viewing chambers, there is no right place, nowhere you can stand to make the illusion vanish, and there is nothing but what you see. However disquieting the initial experience of the viewing chambers might be, this disquiet is not the same as the agitated curiosity that seeks to unveil the mysteries of nature or pierce the veil of illusion. If you do experience disquiet and anxiety in the viewing chambers, this probably has more to do with your lingering involvement with the things and objects of our everyday immersion that have been taken away than it does with any positive experience of something terrifying. Confronted with pure surface seen in a vision that stands in no need of correction in order to see reality, your gaze becomes not curious so much as admiring. Can we give ourselves over to this passion, if only for a moment?*

*A rectangle and a cube, pure geometry. Simple? Most evident? Distinct?*

## Back home (Lexington, Virginia, October 1, 2005)

*These radiant things, like ephemera, are fragile: the smallest twist of the switch will destroy them. The effort to illuminate them clearly or to shine a spotlight on them will cause them to vanish. If you turn on the lights, they go dark. You might be tempted to neglect these radiant visions, dismissing your observations as what some in philosophy call intuitively "inadequate" or not sufficiently evident. They mean by this, roughly, that what you claim to see, what you say you saw, is just a word, concept, or idea that cannot be confirmed by enough experience to count as objective or as evidence that could be presented to others; you can talk about it, but your words do not have enough data or given to lend them substance. There certainly were friends, relatives, and professional acquaintances who sounded very much like these philosophers when they advised me to neglect the appeal of visiting these dark rooms, staring at almost nothing, nothing more than a tiny, shining light.*

*But the viewing chambers taught me to be observant and not neglect the appeal of these fragile, barely existing things, things that shun the spotlight. Like the loves that Bernard Stiegler claims only consist in my unique existence, these insubstantial things (nothings, maybe) appeal to me, demanding that I watch over them patiently. It is my decision to wait here in the dark, to wait on them and for them, my observance, countering my negligence, that lets them consist in anything at all. Let them appeal to me, I tell myself against the advice of those clear-thinking, stable friends and relatives, but it's not so easy in a disenchanted world to let things be appealing and to admit the appeal even of appealing things—easier and better to stick with the non-appealing yet adequate or evident objects I manage everyday and can give an account of to others.*

*Turrell himself notes that most of the time we are not so observant and avoid letting such situations appeal to us. We live most of the time in the world of certain evidence and solid objects that make little or no appeal to a responsibility for those things that consist only with each of us. The intimacy of being bound up together in this con-sistance is too much to bear. Easier to live with what exists "objectively" without us and our choice. We live in the clear and distinct world in which no double shadows objects with doubt. In this world, Turrell claims,* "You are confronted with the evidence and say: 'In light of these facts, I can only decide in this direction,'" *which is no choice at all—no responsibility need be taken when you do the only thing that can be done, walk the only path that appears. But Turrell's viewing chambers offer training in a situation that is perhaps more difficult to bear, one in which, he suggests,* "you do not make a decision that is grounded in exact proofs," *or in certainty and adequate evidence. Indeed, as Turrell continues, even those things that do appear in an adequate thought, with sufficient evidence to be counted as objective knowledge, can still be disregarded, their appeal reduced to the unappealing, if we are negligent.* "Everybody thinks that we live in a rational world, but this is not true.... We are capable of forgetting certain facts; for in reality, they are not so important in our eyes."[12] *The power of objectivity to compel corresponding action, Turrell implies, is a myth, one meant to deny the enormity of our responsibility for letting things fall into oblivion or saving them from oblivion. I must remain observant and not neglect the things that appeal to me if their evidence, however great or small, is to count. This burden on my observance is all the greater the more fragile the appearances are, the quieter their appeal; the claim of their tenuous existence is ever so precarious and not likely to count for very much unless I take it into account.*

## Becoming observant: James Turrell and the mystical cosmos

Here, in the opening of these viewing chambers, is a light that does not illuminate and that does not bring something into focus or let it appear distinctly. Here is a light that, the artist says, "is not so much something that reveals as it is itself the revelation." Turrell's viewing chambers become something like the place where we take a "step back" into this other light—one that shines without prior illumination and that is itself a reality to see. When light itself becomes revelation, what we encounter when we are observant in such light changes too: it is no longer the solid and stable existing object of which we are certain, but a mysterious presence with an unnameable appeal that draws us into light without end.

In making us observant of this light, the viewing chambers stage or enact the paradoxes of theological vision as described by certain of the religious, especially those often called mystical theologians. In Dionysius the Areopagite, for instance, a theologian often recognized as a founding father of Christian mysticism, the theological genesis and structure of the universe is expressed in terms of light—not a light that lets us see other truths to be revealed, but a light that is itself the truth or revelation of the divine reality of the cosmos.

When I propose that Turrell's viewing chambers stage or enact the paradoxes of theological vision, I do not mean that they confirm or disconfirm, defend or refute, the dogmatic or propositional contents of Christian faith. I also do not mean that they contain iconographic content drawn from an acknowledged historical religious tradition. Turrell's work is remarkably devoid of such references; indeed, it may strive to be devoid of almost any reference whatsoever to anything outside the work. What I intend to focus on instead are experiences of human being and the world, self and reality. Turrell's work puts us in a world like that described by mystical theology, and it makes us resemble the human subject of such theology. Together James Turrell and mystical theology might help us elaborate an anthropology and a cosmology of who and what comes after the subject and object of modern disenchantment.

## THE COSMIC LIGHT SHOW: MYSTICAL COSMOLOGY

The mystical theology of Dionysius holds that the cosmos and the things in it are the ecstatic structure of a divinity that is itself by proceeding out of itself so that all might return to it. This model repeats the basic schema of cosmology found in Dionysius's Neoplatonic predecessors: the universe and all the things in it are understood according to the triad of procession, return, and remaining in itself. This triad is not just a diachronic sequence or three steps in a series; it is also synchronic, a structural account of the nature of reality at each and every moment. Divinity, then, is itself not by keeping to itself and maintaining the strict borders of its secure identity but by diffusing and revealing itself in and as creation in order that all might be gathered back into it. This implies that, on some level, the universe and each of the things in it is a revelation or theophany. As theophanic revelation, the things we see will show us the way back to the hidden divinity.

Within this schema, divinity and its relation to the cosmos is best understood in terms of light. "[The divine light] works itself outward to multiplicity and proceeds outside of itself as befits its generosity, doing so to lift upward and to unify those beings for which it has a providential responsibility; nevertheless it remains inherently stable and is forever one with its own unchanging identity."[13] The language is complicated, but the point need not be. The cosmos, as a whole and in all its multiplicity, is an overflow of divine light *proceeding* out of itself so that all things might *return* to divinity by being gathered and uplifted into unity with the divine light as they enter its light. Everything is indeed illuminated—and, even more, illuminating: both shining like light and enlightening us.

Importantly, however, even as divinity radiates or flows out of itself in the light that gathers all into unity with the divine light, it *remains in itself*, since what it itself is is this radiating. Light, by definition or essentially, emits a ray or shines a light, and in this shining it remains in itself. This will have important consequences for what it means to see the light: since light always remains in itself as it radiates or flows out, a mystery (the in itself) remains hidden in the revelation (uplifting for us), a darkness keeps in itself at the heart of all the illumination.

This light is therefore different from the light imagery that might be more familiar in today's usage in that it does not have a moral, personal, or inner significance (as when we speak of an inner light that eliminates doubt and makes for clear decisions) but, rather, a cosmological sense. Though Turrell, raised a Quaker, has often cited his Quaker grandmother's injunction to "go inside and see the light" as inspiration for his work, I cannot but feel that the light of which we become observant through his work is external, cosmic, "objective," or real—like the first light shining in a darkling that is creation and created things, according to the mystical theologians.

Equally important, the light into which we step back in a viewing chamber is different from the light of enlightenment or illumination that clears a space or world where objects appear distinctly. If the cosmos and the things in it are the radiance, flow, or light that manifests this light that remains hidden in its shining revelation, light does not simply clarify things but constitutes them. The universe with all the things in it (God, the world, the human soul, and all things in general, in Wolff's terms) is a vast light show, a vast show of light showing the mysterious divine light. We see the light, not objects in the light, and all things present themselves shiningly to us.

However much the great "outpouring of illumination" might be a revelation of God, the world, the human soul, and all things in general, these things of the all visible mystical cosmos are not to be seen distinctly—precisely because they are revelations of divinity. Theological vision, in aiming to be lifted up to the divine light, does not see distinctly, not even and especially when it sees in light of the divine. Theologians and scholars working in the Dionysian tradition saw well that when the divine is light, it is immanence that distinguishes, paradoxically, the transcendence of divinity. God as light transcends or is distinguished from all things precisely by his immanence as the light that shines in and as them; this cannot be said of things, which are only the shining of a light that is not them—such that it is well to say that God is distinct by being indistinct from all things.[14] When God is distinct from all things by being indistinct from them, divine indistinction shadows each thing we see, like a halo blurring its edges. Theological vision, in turn, as it is lifted upward to see divinity, traces all things it sees back to their indistinct origin in the divine indistinction that in-distinguishes things, as it were.

Importantly, this indistinct origin is dark and invisible, a lost cause at the heart of the universe of effects. It itself being the only source of light, there is nothing that illuminates it, and it cannot be seen clearly and distinctly in the things where it shines forth. As Dionysius puts it, "The fire which warms and burns is never said itself to be burnt and warmed. Similarly, it would be wrong to say . . . that light itself is enlightened." Hence, the theological process of return is one in which "we need to rise from this outpouring of illumination so as to come to the simple ray of Light itself. . . . This divine ray can enlighten us only by being upliftingly concealed."[15] Theological vision thus leads us back to the origin that is our goal by following a light that illuminates us in darkness.

## RELIGIOUS MOVEMENT INTO THE DISTANCE

Mystical theology understands the relation between divinity and the world in such a way that a theological vision means seeing the great light show of the universe in the light of a divinity that shadows each thing, as it were, inseparably, like their halo. Human vision becomes observant not when it sees something solid or distinct in the clarity of light, but when it sees in and through distinct things the indistinct and invisible origin and end, the light, that shines darkly in them. In this theological vision, the cosmos appears to the human being both as divine light to see (the universe is a theophany of light revealing God, who is an invisible light) and light that must be unseen precisely because this light veils the dark light of the transcendently absent divine light. Human being is left with the ambiguous greatness of occupying the unstable and uncertain position where it is all seeing in a totally brilliant universe of light, yet sees nothing clearly or distinctly. "There is no object in my work. . . . There is no image within it," as Turrell says, yet how much more do we see when we look through it toward this nothing.

In the great light show of the mystical cosmos, as in Turell's viewing chambers, things are bright; they present themselves brilliantly as revelations of light that is divine. But these revelations are overwhelmed or saturated by their origin and end in an invisible light that exceeds them—overwhelming them in mystery and saturating them in what might also be interpreted as their aura. As defined by the critic Walter Benjamin, aura refers to "the unique phenomenon of a distance, however close it might be."[16] The visions we receive in Turrell's viewing chambers, as in the mystical cosmos, present themselves to us as light that is itself a revelation or presentation; in this sense, they embody a movement of drawing near. But this revelation or presenting does not ensure their ultimate availability for the eye, mind, or hand that seeks to lay hold of what is revealed or presented before it. A mysterious presence, the in itself of the light that stays itself by shining, saturates it and is indistinct from it. However close to hand the light might be in its revelation, be it Turrell's lightbox or the things of the mystical cosmos, it keeps its distance, never letting our measuring, calculating eye or hand come to rest on a distinct edge, never letting us get a handle on it—perhaps like a lover who is desired all the more the more present he or she is, and if he or she is not, then the love is over, even if the object remains.

When observant of the aura of things, seeing becomes a religious movement, of a certain kind—a movement into the uncrossable, because without end or term, distance where the invisible saturating the visible is not neglected. Hence the theological importance of aesthetics, as well as the aesthetic importance of Dionysian theology. Aesthetic experience of the cosmos as a whole and in each of its parts affords a means of making the uplifting religious movement into the distance toward the invisible light.

The influential Catholic theologian Hans Urs von Balthasar has offered a provocative interpretation of Dionysian theology that stresses this intertwining of the aesthetic and the theological. For von Balthasar, theological observance turns on the fact that for Dionysius the cosmos and the things we see in it are "the manifestation of the unmanifest." The phrase is twofold. Understood as the "*manifestation* of the unmanifest," it means the cosmos is a totality of beautiful things for an aesthetic to see, precisely insofar as it is the radiance of divine light. The light we see is a manifestation or "becoming visible in reality—not as *maya*, mere seeming illusion, but always as (real) manifestation of the unmanifest, of the ever greater and ever more hidden God."[17] Just as Turrell rejects the claim that his viewing chambers hold any illusion or trompe l'oeil but are real, since light itself is reality, von Balthasar emphasizes that the light that is manifest in the brilliant mystical cosmos is also real, not some illusion to be banished when seen from the perspective of the absolute. In insisting on the reality of the images and objects seen, theological observance is an affirmation of the aesthetic: its gaze comes to rest joyfully on the beauty of things manifest through the revelation of divine light.

But there is a danger posed by the dazzling light of this beautiful and total manifestation: namely, the risk of being held captive by the objects seen in the light, held up by the images and pictures one holds to with a gaze that grasps the beauty it sees. Settling comfortably with the objects it sees distinctly in clear light, it forgets the invisible halo or aura of things and, coming to rest with the objects it measures and counts on, stops moving into the distance opened by the divine mystery. As what is seen in the light becomes solid, it no longer lets us see through it to the invisible light—we lose sight of what cannot be seen.

The doorway becomes a wall, the window a façade (fig. 24).

This leads to the second sense, inseparable from the first, of von Balthasar's twofold phrase. The beauty of the universe understood as a cosmic revelation of light is also "a manifestion of the *unmanifest*." "Were the external splendor of the beautiful not the splendor of a mysterious depth . . . then it would not be the beautiful and would not awaken reverence before 'the sacred mystery made manifest.'" Vision becomes observant of the beauty of the world, von Balthasar suggests, when it "is grounded in the worship of what is not manifest."[18] Here, mystical vision saves us from becoming stuck by dislodging, disembedding, or uprooting us from our anchor in the solid and stable, the certain and secure, the objective. This aesthetic saves us by saving the invisible from oblivion, as if our fates were joined to that of the invisible. The vision of the divine directs us toward the invisible aura or presence of visible things by setting us on a path through and beyond manifest images and objects to their unmanifest source or origin.

The wall becomes an open door that admits us into a passage with no end in sight, the façade a window that gives onto the distance and the invisible. We dwell only ever in the distance. *Looking at* becomes *looking into*, as Turrell puts it (fig. 24).

When theological observance of the mystical cosmos does not neglect the invisible and at the same time remains a vision of the radiant splendor of beautiful things, it stands in a precarious relation to the aesthetic and

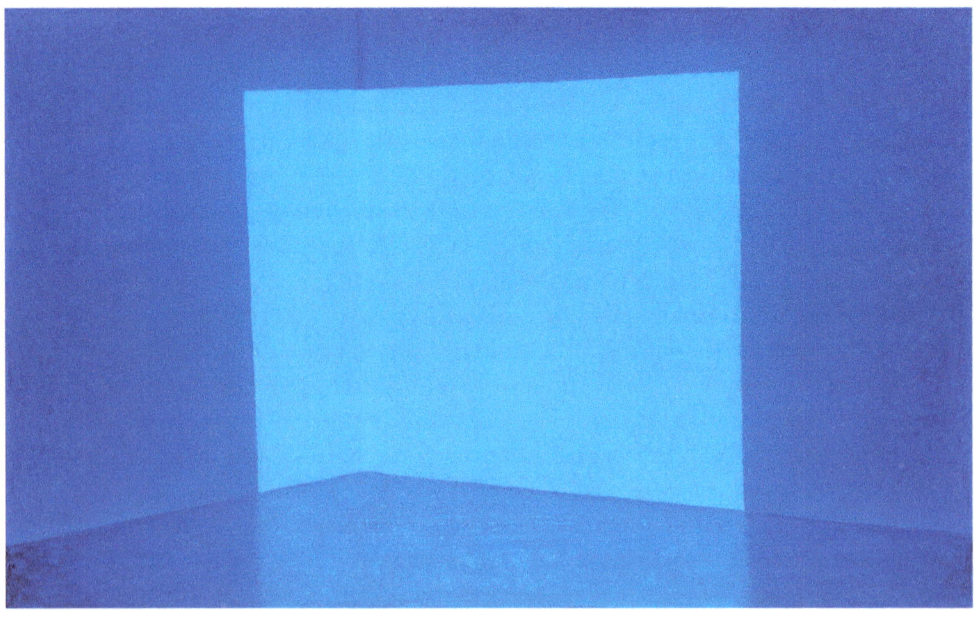

FIGURE 24. Cynthia Hooper, *Blue Wall or Doorway*, oil on board (2011). Photograph: Cynthia Hooper.

to images, objects and pictures, both affirming and transcending them, seeing both a solid and stable wall marking the limits of a totally visible totality and, through it, a doorway inviting us beyond all.

The name von Balthasar gives to this tenuous, fragile, and ambiguous look into things is *wondering admiration*: "The more deeply our wondering admiration experiences the unmanifest God, and does not simply know him... the more the aesthetic relation is transcended." But this transcendence of the aesthetic does not leave it behind, von Balthasar continues: "the more the aesthetic relation is transcended,... the more the truth of the aesthetic emerges." Wondering admiration is this religious movement into the distance, as the universe grows darker the more light it becomes and lighter as we move into the darkness. Our admiration of the things we see grows deeper the more we see because the more we see of things when we are observant the more the invisible grows.[19] Things grow deep and ever deeper when we do not neglect the invisible that shadows and haloes their brilliant shining.

The more deeply we observantly look *into* the wall, the more deeply we go through the doorway, and once into the light there is no end in sight, as the back wall has been overwhelmed in the unlimited, faceless distance it opens and reveals to us.

## SEEING THROUGH: BETWEEN ENCHANTMENT AND DISENCHANTMENT

Standing observantly before *Danae* or *Ondoe Blue* (represented here by Hooper's illustrations, figs. 25 and 24, respectively) or any of Turrell's other lights that oscillate ambiguously between wall and opening, solid surface and endless depth, one can reach no point from which the mystery is banished. Didi Huberman explains works like *Danae*: "The eye has been lost and continues to be. Discovering that one is before a gaping opening is of no help: the mystery is transformed but remains, and even deepens profoundly. First because... if the bit of [blue] is an opening placed before me, the *before* indicates a distance and a separation, in short, an *arrêt*; the *opening* suggests to me a spatial continuity, in short, an appeal or call [*un appel*]."[20] Unlike the objects and images placed before me so that I can be all the more secure in my control and dominion over the objective world, what is placed before me here is an opening that calls or bids me to draw near what might lie on the other side by passing through the opening—just as the things we see as revelations in the mystical cosmos invite us to penetrate them more deeply as ways to unseeingly see the invisible. Standing observantly before *Danae*, I cannot see a way out of the thing into which I look, as one can sense from Cynthia Hooper's illustration. I

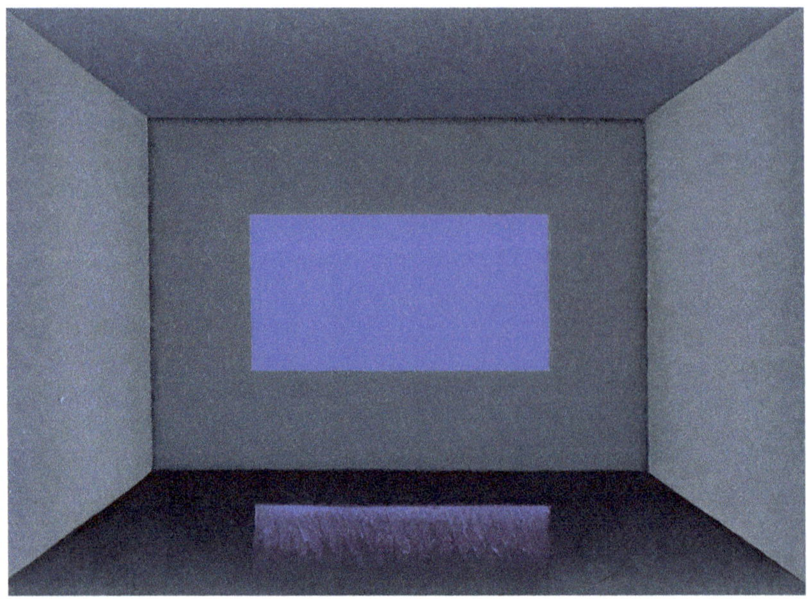

FIGURE 25. Cynthia Hooper, *Blue Volume of Light at a Window*, oil on board (2011). Photograph: Cynthia Hooper.

cannot see an end to the adventure or mystery, a somewhere or someone, smiling, at the end of the path. It appears as if these spaces contain the uncontainable, measure the immeasurable, like the theophany that is the mystical cosmos—manifestation of the unmanifest containing the infinite that cannot be contained.

A unique form of construction produces this effect in me. Didi Huberman explains how Turrell makes these "frames for the unlimited" or "places for aura, for the play of the open and the frame, distance and nearness... tiny cathedrals where man finds himself walking in the color," hardly a light that is clear and clarifying. A bevel, carefully cut to a sharp angle on the wall framing the shape of light, makes the light stand out by defining the edges that secure a distinct place for it. But this distinct cutout, this form taking shape before you, is presented against a background of the same color. "In this way," Didi Huberman concludes, the color is "cut out and distinct in front (as wall section) and infinite in back (as deprived of visible limit, another effect of the back wall). The physical opening poses an obstacle, and the concrete wall (in back) presents to the eye only an unlimited opening, a desert of color.... The opening makes for a limit; the closure abolishes it."[21] Before you, the color is a distinct and vertical surface. Yet, you can see through it the unlimited color it contains.

When the back wall can produce the effect of opening and limitlessness, we cannot be sure there is an end to the beckoning things our gaze enters when we listen to their appeal, heed their bidding, and take a "step back" from the solid and stable objects revealed in the light that enlightens. It's like the mystical vision that saves us by saving the invisible halo of the concrete things we see adequately and certainly. Taking this step back, we go tentatively, hesitantly, never beyond a shadow of doubt, but into something rich and strange.

Like man in the Dionysian universe, who must both see and unsee the universe, who must be both charmed by the beauty manifest in the cosmos and freed from the hold or spell of this cosmic manifestation in all its beauty, one experiences a sort of suspense at the enigmatic visions provoked by Turrell's work. Do I see it, or do I see through it? Can I see through it or do I only see through it, unendingly?

# 4 : James Turrell, Skyspaces

## OPENING AN EYE TO THE SKY

### Clearing on earth—to see the sky

*Lucem post nubila reddit* works as an image of security and stability because of the clearing in the clouds. This is even more true of "The Apotheosis of Electricity." We come to dwell, be it in the town set in the ordered landscape or the safe harbor to which a light clears a way through stormy seas, on the ground of a clearing, where we see the sky and receive the light in it. Without the clearing, it wouldn't matter if the sun was smiling or not, if it was light or dark; we would live beyond this difference or play of opposites.

Today, at the beginning of the twenty-first century, the clearing where we live sprawls everywhere. In it, we have built the global city. As urban sprawl clears away forest and wildlife, along with darkness and clouds, almost everywhere on the face of the earth has been cleared for men to dwell. On the ground of this sprawling clearing, we build and we build, a city that encompasses the globe, a global city, until the open clearing has become full of what we have built.

And as it fills, the opening closes. We no longer live in view of the sky; roofs spring up everywhere, and we strain to see out of the deep canyons of our cities. Most of us live most of the time inside, at home even when away or at work, without giving much thought to the open sky.

The expanding city threatens what Robert Harrison, in *Forests: The Shadow of Civilization*, calls "the edge of opacity," the dark forests that he implies are not opposed to the clearing but give it its possibility. Harrison could also have referred to the clouds, whose thick nebulosity makes the clearing by surrounding it. "However wide the circle may get through the inertia of civic expansion, it presumably retains an edge of opacity . . . where the human abode reaches its limits. . . . This edge is generally called a province. . . . The containment of the province" is the enabling limit that lets the clearing remain open.[1] Without this limit or edge (forest or clouds) to keep the clearing open, one loses the sky too, which vanishes as the clearing becomes sprawl.

I hear this as a passionate plea for the liminal figures that the anthropologist Victor Turner long ago in passing called "edgemen"[2]—those living on the edge. The peculiar power of those who live on the edge is not that they clear away what blocks the sky (clouds, trees), thus securing us on the solid ground illuminated by a smiling light. Rather, the power of the "edgemen" is that they do the "boundary maintenance" that ensures the survival of the provinces that hold together the clearing.

We need to remain in touch with the provinces and the provincials so that we might keep these edges and save the sky from being lost in the clearing.

* * *

I learned this lesson when my meditation on *Lucem post nubila reddit* and "The Apotheosis of Electricity" took an unexpected turn in 2005, and I found myself in the provinces, at Kielder Forest on the Scottish border in Northumberland, England. We were coming home. I had been in Nottingham the week before, busying myself in the confines of the academic precincts, and had just spent a week vacationing with my family in Scotland. We were returning from the Isle of Skye, very nearly the edge of the earth, a place where the border between ground and ocean grows porous and is lost as earth falls apart in broken rock and boulder at the edge of the sea. We were making haste to Manchester, where we would rejoin the solid world. From the international airport, we were to catch a plane that would carry us through the sky, over the ocean, and almost home. Kielder Forest, though in the far reaches or provinces, put us close enough to Manchester that if we rose before the sun did we could drive to Manchester in time to make our morning flight. From the provinces of England, we would be at our home in Virginia in less time than it took our great-grandfathers to get from here to London. I did not think anything of it—neither of the vast distance that would be consumed by the airplane, nor of the enormous speed at which we would be moving while aboard it, nor of the network of intelligence required to coordinate this return.

Along with forests, lakes, and rivers, Kielder boasts several site-specific works of modern sculpture—including one by James Turrell. A recently converted admirer of Turrell's work, I thought we should make a detour, delay our return home, and linger here for a while—even if that would make our return all the more hasty.

Reached by walking a dirt and gravel path several miles long, Turrell's work sits atop Cat Cairn, a rocky hill with a commanding view of the Kielder Forest. But you don't come here for the commanding view of the landscape. Turrell's work is a viewing chamber or observatory, what he often calls a "skyspace," a hollow dome of sorts with an oculus open to the sky above, resembling the Pantheon in Rome or the hogan in which dwelled the Navajo Aby Warburg met in the "antiquity of America." The oculus is a feature significantly absent from most of the closed, complete, totally built buildings we know—in particular, it is missing from the dome that Aby Warburg saw as the backdrop for his Uncle Sam, "the conqueror of the serpent cult" (fig. 10). Unlike the closure provided by most architectural works, Turrell's skyspace provides a shelter that exposes you, opening to the *profondeur* of the sky and its contingencies.

The forest of Northumberland is not the only place where you can find one. Other examples of Turrell skyspaces are at P.S. 1 in New York, the Henry Art Gallery in Seattle, the Quaker Live Oaks Meeting House in Houston, Texas, and elsewhere. This range of locations brings together contexts that the modern mind does not often associate: the religious or the temple (Live Oaks Meeting House), the wilderness or the natural (Kielder Forest), and the urban museum of high culture (P.S. 1 and the Henry Art Gallery). Seen through the lens of Turrell's work, all of these are brought together beneath the sky that appears when, thanks to these devices, we become observant.

These works have led some critics, journalists, and art-lovers to speak of Turrell as a "sculptor of the sky." He bends it and shapes it, bringing forth novel appearances, but without laying a hand on it. His work is an invitation to the sky to condescend to show itself to us. This invitation is made by offering it a frame, a limit or edge that can contain its immensity and thereby let the uncontainable sky appear. Turrell's work works *around* the sky and is always *about* the sky. Being always about the sky that one is seeing, Turrell's own work is not what one looks at when one is there. You do not look at what he has made, for what he has made is just the edge circling around what is not made: the sky that his work is always *about*.

This sky that is not made is what we are made, patiently, to see.

We see it through eyes opened by the open eye of this oculus, a clearing made not by destroying or banishing (as in the clouds that part or are dispelled) but by working on and at the edges—edges that are being banished or cleared away by *Lucem post nubila reddit* and "The Apotheosis of Electricity" (figs. 26 and 27). He makes a clearing, and in this clearing a difference opens, and we see the sky—as illustrated in a photograph made by Memory Harbour (a pseudonym) entitled *World in My Eyes* (fig. 28).

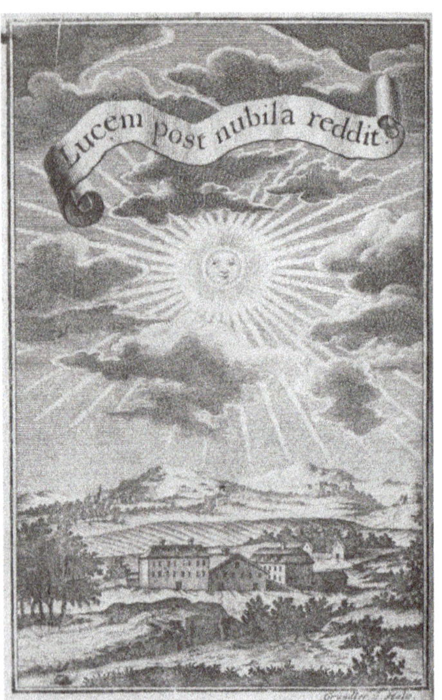


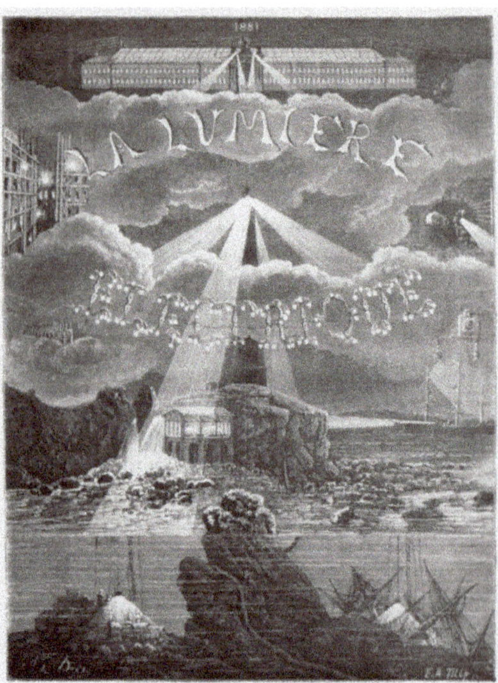

FIGURE 26. Frontispiece from Christian Wolff, *Vernünfftige Gedancken von Gott, der Welt und der Seele des Menschen auch allen Dingen überhaupt den Liebharen der Wahrheit* (1720). Rare Book Collection, University of North Carolina at Chapel Hill.

FIGURE 27. Title page from *La lumière électrique* (1882).

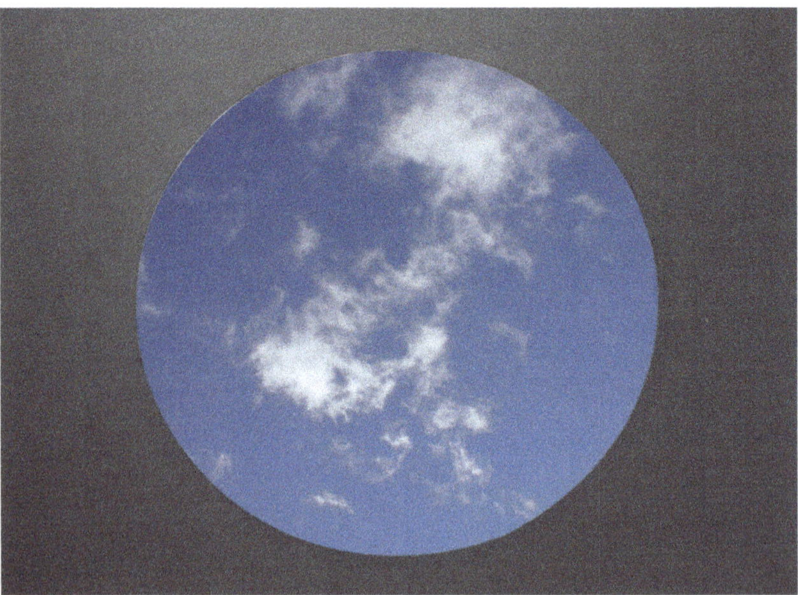

FIGURE 28. Memory Harbour (pseudonym), *World in My Eyes* (2010).

## From giant to man: Vico's clearing

In the history of human being, devising a device so as to gain a clear view of the sky is not new, nor do I make any pretense that my own experience of Turrell's skyspace was a particularly grand version of an old one. We make a clearing in order to see the sky—and also in order that the sky might see us. One of the philosophers and poets, historians and mythmakers, to have meditated most profoundly on this truth was the counter-Enlightenment thinker Giambattista Vico, a famous opponent of Descartes. If Vico is to be believed, the connection between the clearing and the need to see the sky goes back to the beginnings of human history.

In ancient times, according to Vico, "every clearing was called a *lucus*, in the sense of an eye, as even today we call eyes the opening through which light enters houses."[3] These *luci* were fashioned by protohuman creatures whom Vico calls giants as part of the giants' own struggle to see, more specifically, to see the skies and read the future therein. By creative mistaking or misappropriation of the word, the giants' clearing (*lucus*) became the cyclops' eye (*lucus*), which every giant had in the middle of his forehead. Even more significantly, for Vico, this project to "open the eye" so that the giant might see the sky is the struggle that gives shape, literally, to human being.[4]

### THE EFFECT OF THE *LUCUS*: HOMINIZATION

Vico's story of the birth of human being addresses what Ernesto Grassi claims is "the central problem of humanism... not man and his immanent values..., but the question of the original context, the horizon, or openness in which man and his world appear."[5] In addressing the question of *becoming* human or the *emergence* of a world, Vico's version of humanism stands apart from those theologies, rationalisms, and even literatures of the human that assume a fully developed human being. Subject of a creation without becoming, this being never has to *become* human in the way man does when Vico begins his story with the prehuman creature he calls giants.

The giants, Vico relates, were creatures, neither human nor animal, who could become human when their existence and bodies were altered by a clear view of the sky. They were descendants of Noah, who inhabited the forest that sprang up following the retreat of the waters from the face of the earth. Spawned of angels mixing with men, as suggested in the apocryphal book of Enoch, the giants lost their humanity in the wilderness and became unsettled creatures who grew up without spouses or families, forgot the religion of their fathers, and left their dead unburied above the earth. Abandoning each other and their families in solitary pursuit of the food and water provided for them by the natural abundance of the great, dense forest—an Eden that is not a garden because nobody cultivates the soil or cares for the earth—the descendants of Noah, "roving wild through the great forest, . . . must have grown robust, vigorous, excessively big in brawn and bone, to the point of becoming giants."[6]

If the shelter of the wild forest is the scene in which creatures emerge, the clearing open to the sky will be the scene in which these creatures become men. The three institutions that, according to Vico, institute humanity (marriage and the family, burial of the dead, and religion) all emerge in such a clearing. Marriage and the family were not instituted in the forest, Vico claims, because the thick wild affords no place to settle down and because the abundance of food scattered throughout fosters roaming and dispersed living. The lawlessness of the wild runs counter to the respect for generational bonds and monogamy that constitute marriage and the family. Burial in the earth, Vico continues, lays claim to the land to which the human family belongs and institutes the human family as a historical continuity of generations (distinguishing it from the animal family). But this can only happen on the stage opened by a clearing in the forest, where, in Harrison's words, "the family tree supplants the oak tree."[7]

## RELIGIOUS MOVEMENT INTO THE CLEARING

It is religion, the third institution of humanity, that opens the clearing (*lucus*) to the sky.

"Opening the eye" (*lucus*) to the sky, as Harrison puts it, is the giants' response to a chance event, and it is in this response that human history begins, belatedly and after the fact. According to Vico, the eye opens in response to a lightning flash that startles the giants immersed in the thick foliage. Their astonishment provokes them to make a clearing open to the sky in order to see whence came the flash that has already vanished. The lightning flashing out of darkness thus uproots the creatures from the forest habitat to which they were so well adapted.

The story of human becoming is thus launched as a belated and inadequate or inappropriate response to a mysterious bolt from the blue. Lightning, suddenly and unpredictably, flashes in the dark, and the human clearing is made in the trace left by its departure. The beginning of human history is thus split in two: lightning flash and response, out of synch, the one always seeking but never catching up with the other. Hearkening back to this lightning flash, Donald Philip Verene writes, "Without their conscious knowledge, it causes them to begin to make themselves. They begin to make a human world through the experience of something other than themselves."[8] The giants' response incorporates this random event into the clearing, and with this incorporation of the random, the history of men is launched. The contingency of what befalls us from the sky and the vagaries of the weather are very much part of such a history.

As Harrison emphasizes, the giant creatures wandering the dense primeval forest would never "have suspected that beyond the canopies that shielded them there was such a thing as the sky."[9] But "when at last the sky fearfully rolled with thunder and flashed with lightning . . . a few of the giants, who must have been the most robust, and who were dispersed through the forests on the mountain heights where the strongest beasts have their dens, were frightened and astonished by the great effect whose cause they did not know, and raised their eyes and became aware of the sky."[10] When they looked up, however, immersed as they were in the shelter of the great forest, they saw only "the mute closure of the foliage" above their heads.[11] The giants could not see, not even with their own eyes open, the cause of these celestial events and, in this blindness, "pictured the sky to themselves as a great animated body, which they called Jove, the first god of the so-called greater gentes, who meant to tell them something by the hiss of his bolts and the clap of his thunder."[12] In their unseeing vision and ignorance of causes, the giants come to believe, Vico claims, that a body called Jove intended something. These communications remained, however, unseen and therefore illegible so long as the forest canopy, which shielded and sheltered them from the contingencies of the sky, remained impenetrable. In order to see more clearly the communications sent from the sky, the giants open a *lucus*, an eye or clearing, in the forest. The forest then becomes a world, open to the sky and, as such, possessing a horizon. Where forest meets this uncontainable sky, the world includes its beyond, from which a novel and incalculable future might flash.

Prompted by their belief (in Jovian communications), the giants' movement into the clearing where the history of man begins is thus also a religious movement; the clearing where men are made is also a sacred grove or temple. Vico points out that "the ancient Germans, as Tacitus narrates, worshipped their gods in holy places which he calls *luci et nemora*. These must have been clearings leveled in the midst of the forest." He then goes further and connects the clearing with both temples and the practice of contemplation: "[Human ideas] began with divine ideas by way of contemplation of the heavens with the bodily eyes. Thus in their science of augury the Romans used the verb *contemplari* for observing the parts of the sky whence the auguries came or were taken. These regions, marked out by the augurs with their wands, were called temples of the sky (*templa coeli*)."[13] In other words, the clearings where historical man is born were observatories through which the sky might be contemplated and the divine auspices (thunder and lightning of unseen cause) read. Opening the clearing so as to read meanings in the sky is identified as the augur's task, one that he accomplishes thanks to a wand or staff held in his hand. This wand, like the tool we know as an augur, is used to incise, cut out, or otherwise demarcate the borders of a space in the sky, in and through which the augur would then observe or contemplate the signs that might appear in the clearing. These contemplative spaces cut out of the sky by an augur are what is meant by the word "temple"—contemplation and temple sharing a root, *temnein*, which denotes the act of cutting, dividing, or separating. "Opening the eye," or making a clearing where meaning emerges in the sky, here becomes equivalent to constructing a temple for contemplation.

## TECHNOLOGIES TO OPEN THE EYE: A SECOND EYE

Having come into the clearing, the giants, led by the augur carrying his staff or wand, can indeed see the sky, but only when they see it through an eye that is not their own—not one given them by nature, but one made with a wave of the augur's wand.

The prehistoric giants open the eye or clear the clearing with help from Vulcan, whom Harrison reminds us is "the master of technical skill."[14] Their eyes are opened, as it were, by the god of fire and the forge, who uses his skill or craft to hold open the clearing so that the giants might see. "With these one-eyed giants came Vulcan to work in the first forges—that is the forests to which Vulcan had set fire. . . . Vulcan had set fire to the forests in order to observe in the open sky the direction from which Jove sent his bolts."[15] Vico's tale therefore tells us that hominization is inseparable from technologization, the view of the sky in which humans emerge being impossible without Vulcan and the tools and techniques that make a clearing. Technology marks and even makes the beginning of man, its emergence from its giant origins in a body sufficient to itself, robust, and perfectly adapted to the forest environment that provides for it.

If the event of hominization entails seeing the sky, it must also entail adopting this eye that is not one's own. The augur who leads the religious movement into the clearing is, on Vico's telling, never without a wand in his hand, and the temple that this wand cuts out in the sky is never not also a tool for seeing the skies. If hominization is inseparable from technologization, it is also inseparable from religion, and the history of technology and religion are paired in the becoming of human being.

## THE DESCENT INTO MAN

The institution of man, on Vico's telling, involves moving from the shelter of the "forest canopies that shielded" the giants to the exposure of living in the open, under the sky and the contingencies that might befall them from it.[16] For those living under "the sacred canopy" of the forest, the sky might just as well be dark as light, smiling or snarling. Vulcan, in whom fire or technical skill becomes sacred, does not protect the giants under this canopy but throws them into the uncertainties of life in the open, where they are exposed, vulnerable to whatever might come out of the blue—and thus exposed, they become men.

The giants become men when, led by Vulcan and his technologies, they abandon the protection of the forest canopy for the openness of the temple of the sky. This hominization is contrasted with the giantism that prevails in or under the earth. Other giants, scattered and roaming the forests, responded to the lightning flash by seeking shelter in caves, where they remain giants: "Divinity appropriated to itself the few giants we have spoken of, by properly casting them into the depths and recesses of caves under the mountains. This is the iron ring by which the giants, dispersed under the mountains, were kept chained to the earth by fear of the sky and of Jove." The birth of humanity involves a movement that runs counter to "fear of the sky" and emerges from the shelter and security of the cave that conceals into the openness of the clearing that exposes creatures to the sky. According to Vico, the giants were the original case of "autochthones, which is as much as to say sons of Earth. . . . And in the fables the Greeks quite properly called the sons of earth giants, and the Earth mother of giants."[17] Becoming human, however, means leaving this embeddedness in the earth, abandoning the shelter of concealment in earth and cave, or casting off from mother earth, in order to breathe air above earth and live *on* the earth under the open sky. The adventure of human history is launched when the giants, leaving autochthony behind, stick their necks out of the cave and move into the free and clear.

Vico's story makes it quite clear that becoming human involves a "diminution of stature," as autochthonic giants, sons of the earth, "which among the Greeks and Latins," Vico claims, "meant nobles," stoop to the level of man.[18] The opening of the *lucus* is the place for this weakening or diminution, as that is where noble giants, who needed nothing more than their own organism could obtain from what nature provided, are made into humble men, who need Vulcan's aid—the fiery forge of technology—as a supplement in order to see and take care of themselves. Contrary to the much-repeated claim that technology makes men all-powerful monsters, Vico's story tells of the humble beginnings of a technological humanity, a humanity that begins with the humbling effects produced by living under the open sky. If modern man has become a giant, dominating a world that becomes increasingly gigantic as it measures up to the scale of our technological enhancements of ourselves, Vico's story tells of a different beginning.

## THE SPRAWLING CLEARING, THE CLEARING SPRAWLS

What has happened to these *luci*, open to the sky, that make giants into men?

Their fate is described eloquently, yet caustically, by Robert Harrison. In ancient times, he writes, the Mediterranean coast, the cradle of human civilization, was covered with dense forest or lush woodlands. The industrious Greeks and Romans of antiquity cleared places in the midst of this forest enclosure to cultivate fields and build great cities. The cities built in the place made by clearing away the forest were some of the most prosperous on the planet. "Transformed from forests to pasture to cultivated fields, the land around [cities such as] Ephesus became more productive, to be sure." Industry flourished, and an ever greater population was sustained by what farmers, craftsmen, and warriors could make and do in the lit clearing of the city. But "the loss of the outlying forests eventually led to disaster." Observing the current state of the region, Harrison notes, "It suffices to travel around Asia Minor today and visit such cities . . . to see how nakedly they lie under the open sky. There is little in the vicinity to hide the celestial auspices now."[19]

The eye has become so open to the sky that it is blinded and closes.

When the giants complete the project of hominization, when men make themselves at home everywhere in the world by making everywhere in the world a place where they are at home, they lose the clearing whose humbling effect makes them men.

How are we to keep open the humbling project of the descent of man? Can we continue to descend into our humanity?

* * *

If we ascend the hill at Kielder Forest in Northumberland, there is a small, unremarkable device that might help us make our descent. Built by the artist James Turrell, it makes a clearing on earth open to the sky by working around the edges of the profound blue that draws near in it.

## In the open

Kielder Forest (Northumberland, England, September 8, 2005)
*Kielder Skyspace* by James Turrell

*You ascend the mountain, longing to reach the place at the summit where a small stone building with an opening in the ceiling holds out the promise of seeing the sky above. You have come to this mountain not so much for the view, looking out, across and down, from above the horizon, but for a vision, to see the sky. You do not want to look out and see the sun face-to-face, as Wolff did, but up to see the sky. You do not want to bring the clouds down to earth and see them in its order. You want an opening for the sky so that you might see the clouds there.*

*What you find at the top of the hill is not exactly a shelter or a house: the opening in what would be its roof makes it of only marginal use in providing security and safety from the inclemencies of nature or the contingencies of the weather. And it is not exactly a sculpture: hollow, it lacks the solidity and impenetrability of the work of art that you see always and only from the outside. It is instead perhaps a tool: the opening at the top is an aperture that, as in a camera or perhaps a telescope, will help you see the sky. With its assistance, the sky itself and the celestial events it sends might become manifest in the frame made for them by this aperture.*

*You sit on a bench built into a wall that slopes gently back, providing support for the effort to look up through the oculus and receive a vision of the sky. Tipping back your head to look up through the oculus, you feel almost as if you have left your body behind to become a pure eye, receptive to all that shines into it, losing yourself in what you see. You grow dizzy and would fall down were it not for the carved rock and shaped concrete that supports you as you realize this vertiginous prospect. The skyspace holds you here, on the edge of this dizzying moment, looking into an opening that you cannot enter—or is it one you cannot leave . . .*

Rémi Brague, in *The Wisdom of the World*, tells of medieval philosophers and theologians who claimed that man earns his special place among creatures as witness of nature and the cosmos with his erect posture and a rotating neck, which together give him the possibility of looking into the heavens. Many scientists would agree: the distinctiveness of the human species resides in the fact that we walk erect, with hands divorced from functions of locomotion and head freed from responsibility for grabbing and procuring what we eat. According to the medievals cited by Brague, this construction affords human beings the opportunity to realize their singular nobility, for without this physiology, man could not look at the sky and contemplate the heavens.[20] This physical ability to raise his eyes to the sky distinguishes man from the animals who must use their faces to procure food that crawls on the earth or remains rooted in the ground. It also distinguishes man from the angels, who know the highest things "without needing to raise their eyes to the firmament and reading it there."[21] Angels, to realize the nobility of the soul, need neither to venture into a clearing where they can turn their gaze to the skies nor to wait for the clouds to part; they already dwell in the heavens. But men, who dwell between earth and sky, need both—an open clearing and raised eyes—if they are to emerge from their autochthony and come into their humanity. Brague goes on from the medievals to tell of those moderns for whom the erect posture of human being still accounts for human greatness, but now owing to the fact that it affords human beings the privilege of dominating nature. Owing to our erect posture, we have hands that can seize hold of the world and, perhaps even more basic, eyes with a commanding view of this world. For the moderns, "Man is upright not in order to look at the sky, but in order to be able to watch the rest of creation from above it."[22]

At Turrell's skyspace, I take a step back from self-assertive modernity with its perpetual look out toward the horizon to see what comes next. Like Brague's medievals, I cast my head back in order to look to the sky. But in approaching what the medievals take to be the dignity of human being, I grow dizzy and fall back, caught by the benches and sloping walls that support my fall. I do not see the sky by standing tall. If I do stand tall like a giant and attain the highest possibility of what my erect posture affords me, I fall over.

Turrell addresses this when he talks about the phenomenon of celestial vaulting. One of the authors on whom he draws as a source for describing this is the scientist Marcel Minnaert, who explains that when we stand erect and survey the sky, "the space above us does not generally give us the impression of being infinite, nor of being a hollow hemisphere spanning the earth. It resembles, rather, a vault whose altitude above our heads is less than the distance from ourselves to the horizon."[23] Standing tall and surveying all that appears within the circuit of the horizon, you lose infinity and depth, living instead under a flat, opaque roof where what gets into the picture you see is all there is. Turrell instructs us instead to fall or lie down on the earth. Lying prone, he says, we come to dwell under the open sky and see a phenomenon that is inapparent when we look out and survey the world with the commanding gaze that for disenchanted moderns comes with erect posture. This phenomenon is the infinity and openness of distance, a vista into which you look without your gaze coming to rest.

What my own visit to the skyspace let me understand is that human greatness (looking into the heavens, as the medievals said) lies in its capacity for fainting, for dizziness, for lying down—for falling. Turrell's skyspaces support this fall. They bring us to a place where we lose the position that affords us the commanding gaze of Brague's modern man, erect with focused gaze. But they also complicate the position of those who would praise unhesitatingly the medieval by reminding us that the heights of humanity, even according to the medieval schema, are realized in moments of self-abandon and ecstasy, when, with head thrown back, you fall.

*Sitting here, in a supposedly secure place where the stone walls promise to contain whatever vision you might have, you grow a bit uncomfortable. You have bent your neck back or lain prone for so long a time looking up that you have grown dizzy, lost your balance, and sat down in surrender to the whimsy of the sky. In this visionary place, you are surprisingly not in control of the conditions of sight. You dwell here unsettled, out of control, as the sky itself decides what you will see. What you see comes quite literally out of the blue: clouds floating over the edge of the aperture, birds soaring through the frame of the oculus, a leaf turning over and over as it drifts on uncertain winds whose currents take it into the distance.*

*With its aperture open to the heavens above, the device is like an eye. But who is it that sees? I have become a part of the machine such that it is no longer I who see, but the whole device that receives a vision when I enter into it. Am I in charge of this device or is it in charge of me? Or are we so implicated, together constituting a system that sees, that the language of tool or device is no longer appropriate?*

*A strange device, then—one that is about, not securing a vision, but the insecurity of receiving one. Little to nothing remains permanently in the frame of this device. The blue yields to a swiftly passing twilight red; the gray of overcast gives way the next day to swift cloud white. Birds leave as they come; leaves float into view in order to pass over the edge and out of sight. I am helpless to stop their passing. Nothing stays securely in this place.*

*A strange device, again—one that does not make the world from what you know about it but lets it come out of the blue without your knowing what or when. What you look into while you rest here is not something either you or he, James Turrell, have made. Though there is a work, and even a work of art, you have come here not to see it but to see into it and through it. The longer you stay, the less certain you can be of what you will see. The more familiar you become with this place, the more surprises you may chance to see. Residing here for more hours does not mean that you are any more likely to see what you planned on seeing. What will come, and when? Having come, how long will it stay? Once departed, will it come back? Waiting patiently and hoping is about all you can do, though even patience does not guarantee that your vision will be secured. Eventually you will grow tired or bored and leave these provinces for home.*

*If it was not I who was in control of what I saw that day, who was? The sky itself, without smiling face, seemed to exercise its own mysterious intentions, sending what it would from out of the blue. I recall the words of Georges Didi-Huberman, who claims that* "what we see looms over us, literally, and in this sense what we see sees us, since these works are nothing other than architectural oculi."[24] *The oculus by which I thought I would see turns out to be an eye that sees me as I sit patiently awaiting what it sends.*

* * *

In opening this clearing where distance draws near, Turrell's art separates what modern disenchantment often connects—seeing from controlling, touching from mastering, and perhaps therefore knowing from manipulating. In Turrell's work, seeing and knowing are best understood as something like contemplation—a vision that does not grasp what it sees but rather admires it or draws intimate with it in the distance.

## Cherishing the blue

What did I see, that day in that place in Northumberland? The blue sky. Yes, the sky which is itself nothing, pure depth and profundity, pure *profondeur*. A strange thing to see, for it is nothing at all. Though you can see it, you cannot locate the sky (say where it is) or measure it (say how far away it is).

### "THE BLUE OF DISTANCE"

I was looking into what Rebecca Solnit has called "the blue of distance," a blue that she reminds me is made up of all the light that gets lost and scattered on its journey from the sun to us. Blue, she says, is the light that "does not travel the whole distance from the sun to us . . . the light that does not touch us . . . [the light] that gives us the beauty of the world."[25] The beauty of the world comes from this bending of light as it swerves on its journey through the void, getting lost in the distance along the way. This lost light is something to which we remain oblivious when looking at

Wolff's *Lucem post nubila reddit*: all the rays there move directly from their source to their end, never straying from the straight and narrow path of focused illumination. Seen in the white light of full or direct illumination, Wolff's world of solid and stable things might appear clear and distinct, but it offers little charm or aura and is not very beautiful—and this is owing to its neglect of the lost blue.

First seen in the work of European painters of the fifteenth century, Solnit claims, the "blue of distance" appears as a narrow, sometimes wider, band that gives "depth and dimension to their work." This blue is where the world of clear and distinct objects edges off toward the faraway and gets lost in the distance, according to a lesson taught by Leonardo: "make the first building... of its own color; the next most distant make less outlined and more blue; that which you wish to show at yet another distance make bluer yet again." The blue of distance introduces a third, intermediate, or borderline realm between the brilliant purity of heaven's white or golden light and the refracted splendor of that light as it appears on the "many colored earth below." Between the two realms (heaven and earth) where one might expect solid and stable objects to appear clearly and distinctly is the "faraway blue realm that is neither, not part of this Christian duality," a realm where things appear, as Leonardo said, "less outlined and more blue."[26]

Taking the medieval icon or devotional image as emblematic of art before the fifteenth century, Solnit claims that before depicting the blue of distance "artists had not been much concerned with the faraway in their art. Sometimes a wall of solid gold backed up the saints and patrons; sometimes the space curved around as though the earth were indeed a sphere and we were on its inside."[27] This solid gold wall and the characteristic flatness or lack of depth in medieval painting, according to Solnit, ensured that the saints never got lost or drifted off into the distance; they would instead stay safe and secure in their place in the heavens and, perhaps more importantly, remain accessible to the devotee who always knew where to look for them. This world, Solnit continues, is not unlike the mental landscape of children: "There is no distance in childhood: for a baby, a mother in the other room is gone, forever, for a child the time until a birthday is endless. Whatever is absent is impossible, irretrievable, unreachable. Their mental landscape is like that of medieval paintings: a foreground full of vivid things then a wall."[28] Beyond that wall, oblivion. Whatever passes to the other side passes into the void, is less than nothing, not even an absent thing. On this side, however, in the brilliant world of omnipresent gold or all-revealing white light, nothing is ever lost or passes away; for if the light is everywhere present, then there is no place that is not illuminated and so no place to get lost. If something is not here, in the clearly illuminated totality the child sees before it, it simply is not and therefore cannot even be lost, absent, or missing. The logic is impeccable, the security purchased unshakable, and the sense of wholeness irrefragable. Oblivious to oblivion, not seeing what is not here to see, one can be confident that all there is can be within reach.

But, Solnit suggests, the discovery of the blue of distance, or Harrison's "edge of opacity," offers an intermediate realm in which less vivid, less solid, less stable things might be spared oblivion and therefore remain real, however far off or absent or... dead. "The blue of distance, Solnit claims, comes with time, with the discovery of melancholy, of loss, the texture of longing." With the discovery of the realm of the blue, the things that pass out of the clear light of the foreground move into the realm of distance, where they lack solid and stable reality and yet are not consigned to oblivion. We are not oblivious to what abides in the distance, even if it is too far off to be reached objectively or seen clearly. Tinged with blue, these things we never forget, like our memories of the dead, "take on the color of where you are not... and the color of where you can never go."[29] This is the "blue of distance." It is, or can be, very beautiful for those who do not neglect it but devote themselves to the things it colors.

In the blue of distance, things are a long way off. Our longing, Solnit claims, is the way to keep open this "long way off" and so to sustain the distance in which things are spared oblivion and the world grows beautiful. The challenge, she suggests, is to cherish this blue, to remain observant of it or to always keep the distance near and dear, to your heart. Such devotion entails the sustenance of longing, of looking into the blue where things remain a long way off—perhaps becoming blue yourself. Our devotion to distance is made difficult by the dominance of consumption as a mode of life that pretends to satisfy desire and fill our longing with ever-ready objects, and it is made difficult by the acquisitiveness that aims to keep things out of distance and so to prevent the pain of longing. But for Solnit, unlike for the consumer or the miser, the blue of longing and of distance are not problems to be solved. "I wonder sometimes whether with a slight adjustment of perspective it could be cherished as a sensation on its own terms, since it is as inherent to the human condition as blue is to distance? If you can look across the distance without wanting to close it up, if you can own your longing in the same way that you own the beauty of that blue that can never be possessed?"[30]

Solnit knows very well that this longing is the question of love. For it is love that stays intimate with what remains in the distance; it is love that cherishes the blue and is not oblivious. Citing the mystic Simone Weil, she says, "Let us love this distance, which is thoroughly woven with friendship, since those who do not love each other are not separated."[31] With the intimacy of love and friendship comes distance, and that is not oblivion.

* * *

How can we cultivate a taste for the blue that Solnit claims is inherent to the human condition? Turrell's skyspaces are a response to this vocation to cherish the blue, to remain observant of the distance. They bring distance near, where we can keep it dear to our hearts, so near and dear that it at times becomes the skin or firmament of the heavenly vault we see stretching over the oculus.

Turrell has said of the Roden Crater project, his life's work, that as visitors emerge from tunnels inside the crater and ascend to the crater's cone they will see the celestial vault: "You'll get this sense of closure, although nothing physical is there."[32] It is almost as if by submitting to the demands of Turrell's devices you see the firmament return. The blue of distance materializes.

And yet, however much the blue materializes, the celestial vault that encloses the place is also the aperture that opens it. I wish Turrell had not said only that you get a "sense of closure" but had also spoken of the opening. The blue that might, like the firmament, enclose this place, make it distinct, is also the beautiful blue that injects distance and the unlimited into the distinctness of this chamber too small to contain it. Distance having drawn near is not distance overcome but, rather, distance made unsettlingly intimate.

## Kielder Forest (Northumberland, England, September 8, 2005)
*Kielder Skyspace* by James Turrell

*The invisible and unending blue sky seemed on that day in Northumberland, when I adopted that strange posture beneath the frame of that strange oculus, to have drawn near.*

*My eye finds to see what it will see by looking into this other eye, this oculus, and seeing what appears there as given to see. Looking into this other eye, I and the things of the world enter the intimacy of a gaze, an intimate gaze, or a gaze intimate with what it sees, however far off and especially because far off.*

*What draws into the nearness or intimacy of looking into this other eye? I saw passing clouds, shifting forms rising and collapsing. I saw a leaf turning over and over, adrift on uncertain winds, and birds. Clouds, blowing leaf, birds, even an airplane—all drew near to me in the eye designed to receive them, yet none were contained by the limits of this container. I became intimate with things in the distance of the blue sky as it took shape in the oculus.*

*The simplicity of such a simple vision of things can be the hardest to achieve.*

## "LOVELY BLUENESS"

In a late work written after returning from the asylum, the poet Friedrich Hölderlin tried to make his own home in a place under the blue sky.

Looking into what he termed the "lovely blueness," in which he saw "the steeple blossoms," Hölderlin asked, "Is God unknown? Is he manifest like the sky? This rather I believe. It is the measure of man."[33] For a long time, I wondered if the two questions were posed as alternatives. If I answer "yes" to one, must I answer "no" to the other? Or if not synchronous alternatives, perhaps a series in which, say, a negative answer to the first leads to a positive answer to the second: No, he is not unknown; he is known. How? Because he is manifest.

Yet another reading is possible. I suppose I should have known it all along, but it was taught to me at the skyspace in Northumberland, where I saw the sky and learned what it might mean to be "manifest like the sky." Perhaps the answer to both questions is "yes": indeed God is unknown, and yet he is manifest. "The god who remains unknown must by showing *himself* as the one he is appear as the one who remains unknown. God's *manifestness*—not only he himself—is mysterious," Martin Heidegger writes in an important commentary on Holderlin's poem.[34] Such an unknown God who is manifest mysteriously, or a God who is manifest yet remains mysteriously unknown, appears if you believe. "This rather I believe," says Hölderlin. It is belief that holds God to be both unknown and manifest; it is belief that maintains (rather than dispels or sees through) the mysteriousness of manifestation. While the convinced religious are often certain that they know God, whose work is manifest all around them, those who do not know God still have to believe and in their belief hold an unknown God who manifests this mystery.

Of course. Belief can hold both. But I am not what most people would call a believer. Is there for me an experience of such belief? What would it mean for me to experience such belief? Where is such belief born? Unknown and yet believed to be—this makes sense to me if a being can be manifest like the lovely blueness of the sky. It all hinges on an experience of the sky and its "blue of distance." According to Heidegger, "God's appearance through the sky consists in a disclosing that lets us see what conceals itself, but lets us see it not by seeking to wrest what is concealed out of its unconcealedness, but only by guarding the concealed in its self-concealment. Thus the unknown god appears as the unknown by way of the sky's manifestness."[35]

Into such a sky, I believe, a steeple might perhaps blossom and a dwelling place be marked by the sacred. There will be no steeple without the sky into which it rises, and the "lovely blueness" of the sky will fall into oblivion if the steeple does not rise up to draw us intimate with its distance. The steeple of the church might make the believer, not the one who knows what he believes, intimate with such distance, but it does not cross the distance or cross it out. The steeple does not satisfy our longing; it extends it, stretching higher and higher into the distance that is the sky, exposing us ever more to the lovely blue that colors the world with its beauty.

A skyspace recalls this steeple.

Hölderlin saw in the approach of the lovely blueness of the sky "the measure of man." It is the mystery of the sky that becomes the measure that puts man on earth. This is "perplexing," Heidegger observes, and "inconvenient."[36] What good is a measure that remains mysterious or "manifest like the sky"? What can such a measure measure? For a measure to serve as a standard for anything, shouldn't it be palpable, graspable, within reach, so that it can be laid alongside what it is to measure? Shouldn't it be more known and more accessible than that which it measures? What does it say about man if his measure should be the lovely blueness of the sky's distance, a measure that is absolutely incommensurate with what it nevertheless measures? Mircea Eliade, the great phenomenologist of religion, said something similar: "Beholding the sky, he [man] simultaneously discovers the divine incommensurability and his own situation in the cosmos."[37] I am measured, according to both Hölderlin and Eliade, by a mystery. Unlike those things which admit a measure commensurate to them, the portion measured out to me is one of which I remain uncertain. I find my place or situation by opening myself to the manifestation of a distance that I cannot cross or measure. My position thus becomes one in relation to a mystery, which leaves me, inflecting Eliade perhaps in ways he did not intend, ever uncertain of where I am.

* * *

Rising into the intimacy of Turrell's skyspace, I come to dwell on earth by experiencing what "manifest like the sky" might mean.

Kielder Forest (Northumberland, England, September 8, 2005)
*Kielder Skyspace* by James Turrell

*Where are you, here in this place where you have come to be? It is not like the distinct locations of your everyday, workaday world, where clearly defined limits or borders set each in distinct relation with the others. You see the distant sky, for instance, in this place without this sky being contained by the limits of a definable position. Though you can see it, you cannot locate the sky (say where it is) or measure it (say how far away or how big it is). Like the ancient temple, this clearing in Kielder Forest is a container or receptacle for what exceeds it; it cannot hold or keep what it receives from this distance.*

# 5 : Andy Goldsworthy, Works

## TO DWELL CREATIVELY WITH EARTH AND SKY, WIND AND WATER

### Clearing—place of clarity, clarity of place

Consider again the two images with which I opened this book: *Lucem post nubila reddit* and "The Apotheosis of Electricity" (figs. 2 and 3). The first, the frontispiece to Wolff's *Reasonable Thoughts on God, the World, the Human Soul*..., depicts the dawn of a new day when clouds will be banished and "all things in general" will appear clearly and distinctly in the clearing made by the light of the smiling sun. This clearing opens a place where man can take a stand on solid ground surrounded by things that have come to rest in places familiar to him. The clearing is, the picture shows, where he builds his home.

In "The Apotheosis of Electricity," the place of the sun is held by a great electric factory that assumes the work of shining a light that clears away clouds and makes a secure harbor to which ships can come home. This image teaches us about the important role that human industry, work, and technological invention play in making and holding open the clearing where things and men might come to rest on solid ground. Reflecting on the meaning and experience of these human technical capacities, Martin Heidegger wrote, "If man tries to win a foothold and establish himself among the beings [*physis*, commonly translated as *nature*] to which he is exposed... then his advance is borne and guided by a knowledge of them. Such *knowledge* is called *technē*.... From the outset, [*technē*] is not, and never is, the designation of a 'making' and a producing; rather it designates that knowledge which supports and conducts every human irruption into the midst of beings; it always means... the disclosing of beings as such."[1] Not fully rooted in nature himself, man must contend for the ground on which he can "win a foothold" and stand amid the profusion of the things of a nature that fills and overfills the planet. This nature generates things like the sea, tossing this way or that, ever fluctuating and turbulent, indifferent to the human who would dwell there. *Technē* is the irruption of man in this nature. It is, first, the work to establish stable ground or clear an opening in which our technologies can, next, build or make a human world and its objects. In other words, as Heidegger puts it elsewhere, "whatever can look and turn out now one way and now another" is brought to lie here before us by a technology that lights the way to solid ground.[2]

Just as surely as the clouds in these pictures must part for the clearing to open in which "all things in general" can appear, the flowing rivers and stormy seas (in which things might "turn out now one way and now another") must be pushed aside, marginalized, or forgotten when man comes to take his stand on solid ground. What these pictures of clouds clearing put forward as the ideal place of human dwelling appears to be an earth devoid of rivers and tides, solid and stable ground where one need not trouble oneself with what drifts ashore or falls from the sky.

* * *

A clever reader will have noticed that my discussion of these images throughout this book has traded on two related senses of *clearing*: one relates to clarity and the operation of a light in which things might be seen clearly and distinctly; the other refers to a place, an opening or a field, in which men can build and dwell. The two senses are of course not unrelated—we saw them working together in our reading of the imaginative science of Giambattista Vico, where the giants burn a clearing in the great dark forest so as to see the light of the sky. Someone who has read widely in twentieth-century philosophy will also know that I draw both senses from Martin Heidegger's work. And a reader who has taken the time to reflect, even briefly, on the modern science of paleoanthropology will know that this science claims a human world emerged when our ancestors left the dark forest and the trees for the savannah, where a clearing open to the sky emerged amid the jungle.

It is on the second sense, *clearing* as place or opening where human being emerges and comes to dwell, that I will now focus. I will do so by looking at the work of the artist Andy Goldsworthy. How can his work illustrate a way in which human beings might come into the clearing? As Goldsworthy advances into the clearing, he does so with his hands, the primal operator of *technē*: his hands open and they hold open a clearing in which a world, humanly constructed and artificial, emerges amid the earth. His hands make a world that is quite different from the one pictured in our images of modern disenchantment, and, as we might expect, different sorts of things will get into the picture when Goldsworthy has a hand in it. The world that Goldsworthy creates, in part, comprises what Michel Serres describes as "forms very near to the fluxes engendered by rivers, the tide, gusts of wind, and liquid pools. The work does not stay."[3] Or, to borrow the title of the popular documentary film about Goldsworthy, his work opens a world replete with "Rivers and Tides."[4] There, in Goldsworthy's world, we dwell not on solid ground but nevertheless profoundly in a place, alongside things that do not stay permanently and are often far from stable, in flux and fluctuating because engendered or created *with* the waters and the winds. *With*: that is to say, *out of* or *from* the river and the wind, but also *in partnership with* the river and the wind. Waters and winds, earth and sky, prove to be both elemental natures that emerge in the work of art *and* creative forces at work in the thing's emergence.

If "The Apotheosis of Electricity" shows us a clearing made for man who cannot abide the impermanent and unstable—a world that excludes rivers and clouds, winds and storms, and all that might be borne aloft or cast adrift on their fluctuations and turbulence—Goldsworthy's work shows us what might get into the picture, and flow away, when our hand guides the clearing. We dwell there with created things that are not secure but adrift; we abide with things-made that do not stay but float; we reside with thingly works that come to be by scattering themselves in the wind with which they are created.

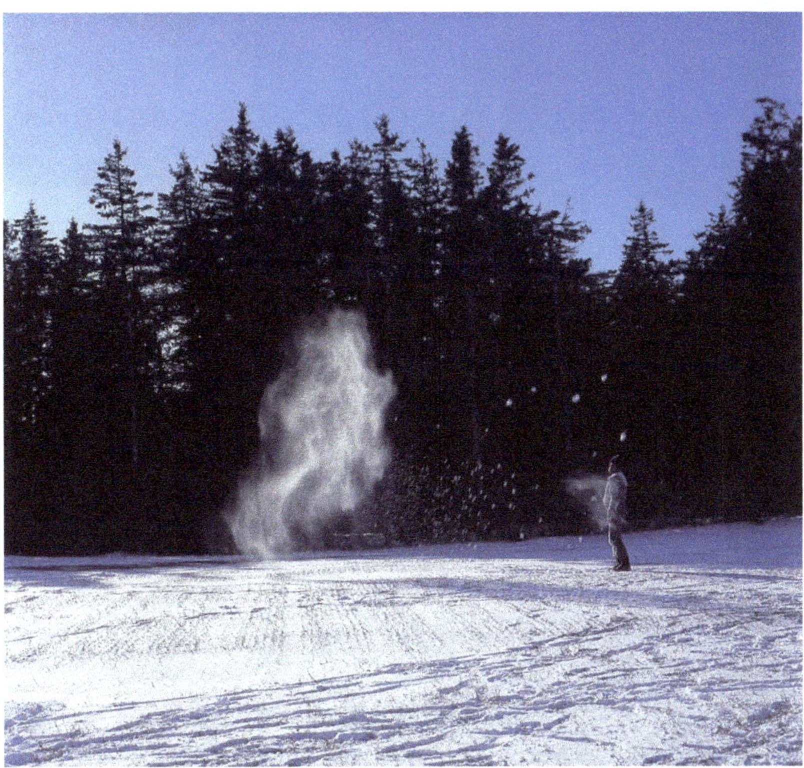

FIGURE 29. Andy Goldsworthy, *Snow / sun / wind / throws / 7 February 1999*. Photograph by Mark Austin.

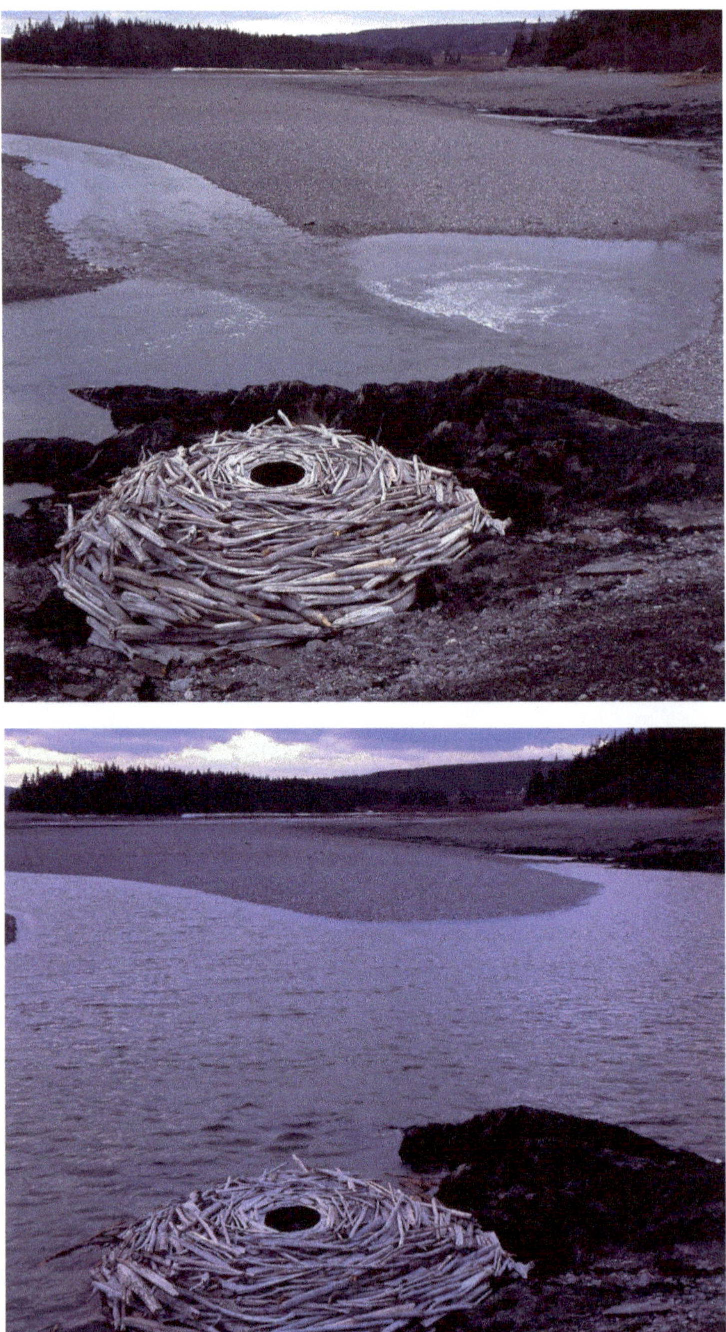

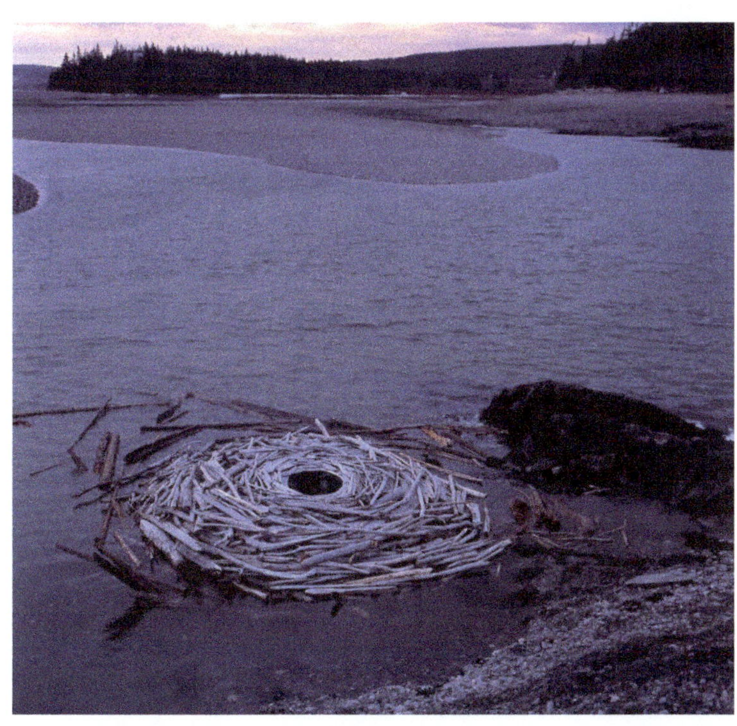

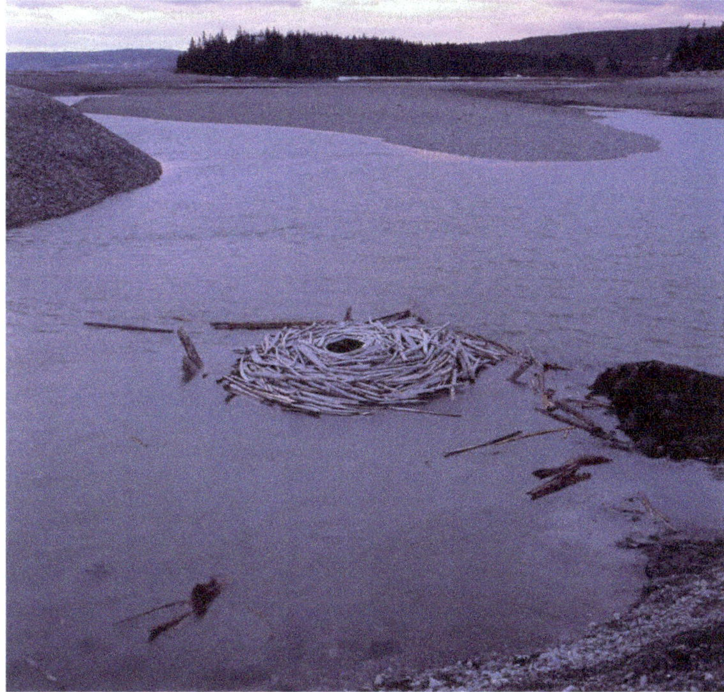

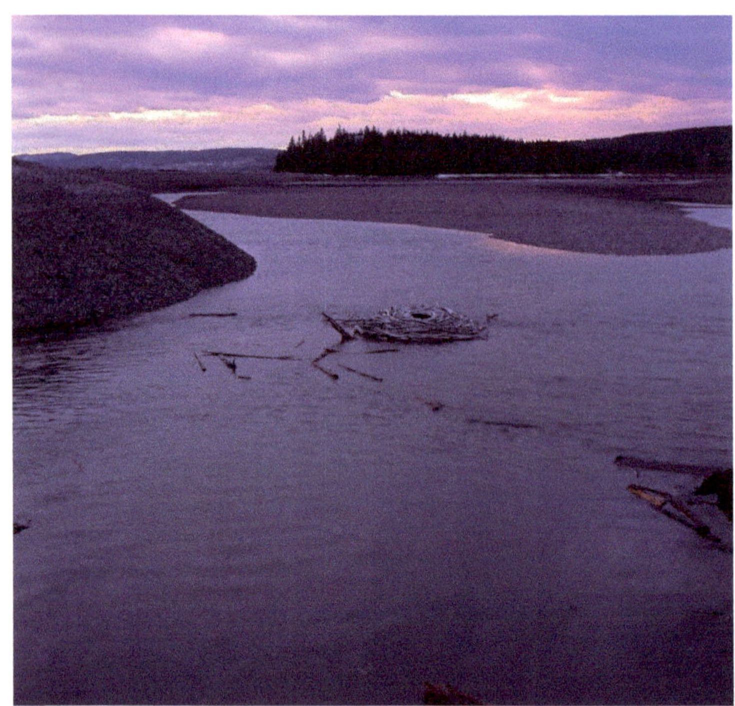

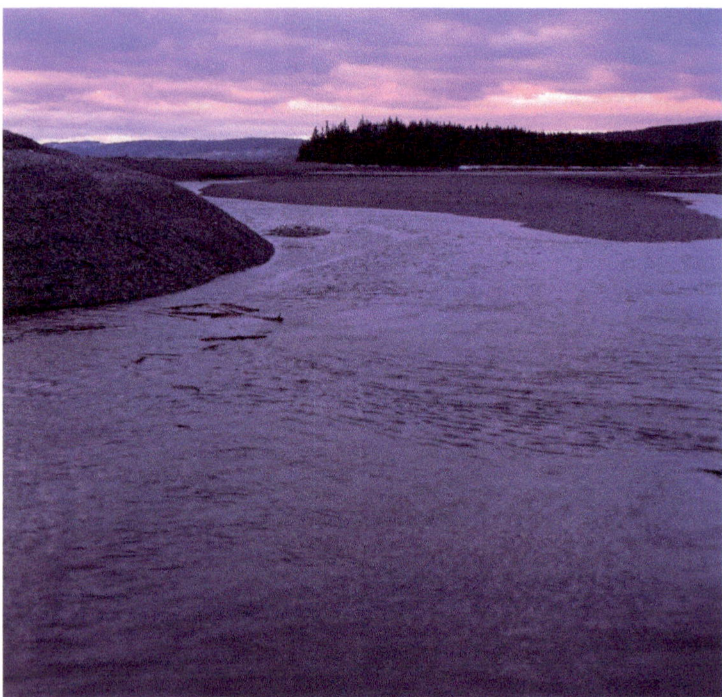

FIGURE 30. Andy Goldsworthy, *Stick dome hole / made next to a turning pool / a meeting between river and sea / sticks lifted up by the tide / carried upstream / turning / 10 February 1999*. Photographs by Andy Goldsworthy.

## A hole in nature

It is not uncommon for both his admirers and his detractors to think of Goldsworthy as a wooly romantic, a back-to-nature type fleeing human culture and the work of making, avoiding technics altogether in favor of rootedness in nature, place, and the earth. This interpretation is suggested by the fact that Goldsworthy works almost entirely with the givens of a place, bringing very little, almost nothing, to the site where he creates. Bark, leaves, and rocks found on-site are his materials; colors are provided by clay found at the bottom of a stream or from roots uncovered beneath the soil; thorns serve as fasteners in place of industrially produced nails. As one critic summarizes, Goldsworthy is "almost puritanical in his insistence on using materials like sticks, stones, leaves or water found on site to create often ephemeral works that minimally affect the environment."[5] Early in his career, this puritanism entailed not even tearing leaves from trees but waiting for them to be given to him as the passage of time, the inevitability of death, and the natural process of entropic decay brought them to the ground. Only then would he claim them.

In taking what a place offers or gives, Goldsworthy's work is attuned to what he speaks of as the "energy of a place" or the "tremendous potential" here. But it would be a mistake to conclude from this connection to place and nature that Goldsworthy teaches us nothing about the human creation of a world or about the work of art and the role *technē* plays in the birth of a world and its artificiality:

> I remember overhearing a comment by a member of an audience waiting for me to give a lecture who was trying to explain my work to the person next to him and saying that I use only natural materials and no tools. My commitment to what are described as "natural materials" is often misunderstood as a stance against the "man-made." I need the nourishment and the clarity that working with the land with my hands gives me, but at various times I have made use of light and heavy machinery. . . . Pretending I could do without tools when I need them would be a lot like pretending I could swim to America.[6]

If Goldsworthy has much to teach us about how we might have a hand in opening a clearing where a world emerges, he will have equally much to teach us about this hand's relation to technology and the tools it holds. I will consider that soon enough. One thing that is clear for now, though, is that Goldsworthy rejects the idea that the work of art, human making, and the artificial or man-made have nothing to do with dwelling in the places he inhabits. Dwelling in a place is not entirely and only about nature, even if it does involve working with natural materials.

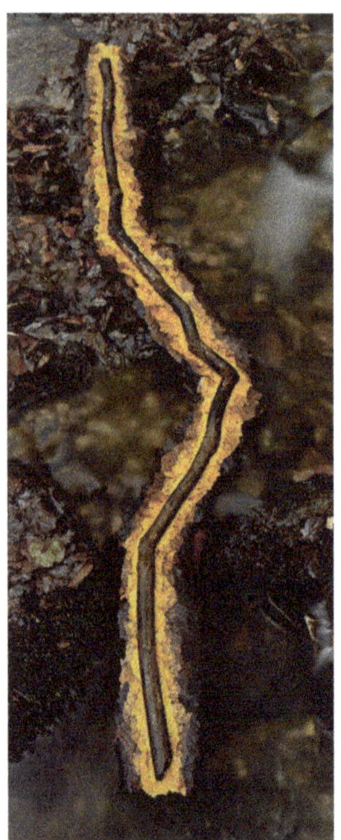

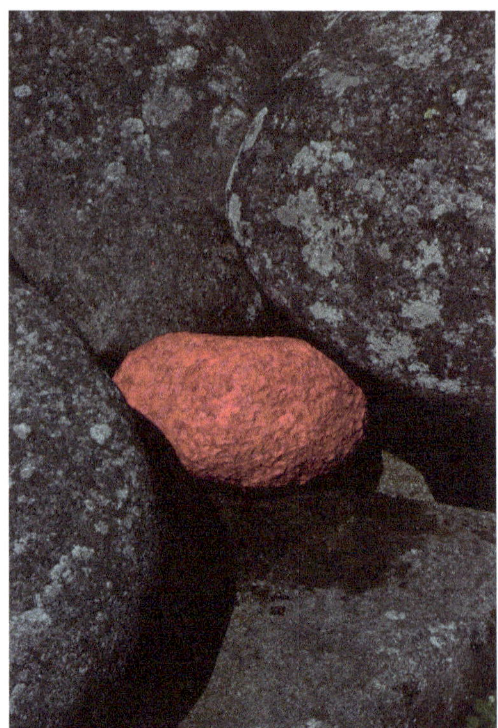

FIGURE 31. Andy Goldsworthy, *Elm sticks / laid on elm leaves / held above the stream / by elm bark. Townhead Burn, Dumfriesshire / 22 November 2002*. Photograph by Andy Goldsworthy.

FIGURE 32. Andy Goldsworthy, *Poppy petals around a granite boulder*. Photograph by Andy Goldsworthy.

Nature in our modern sense never made yellow form like these leaves do, and elm sticks float on bark above a shallow, running stream like that (fig. 31), and it never made a rock as red as poppy petals like this one (fig. 32). While these works might "minimally affect the environment," they do mark a disturbance or unsettling irruption within it. These are, the same critic wisely continues, "works of magical artificiality," and while they "might well be about nature, they are not natural."[7] Human craft, industry, and creativity has had a hand in bringing to light what gets into the pictures we see here. These things have been made, not given. The nature of things has not been left to realize her own ends, "to turn out now one way and now another" but has received a hand; human work and Goldsworthy's own peculiar industriousness have shepherded it this way rather than that.

What Goldsworthy exemplifies, then, is a way of human being, in Robert Harrison's words, "not in nature but in the relation to nature." "We do not inhabit the earth," he continues, "but inhabit our excess of the earth.

We dwell not in the forest but in an exteriority with regard to its closure."[8] The work of art, with *work* taken in an active sense, is the way in which Goldsworthy establishes himself there as a human being in relation to the earth or nature which he exceeds. What emerges in this relation—the work of art, with *work* taken in a nominal sense, as result or outcome, artifice—is what we might call a world, other than but related to the earth with which it is made.

This relation, or world of art, in which we dwell (the opening or clearing in nature) is lost by those who are fully and unquestioningly part of the picture set up by modern disenchantment. If nature is so clarified as to be reduced to raw material, then no relation is possible since, inert, it can only be manipulated or dominated. Commenting on the man and nature that come to light in Wolff's *Lucem post nubila reddit,* the theologian Karl Barth asserted, "The abundance of things provided [by the light of the smiling sun] is in the eyes of [this man] a mass of raw material, of which he believes himself to be the master. This material he confronts as he who has all the knowledge: knowledge of the form, the intrinsically right, fitting, worthy, beautiful form for which all the things provided are clearly intended to be the material." In the world produced by human mastery over, not relation with, nature, nature, if the term holds, "has been put to rights and formed in accordance with man's sensibility and enjoyment... the stream as a fountain, the lake as a clean and tidy pond, the wood as a park reduced to visible order, the field and the bushes and flowers as a garden, the tree shaped with the garden-shears."[9]

This fully human world, in which forest has become park and stream fountain, is the dream of many modern urban- and suburbanites: the city, built on ground made of concrete, where we might be emancipated from the earth and approach the freedom and autonomy imagined by much of secular humanism. In this dream of the city, the freedom to make and to build is unlimited because no longer in thrall to, or enthralled by, surrounding forest, fluctuating cloud, or turbulent river. Antoine Roquentin, in Jean-Paul Sartre's novel *Nausea*, imagines the security of such a world:

> I am afraid of cities. *But you mustn't leave them*. If you go too far you come up against the vegetation belt. Vegetation has crawled for miles toward the cities. It is waiting.... *You must stay in the cities* as long as they are alive, you must never penetrate alone this great mass of hair waiting at the gates.... In the cities, if you know how to take care of yourself, and choose the times when all the beasts are sleeping in the holes and digesting, behind the heaps of organic debris, *you rarely come across anything more than minerals, the least frightening of all existents.*[10]

Even if an undercurrent of awareness seems to have awakened Roquentin to the pavement cracking beneath his feet, he seems unable to accept the possibility of not living the dream of urban freedom.

Scorning Roquentin's advice, Andy Goldsworthy ventures beyond "the gates" and does not build his most famous work in the city—or even the park or garden. He works in difficult to reach, hard to manage, and sometimes out of control places where the nature he encounters has much more to it than the merely mineral, "least frightening of all existents." His work drives him to a rugged seaside beach on the edge of earth and water, into the turbulence of rushing rivers, and to the extreme end of the earth, to the North Pole, to create work with ice. He even traffics with holes, where Roquentin fears "all the beasts are sleeping" (fig. 33).

If making or staying in the city represents one way to put an end to the disturbance of dwelling in the relation with nature, this relation is also lost by those who want nature untouched and unscathed. Defenders of the uncleared earth often seem to deny a human relation with nature in their effort to protect it from contact with human operations that would represent, they argue, a contaminating foreignness. Nature, in this view, remains sacred and hale, whole, something not to be touched, handled, or broken into, to the point that it loses any relevance to us because we no longer have any relation to it—lest its absolute sacrality be reduced to a sacredness that is relative, because relative to us. Sometimes this protection of nature's absolute sacrality takes the form of returning man to his supposed oneness with nature. Nature, as absolute, cannot admit anything as relative to it, so man must be part of this great unity; there cannot be anything more to the human than the natural and, indeed, the human must be reducible to this nature. Surely, making man one with nature eliminates the possibility of any relation, which necessarily implies separation—and without any relation, how could the great unity have been so disturbed by man, as many defenders of nature's holiness insist has happened. The defenders of nature's holiness should take a minute to recall that God died, too, as much from his remoteness and abstraction as from a descent into immanence and human science.

Andy Goldsworthy does not leave nature untouched. Far from it: he touches it all the time, creatively manipulating it. In his hands, human creative work does indeed come into nature, disturbing it and shaping it, but not exactly from the outside. His work is an opening or break in nature. Perhaps this is the importance of the holes that were some of his earliest work and remain an ongoing theme. With the irruption of humanity, Goldsworthy's work suggests to me, a hole or break is made in the midst of nature—signaling the emergence of an excess or stranger in its fullness.

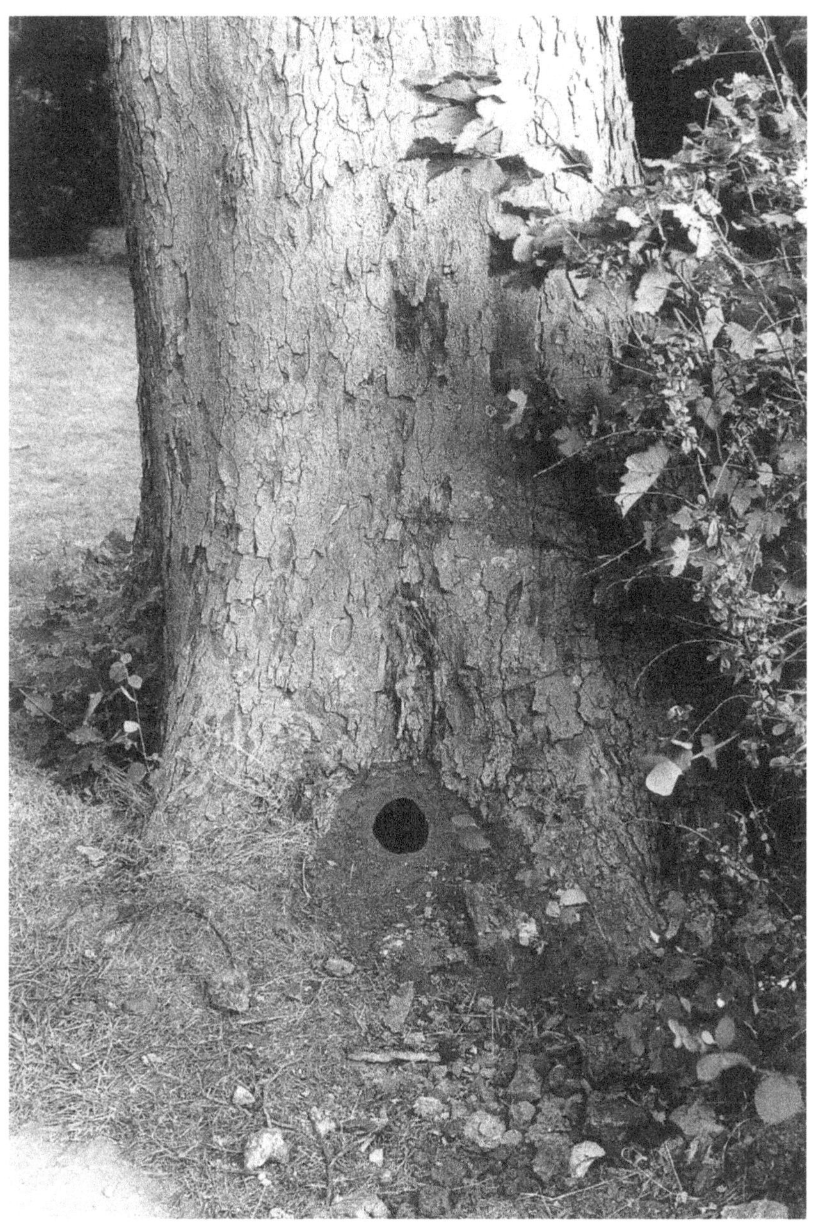

FIGURE 33. Andy Goldsworthy, *Yorkshire Sculpture Park / September 1983*. Photograph by Andy Goldsworthy.

## In praise of his hands

If you ask the people who love Goldsworthy's work what makes it so special, one of the first things you hear is "his hands, the things he can make with his hands!" Indeed one of the images from *Rivers and Tides* that lingers most impressively in my mind is from the opening segment, in which we see Goldsworthy at work on a frigid morning manipulating delicate icicles with bare fingers, exposed through the ends of thin gloves with cut-off tips. He has been there, he tells us, since before the sun rose, working with ice to make a twisted, snaking sculpture. He warms the ice with his hands or uses his saliva to melt it just enough and then gently holds it while waiting for the cold to refreeze it in place. The work could not be built in the light of the sun, which would warm the ice ever so slightly, to the point that it would not refreeze. Nor could the work of art happen if his hands were entirely covered; he needs the dexterity of bare fingers to manipulate, however painfully, the icy things available to him in this place hardly warmed by the light of the sun. A complicated partnership, a fraught romance.

The importance that the supposedly naïve man in the street attaches to Goldsworthy's hands is confirmed by the title of a critical retrospective of his sculpture from 1976 to 1990: *Hand to Earth*. A human being, a man, exceeding nature, advances into nature; or—since "nature" is likely to be taken abstractly or conceptually, and "man" as mind or language—a *hand* reaches out into *earth*, clearing an opening where the work of art might create a world and a man, Andy Goldsworthy, might dwell for a moment. If Harrison is right that "we dwell in the relation to nature... [and] inhabit our excess of the earth," hands embody this excess; they are the bodily way this relation is enacted.

What happens when this hand reaches out to the earth? What is brought to light or comes into the clearing? How does this act of opening a clearing or clearing an opening (making a hole in earth) differ from other ways of doing so? And how does this hand make a different humanity of man as it leads into the clearing where humanization happens?

### UNSPECIFIED SPECIES: THE MAN WITH HANDS

Many thinkers claim it is the unique dexterity of the human hand that specifies the human species. Thinkers as diverse as the fourth-century theologian Gregory of Nyssa and the twentieth-century paleontologists Richard Leakey and André Leroi-Gourhan come together on this point—all suggesting that the capacity for language and reason, which many philosophers and humanists take to be definitive of *Homo sapiens*, is made possible by the human hand. As Gregory asserts, "If man were destitute of hands, the various parts of his face would certainly have been arranged like those of the quadrupeds, to suit the purpose of his feeding.... If then our body had no hands, how could articulate sound have been implanted in it."[11] Centuries later, writing in a very different context, the paleontologist Leroi-Gourhan will cite the text of Gregory as an epigram to his great work, *Gesture and Speech,* and remark: "There is little we can add to this quotation except perhaps by commenting in the language of the twentieth century upon what was already evident sixteen hundred years ago." He goes on, over several chapters, to argue that the development of a human brain, that is to say, a brain with the capacity to use spoken language, depends on changes in the anatomical structure and organization of an organism—changes *not* designed to enable language but which make it, unintentionally, possible. These changes are chiefly those associated with upright posture and the consequent liberation of the hands from the specific task of locomotion. "Bipedal posture and a free hand automatically imply a brain equipped for speech."[12] Gourhan's contemporaries Richard Leakey and Roger Lewin concur:

> The development of language becomes feasible when appropriate selective pressures are operating: a mouth that is adapted to help procure food, carry objects, and threaten or exert aggression is unlikely to be able to articulate complex sounds. By our definition, competent manipulative hands and a sophisticated language are essential faculties to a cultural animal.... [But] in a very real sense we owe our capacity for speech to the higher primates reaching out [with their hands] to analyze their three-dimensional world.[13]

The hand, it seems, frees us to be the rational and linguistic being that we are: without hands we would need to use our mouths and tongues for grabbing, not speaking; and the posture that accompanies the free hand implies a brain capable of language and reason. Whether one is a paleontologist or a mystical theologian, the human hand thus appears as something like the condition for the possibility of the language and reason that specify man.

But if the hand conditions human specificity, then human being is specified by its lack of specificity. What makes the human hand unique is its indetermination for specific tasks or purposes; the hands are free and freeing. When forelimbs are no longer necessary for locomotion, they are liberated for other and undetermined tasks. Observing that the human hand has a sophisticated ability to grasp fine or delicate things precisely, whereas the hands of other animals and prehumans have either a simple precision grasp or only a power grip, Leakey and Lewin write, "Later in the evolutionary progression the precision grip began to emerge, reaching extreme sophistication in humans. But, in spite of this specialization, the human hand has not lost its basic general abilities, such as the power grip and prehensibility... the human hand is extremely functionally flexible."[14] In its extreme flexibility, the human hand breaks out of any specific, fitted niche in nature and detaches human beings from fascination with an environment in which they would be rooted. The hand makes us a stranger, a foreigner, a hole, without proper place.

Aristotle, in ancient Greece, gave eloquent expression to the ambiguous greatness conferred on man by his free hands. Lions are strong; horses are fast; turtles have shells, eagles wings with which they fly—while man is born only with his bare hands, the hands by which he is bare. And yet,

> much in error, then, are they who say that the construction of man is not only faulty, but inferior to that of all other animals; seeing that he is, as they point out barefooted, naked, and without weapon of which to avail himself. For other animals have each but one mode of defense, and this they can never change.... But to man numerous modes of defense are open, and these moreover he may change at will; as also he may adopt such weapon as he pleases, and at such places as suit him. For the hand is talon, hoof, and horn, at will. So too is it spear, and sword, and whatsoever other weapon or instrument you please; for all these can it be from its power of grasping and holding them all.[15]

Observing human being naked, barefoot, and without weapon, lacking in a specific gift or talent that would, by nature, protect him and establish a place for him in nature, Aristotle points to the hand. It is this that converts human destitution into a wonder. To this, the naked hand, with its astonishing lack of determination, he attributes the flexibility and adaptability, multiplicity and variability, of man.

The poverty or destitution of man ("barefooted, naked, and without weapon") becomes on Aristotle's reading the source of human being's creative capabilities. "The hand"—lacking a specific function, good for nothing in particular—"is not to be looked on as one organ but as many.... [making man] the animal of all animals the most capable of acquiring the most varied arts." Aristotle here sees the specifically unspecific nature of the human hand as the ground of creativity and art, making man the most capable place for the emergence of a world and the artificial. By its arts, which are many, not just one as would be the case if the hand fit into a determinate niche, the human hand opens many possible worlds, enabling man "to adopt such weapons as he pleases and at such places as suit him," and it itself takes on a multiplicity of forms ("talon, hoof, and horn, at will"). The indeterminacy of human being could not be represented better than by these hands.

It is because the hands fit man to no place in particular that human being must use its hands to build the many worlds that will house its uncanny, disturbing strangeness on earth. Goldsworthy's work exemplifies this, with the extreme multiplicity of its media (stone, leaves, bracken, water, clay, wool) and its forms (spirals, circles, zigzags, webs, horizontals and verticals). The critics rightly remark on the range of his work, on how much he has made, and how varied it is. One can also note the multiplicity of sites and places where he has created: pastures in rural Scotland, frozen fields at the North Pole, forests in upstate New York, museum spaces throughout the world, warehouses in the industrial sections of major cities. Though he might talk about the need to feel connected to place, the work he does with his hands has meant that place is always plural, that his connections are never exclusive or definitive, settled or permanent.

Lest we think that the world opened by the human hand is natural, in contrast to the one made by machines, which is artificial, Aristotle reminds us that "the hand is not to be looked on as one organ but as many; for it is, as it were, an instrument for further instruments... of all instruments the most variously serviceable."[16] Hands are instruments, that is, of the breakout of the technological, the artificial, and the nonnatural amid nature. As the philosopher Bernard Stiegler puts it, "The hand is the hand only insofar as it allows access to art, to artifice, and to *tekhnē*."[17] As soon as a being with hands emerges on earth, there is the potential for tools and technology—the hand being "an instrument for further instruments"—and hence also for the earthly excess of a world in the work of art, human creativity, and the artificial. Leroi-Gourhan, the paleontologist, concurs, bringing Aristotle's metaphysical propositions back to what twentieth-century science had to say about the emergence of human being on earth: "The Australanthropians seem to have possessed their tools in much the same way as an animal has claws. They appear to have acquired them, not through some flash of genius which, one fine day, led them to pick up a sharp-edged pebble and use it as an extension of their fist... but as if their brain and bodies had gradually exuded them."[18] Indeed, there is nothing in the fossil record to suggest that there ever was a human hand that did not hold tools; we never find an organism with these hands in the absence of the inorganic tool that "their brain and bodies had gradually exuded."

If human anatomy has as its corollary the technological, if we regard "tools as being a 'secretion' of the anthropoid's body and brain,"[19] then the hand that identifies human being is also what makes it ever not itself. In Aristotle's words, "the hand is talon, hoof, and horn, at will. So too is it spear, and sword, and whatsoever other weapon or instrument you please; for all these can it be from its power of grasping and holding them all."[20] The very power by which the hand asserts itself by nature, grabbing and holding, is what undoes it and its nature, transforming it into another instrument, artificial and other than itself. The hand always holds a tool, by which it becomes spear and sword, talon, hoof and horn, making a human being something other than the human it is. "Chopper and biface seem to form part of the skeleton, to be literally 'incorporated' in the living organism."[21] One therefore cannot look at the technological or the artificial as a fall from original purity or unity with nature.

## COUNTING ON OUR HANDS

An exhibition entitled *Writing on Hands: Memory and Knowledge in Early Modern Europe*, organized at the Trout Gallery on the campus of Dickinson College and curated by Claire Richter Sherman, offered visual demonstration that the hand represents the technical already inhabiting nature in human being. The exhibition collected images of the human hand as depicted in early anatomical renderings, religious works, astronomical charts, musical scores, and other contexts. Looking at these pictures, one is struck by all that we can do and have done with our hands. Not only do we make all that we make with the tools we hold in them, but we speak with our hands (sign language), divine with our hands (chiromancy), count with our hands (as children, and many adults, do math), and use our hands as memory devices (the Guidonian hand used by monks to memorize complicated chants). Indeed, we have even used our hands to chart the path to salvation, in monastic diagrams and manuals (literally) for the spiritual life. Sachika Kusakawa writes in the exhibition catalog, "In Western Europe the hand had once been a reliable instrument for reckoning numbers, symbolizing a skill that orators considered a mark of accomplishment. It has also been a memory pad, facilitating the task of 'calculating' the most important date of Christianity."[22] Today machines perform all these tasks, especially those of calculation and archiving memory. We need not conclude from this, however, that today's calculating and archiving machines entail an alienation from our organism or our bodily envelope. Rather, we could look at these images as showing us that our hands are the first tools on which we could count. I am not first free of tools, such that I fall into technology; rather I am joined from the start with a tool, at my hand, an instrument for instruments.

But with the apotheosis of electricity and modern technologies, something surely has happened to these hands and their relation to technologies and calculation. As Kusakawa observes, "When methods of communication and instruction began to change, and when cultural values began to shift, the hand ceased to be the tool that people in western Europe counted on." All the procedures that we can do and have done with our hands are, with the apotheosis of electricity, ones that are now done, when they are done, by machines. What "The Apotheosis of Electricity" shows is the moment noted by Kusakawa, when "the hand ceased to be the tool that people in western Europe counted on." With the apotheosis of electricity, a world comes to be in which, believing that we can't really count on our hands, we no longer count on them; they are not as reliable, as efficient, or as fast as the technologies that replace them. An age obsessed with repeatable results, efficient production, and getting things done quickly so as to do more things cannot count on human hands. Better to get the tools out of human hands, transfer their control to machines, which can be managed by the merest flick, click, or wave on the touchpad or joystick.

The beauty of Andy Goldsworthy's work reminds us, even so, what it might mean to count on our hands, to count on them to open a world in which things appear, brought forth by the delicate, fine touch of a human hand. This is precisely not to say that his handiwork roots us in the earth or even that it returns us to unity with nature, for hands are instruments with which we count and on which we count; they are nature's way of introducing calculation and the technical onto the earth. Goldsworthy has said, "My commitment to what are described as 'natural materials' is often misunderstood as a stance against the 'man-made.' I need the nourishment and the clarity that working with the land with my hands gives me, but at various times I have made use of light and heavy machinery.... Pretending I could do without tools when I need them would be a lot like pretending I could swim to America."[23] His hands, "the instrument for further instruments," have at times taken hold of a blowtorch or manipulated a crane to lift large boulders; they have sketched plans and designed projects. But Goldsworthy never lets the instrumental and the technical, the work and creation, the man-made and the artificial, get out of hand. Even when a blowtorch is used, it is worked by hand.

This is perhaps what distinguishes his advance into nature from the clearing made with "the apotheosis of electricity." The trick to dwelling in the relation with nature, he shows us, is to keep our hands on the tools we use to hold open the clearing. Let's not come unhinged and disarticulate the joint of hand and tool—giving credit to the tool alone for what the hand can do when it takes hold of it. The apotheosis of electricity, then, might mean that modern technologies have become detached from a hand that manipulates them with the precise and delicate operation of human being. As we click, switch, type, or wave our way through a world of our own making, we seem to have forgotten how to be the being with a hand in the creation of a world.

Much of the charm of Goldsworthy's work resides, I suspect, in the way it marries care and delicacy with uprooting and disturbance, a marriage effected in his hands. As the primal operator of the human advance into nature, the hand uproots; it turns over and overturns, discovers and unearths. Goldsworthy's hands are dirty: they uproot bracken in order to discover the burnt umber of the stalk buried in the earth; they crumble rock in order to release the red iron pigment; they move rocks deposited in forest, beach, and meadow. And yet, though the hand uproots and breaks open the earth, one sees in Goldsworthy's work of art a dedication to the careful work of making a world by hand. The world made by hand is in a wonderfully delicate and enchanting balance—like one of the cairns we see him build on the beach in *Rivers and Tides*, poised just at the tipping point, where a stone placed a centimeter to one side pushes it over the edge and brings the whole pile down; or like the web of twig and bracken held together only by thorns and hanging from the limb of a tree so delicately that the slightest gust of wind or too-firm touch will cause its collapse. What characterizes his hands is not so much the power of their grip as it is their touch. "I was able to pick the icicles and the pieces [of ice] up not by gripping or holding, but just by touching them."[24] Such a hand is capable of the careful work and fine manipulation that takes care in a world in which fragile beauty is not neglected.

As the paleontologists remind us, "fine manipulation with the fingers has implications beyond simply being able to pick up small food morsels.... [The thing handled] is not merely a small part of a larger intact pattern.... The opportunities for learning about the world, rather than simply reacting to particular shapes in preprogrammed fashion, are enhanced enormously."[25] Because man has dexterous hands capable of fine manipulations, his world is broken into movable and re-movable fragments and is not a completed whole or programmed history into which he must fit. The world of a man with hands is a world in bits and pieces of incompletion that can and must be fit together. The precise touch of the human hand, unlike the power grip which alone some apes possess, can get a fine, delicate hold on fragile things in a world of incompletion.

Fragmented and not preprogrammed, the world that opens with the hand is not already completed actuality, but possibility and potential. Hence as Goldsworthy advances into the earth with his hands, he sees what he often calls "the incredible potentiality of the place" or "the energy of the place." He does not see a world already actual, present and presented to him; rather he sees the multiplicity and richness of possibility, there in that particular place, possibility that spectators or tourists, sightseers, might never imagine. Such possibility is not simply the latent existence of an actuality simply awaiting a cause (the artist). It is not as if the place says to Goldsworthy, you can do this or this or this or this. Rather, "the incredible potentiality of the place" that Goldsworthy opens seems to me much more like possibility as such, possibility as an openness that could turn out now this way, now that, or any other way, but only becomes this or that when, and if, Goldsworthy's work brings it to light—which means that when it comes to light it comes to light as nothing it would have become if left to blossom in its own light.

## "Each work is a discovery"

"Each work is a discovery," Goldsworthy says, as hands un-cover and disclose, remove and uproot from the shelter of concealment in the earth.[26]

Coming into "the incredible potentiality of the place," he introduces strangeness and incompletion into the closure of the earth. His being there means an unsettling disturbance of nature, a disturbance that makes the earth strange and foreign to itself: stones that float weightlessly over uneven ground (fig. 34); ice that steps from rock to rock over a running river (fig. 35). It is as if a hole had opened in the midst of the earth, something earthly that is not of this earth, something natural that

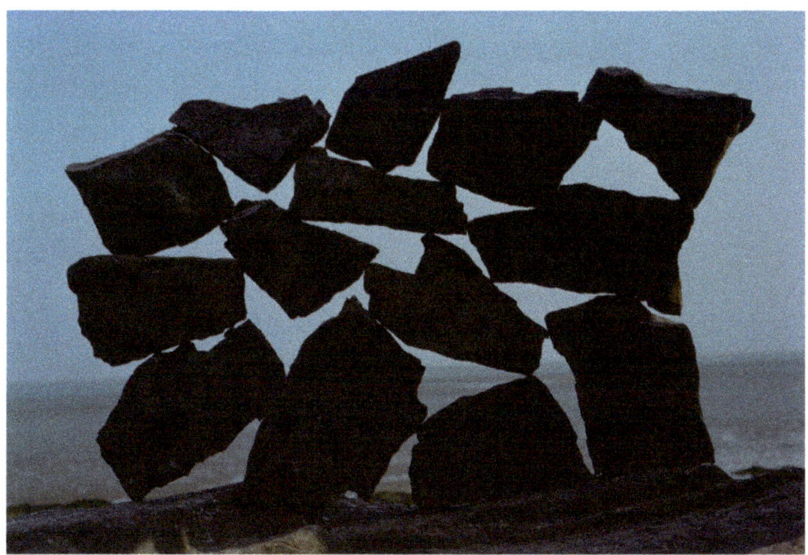

FIGURE 34. Andy Goldsworthy, *Balanced rocks / Morecambe Bay, Lancashire / May 1978*. Photograph by Andy Goldsworthy.

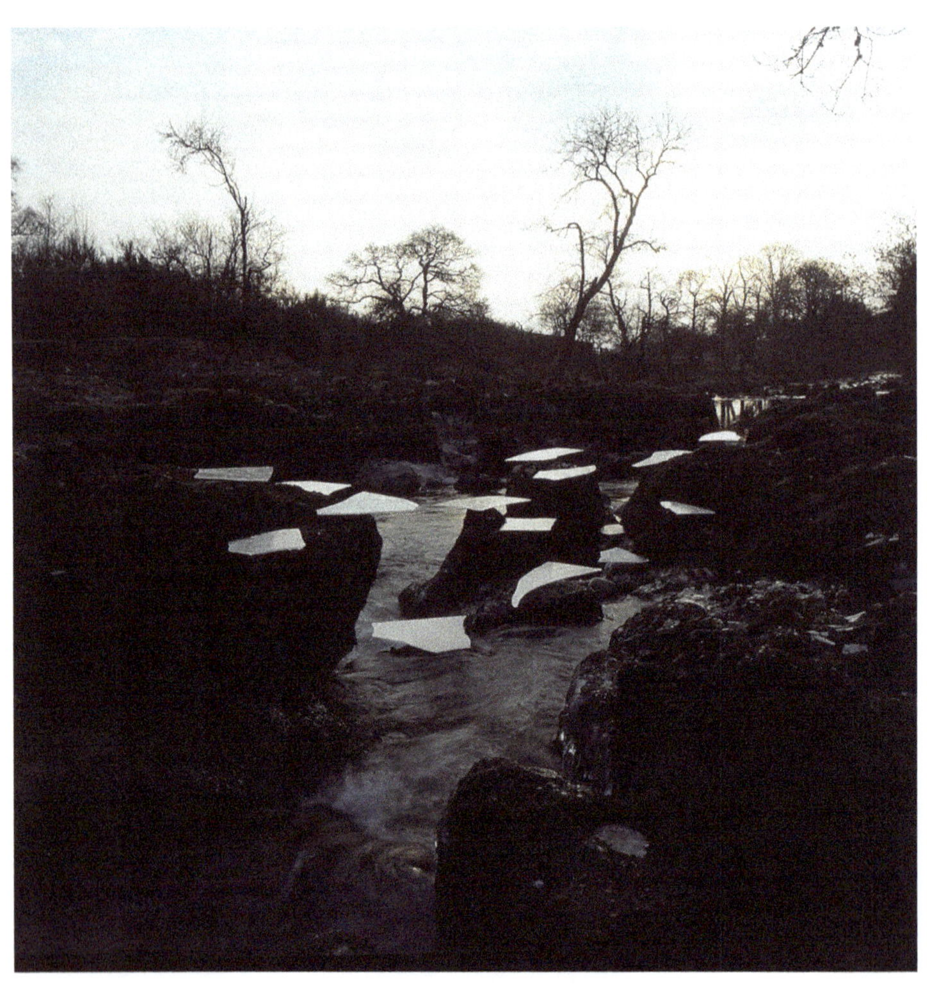

FIGURE 35. Andy Goldsworthy, *Thin ice lifted from nearby pool / frozen to river rocks / melting as the sun rose / Scaur water, Dumfriesshire / February 2004*. Photograph by Andy Goldsworthy.

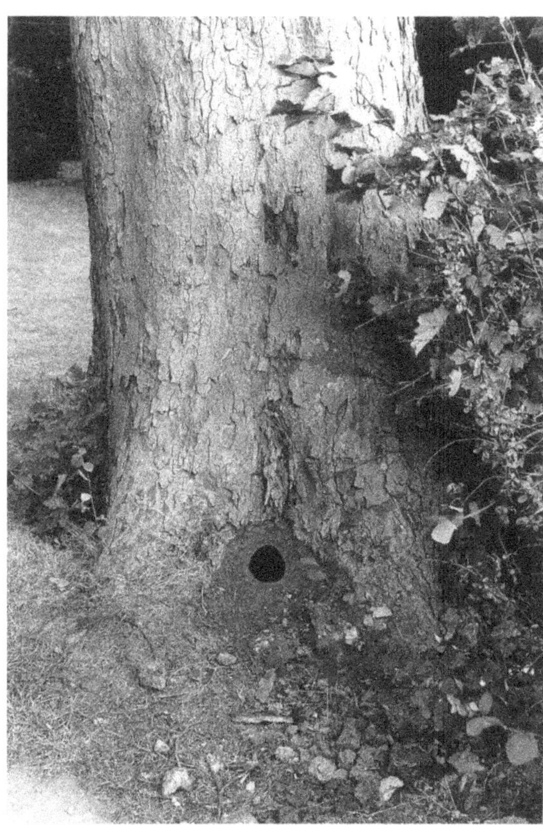

FIGURE 36. Andy Goldsworthy, *Yorkshire Sculpture Park / September 1983*. Photograph by Andy Goldsworthy.

does not belong to nature. In this hole or clearing or opening, something wonderful is brought out of the self-enclosing shelter of the earth and comes surprisingly into the world (fig. 36).

"Each work is a discovery." This suggests that the hand opens a world very different from that opened in modern disenchantment. The world opened by the apotheosis of electricity is one in which "God, the World, the human soul and all things in general" appear clearly and distinctly. Brought to light in this way, all can be seen or predicted in advance of any encounter with or relation to it. This is a mathematical world in which one can hope to calculate each occurrence in advance, before it actually befalls one. Research procedures, or ways of life, whose method conforms to this preconceived plan prove the proper path to arrive safely. "Stick to the straight and narrow" becomes the best advice to produce the desired outcome, to achieve the intended result, to reach the safe harbor.

When "each work is a discovery," not the production of an effect, what is requisite to the work and the world it creates is the unpredictability of what wind and sun will bring, the vagaries of cloud and rain, and sometimes their inclemencies. Though practiced and skilled, Goldsworthy learns what to do from what he discovers when his hand touches earth. Watching him work on-site, one sees that his hand moves hesitantly, tentatively, feeling the weight of the stones in order to learn where to put them. Very often, the work of his hands fails, and the cairn collapses. But at least as often, the hand clears a path to success and brings something unique into being, something difficult if not impossible to repeat precisely because it was made without an antecedent concept, or advance calculation and measurement, by a hand that discovered what to make only after it had made it. Dictated more by what he feels with his hands when he arrives in the place than by what he designs with his mind before entering it, each of the cairns is different and betrays the trace of its making. The hand leaves its mark in the world it creates, precisely because its causality is not efficient enough to erase what it leaves behind.

However skilled, the hand fumbles along, tentatively but delicately, because it does not, in advance, fully comprehend what it will be exposed to or, rather, because it knows enough to know that it is exposed to the outside. Goldsworthy himself is exposed as much as what he dis-covers by unearthing. Working outside with his hands, he is exposed to the elements of the earth: snow and rain, wet and cold, heaviness and darkness, all touch him fiercely, as he acknowledges when he says that the cold takes away heat that once lost cannot be gotten back.

Putting hand to earth, Goldsworthy repeats a gesture with which some claim human civilization began: farming, or agriculture. In contrast to the crudeness of culture made by the efficient production of objects from inert, dead raw material in the laboratory or factory, the culture that is made on the earth through agriculture is a cultivated one. It is created with the earth and sky, the wind and the water, which come into the world in the things that the hand cultivates—like the farmer, or perhaps the vintner, whose work cultivates the elusive *terroir* to make a great vintage in which soil and air, sun and cold, can be tasted. Their work, like Goldsworthy's, creates by *cultivating* the fields (culture as agriculture), unlike that of many experts and academics who make culture by *mastering* their fields. The philosopher Ed Casey speaks to this other origin of the cultured and the cultural:

> *Culture* and *cultivation* were synonymous in Middle English, a reflection of the fact that both words derive from the Latin *cultus*, worship. *Cultus* in turn stems from *colere*, to take care of, till, occupy, dwell. The mention of "dwell" forewarns us of a curious twist in the history of the word *culture*. Despite its current connotation of "higher" learning, this word has profound roots in the land and the soil.... *Agriculture*, a first cousin

of *culture*, explicitly brings together cultivation and land. In fact the English word *culture* first meant a piece of tilled land.[27]

The work of cultivation, Casey suggests, binds our culture to the earth in a way that might even be related to worship (*cultus*), loving care, or careful devotion. Culture and the things of a human world, the man-made, are tied to nature by bonds that must be cultivated, religiously (*religion* being etymologically rooted in the Latin *ligare*, to tie or bind) and agriculturally. The opposite of such a re-lig-ion would be neg-lig-ence: "Whoever has no religion should not be called an atheist or unbeliever, but negligent,"Michel Serres declares;[28] such a person furthers the neglect into which the natural falls when we fail to cultivate it diligently, that is, with loving devotion, according to the old sense of diligence, a sense that underlies much of the monastic life as *de diligendo dei*.

One can admire Andy Goldsworthy's own diligence as he cultivates the places of his dwelling.

## Creative unsecuring

"Each work is a discovery." Indeed, a dis-covery that involves Goldsworthy in some of the processes of nature *at the same time as* it marks the end of earth or nature as intact, unscathed, or untouched by human hands.

### THE MELT DISCLOSES THE ROCK WITHIN

One of the best examples of creative dis-covery or dis-closure can be found in the work *Snowballs in Summer* (fig. 37). How does a thing look and turn out when it comes into the clearing to which Goldsworthy lends his hand? The melt discloses the rock within. As the rock is brought to light through this operation of disclosure, it is more and more exposed—exposed to view by the clearing away of what covers and hides it, and also exposed to hazard and collapse. "Its coming forth is—and is continually threatened by—a coming to pass."[29] Nonetheless, the unsecuring and instability of this disclosure creates a succession of beautiful forms as each moment stands delicately poised and composed.

This way of bringing things to be works *with* time, not against it. Time truly is at work here as the future remains open, but also as time works to make a work. Who knows what will come to be after any given point? Who knows what new form will be disclosed as the slow melt unsecures the rock, continuing it on its errant way? As the initial arrangement of the rock within the snowball is hidden, the future course of its development remains shrouded in mystery until after it arrives, at which point its

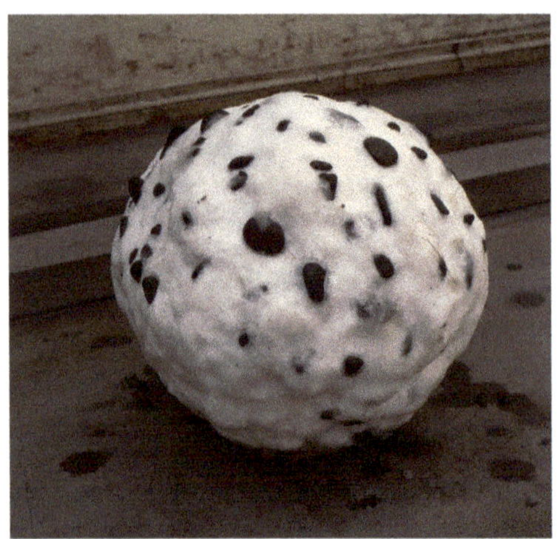
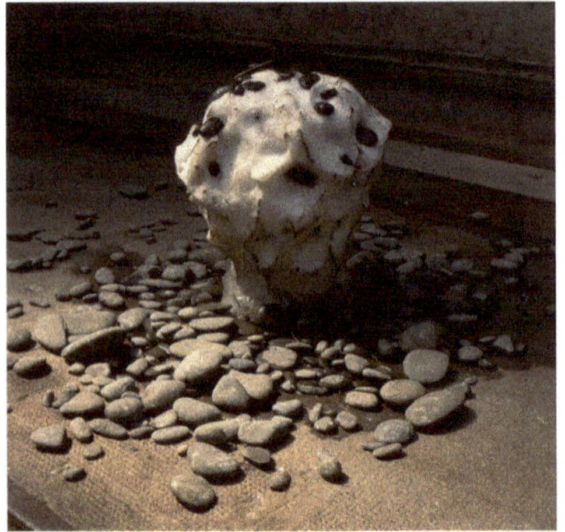

path of arrival might be traced in the photographic record that presents it clearly and distinctly to us. "I will not fully understand each snowball until it has melted," Goldsworthy comments, keenly noting the way that certain knowledge and the objective presence of the thing, a full understanding in the light that reveals, is obtained only at the price of its life or nature.[30]

Goldsworthy comments on this disclosure, the melt that brings something into the open: "When snow melts things hidden slowly emerge—evidence of time laid on the ground. Rocks carried in avalanches, soil crumbling from an eroded bank, bird droppings, feathers, the remains of a kill, fruit, windblown twigs, leaves... caught up in the fall and the movement of the snow. Removed from place and season—suspended in snow and time. Fresh snow falling on old—compressing a layer of debris—to be revealed like fossils in the melt."[31] What is interesting is that for Goldsworthy nature does not specify the place of things but their movement, not their being but their being in time. His talk of nature is not allied to talk of roots, permanent presence, or the security of fixed and unchanging orders: the stone and rock has been displaced and altered with the avalanche and the unceasing flow of the river; even the soil itself, the supposedly solid ground on which we build stable things, has crumbled and eroded and decomposed into the earth—making it too flow for one who sees time from a perspective not limited by the tasks and lifetime of a human individual. Everything moves, and the nature of a thing is more how it falls than how it lies. "Snow and ice is on a journey—it falls from the sky, forming drifts, thawing into the earth or grinding its way through a valley in the form of a glacier. Movement is a part of its nature. Working with snow and ice is touching a force that has shaped

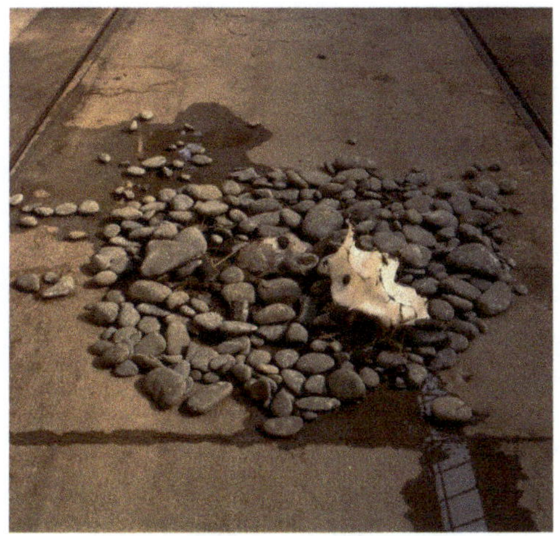
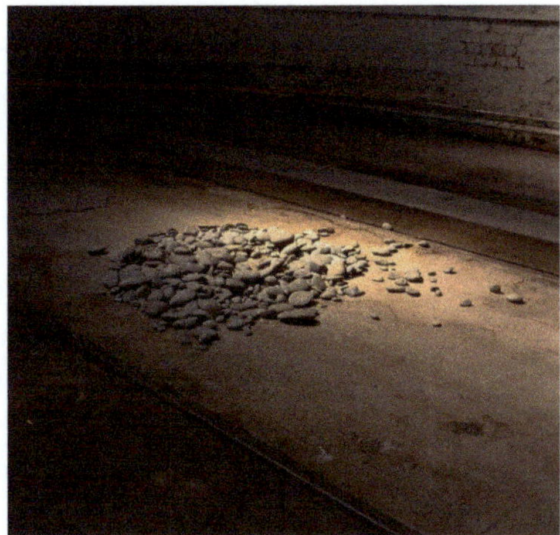

FIGURE 37. Andy Goldsworthy, *Snowballs in summer / Pebbles / Tramway, Glasgow / July 1989*. Photographs by Andy Goldsworthy.

the land."[32] Here we have a flowing or becoming (a journey or movement) that does not befall the solid self of things or of me from the outside, but which is indeed the "self," "substance," or "nature" of the ever-flowing self of things. In a clearing with rivers and tides, not even the land offers a permanent place or has a permanent nature but, rather, has been shaped by the journey of snow and ice.

## UPLIFTED BY THE RIVER AND ADRIFT WITH THE TIDE

The things Goldsworthy creates are created with this nature. He too, along with it, has a hand in navigating the movement whereby something flows and drifts into the clearing of the world, but his hand does not work to grab hold of this movement, secure it in his grasp, and stop it from passing. Heightening the sense in which creation is an unsecuring, Goldsworthy brings no fasteners with him when he comes to the place where he will work: no hammers, no nails, no glue, no rope, nothing that would secure what is made, either to itself or to a place where it might be fixed.[33] His ice sculptures are formed with materials melted in his mouth and then re-frozen by the cold; the poppy petals covering a rock are licked and held in place only by his sticky saliva. Though devoted to the earth and diligent in cultivating the possibility that opens before his hands, Goldsworthy's work does not establish the roots that would fix in place the things he builds or secure them to the ground. Built in a clearing that includes rivers and tides, most everything he makes is carried away and slips out of reach as it is set adrift on the journey of its coming to be in time.

It is no mistake that Goldsworthy often works and builds at the water's edge, on beaches or riverbanks. In *Stick dome hole / made next to a turning pool / a meeting between river and sea / sticks lifted up by the tide / carried upstream / turning / 10 February 1999* (fig. 30), for example, he has built where the river meets the ocean, where the rushing river flows into the sea, empties itself, and is lost. The work builds on the turning pool of water gathered at a bend in the river as it runs its relentless course to the sea. There Goldsworthy has gathered driftwood into a dome, with a hole at its top, an echo of the vortex around which a whirlpool might spin or an eddy might form, momentarily in the turbulence of a stream, before being released with the rushing flow. The thing looks almost like an inverted whirlpool of driftwood being sucked down the hole. The driftwood has achieved a temporary calm, a momentary stability, as it comes to rest in the delicate balance of the fragile dome Goldsworthy has manufactured. Yet it will soon be cast adrift again, when the tide returns, the water rises, and the solid ground is immersed under flowing water.

Seeing the driftwood momentarily at rest in the dome, a passerby asks Goldsworthy, "What is going to happen? What do you expect will happen?" Goldsworthy—the master craftsman, the supposed origin of this work of art—replies, "It's going to float away; it's going to move into the pool there." "Will it stay intact?" "No, it won't, absolutely not," Goldsworthy responds, and serenely waits and watches as the product of his work, lifted up by the rushing river, rises from the ground, casts off from dry land, and drifts away.[34] The driftwood slowly scatters, parts float off, trail behind, and the thing leaves itself behind itself as it rises from the earth and flows out to sea. Everything that rises does *not* converge but scatters and dissipates—the last thing to pass away being the hole that was central to the work. "As the dome separated from the land, . . . I expected the hole to collapse. Instead it floated ever so gently out into the river, where it began to turn"—a hole adrift on the flowing river, turning and spiraling away.[35]

Reflecting on this, Goldsworthy comments, "It feels like it's taken off into another plane, into another world, or another work. It doesn't feel at all like destruction."[36] It is as if this unsecuring that casts adrift is not the work's destruction but its nature, as if the energy or potential harbored in this wood is meant not to be stored but to be released, sent off on a journey in which it becomes increasingly unavailable. With our technologies, we men of modern disenchantment pretend to build things that are permanent, solid, and substantial, resistant to time and its erosions, things that stay intact—and if they don't, we throw them away. Goldsworthy, by contrast, has made a hole, empty, adrift on the flowing river, dissipating slowly until it comes to the sea where it passes away. This drift of things toward complete unavailability in the sea that swallows all becomes, in Goldsworthy's hands, not destruction but creation, the creation of another work—as if the rivers and tides, winds and skies, that he works with remain creative even after he withdraws his hand. He created work with them; now they create with his work, as things drift beyond his control. Irreversible dissipation and inventiveness, an entropic tendency toward unavailability and creativity, go hand in hand in a movement of transcendence, "taking off into another plane."

## THE GIFT OF AN ERRANT JOURNEY

When Goldsworthy puts hand to earth, even when that hand holds a tool, his touch launches another step in the journey that is the nature of the thing. Commenting on the work of hollowing out a granite rock weighing many tons to serve as a massive planter for a tiny oak sapling, Goldsworthy observes that the blowtorch handled by his machine operator "continues the journey these stones have made so far. They have a history of movement, struggle, and change," having been forged in fire at the earth's core, then split by glacial flows during the ice age before being moved and broken by the farmer's plow. "I have great sympathy for anyone caring about stone, but sometimes the level of protectiveness is suffocatingly precious. The stones have come from areas cleared for farms and homes. . . . These glacial boulders have had a long and, at times, violent past—both natural and manmade. . . .Underlying the pastoral calm and beauty of a field is the destructive or creative violence (depending on how you look at it) of stones and trees being ripped out to make farmland."[37] Unlike many who dream of recovering the sacred inviolability of earth and the land, Goldsworthy sees his contact with these rocks not as a touch that damages their otherwise pure, unscathed nature, but rather as a next step in the violent yet natural, uprooting yet creative movement of exposure or unsecuring that is their nature. Indeed, to the extent that the nature of the stone is its journey out of the self-enclosure of the earth, it involves an unsecuring or uprooting, a sending that casts adrift and exposes the stone to contact with all sorts of others (Goldsworthy, for example) whose touch makes this destiny of things sent adrift an errant destiny, the course of the stone's creative decline a swerving path.

Sending things on their errant way, rather than holding them fast in place, Goldsworthy calls his work a "gift." It is what he gives to the nature he works with. The rock cairn he builds on the ocean shore, where it is swallowed by the rising tide only to reemerge from the receding tide, like life itself emerging from the waters—this work, he says, is a gift handed over to the sea, and the sea, he says, "makes the work better than anything I could ever conceive." "I have no idea what the tide will do to it."[38] No idea, better than I could conceive: that is to say, the work is not fully conceived before it is made, and his hands are not mere extensions of his power to conceive or idealize (supposedly unique locations of creativity). His hands are for giving; he touches in order to give away, not to keep.

The creativity at work in work like this thus involves causes other an intelligent maker's own efficiency—the ocean, too, is required for the cairn to come into being; the sky sets conditions to which the icicle sculpture is indebted; above all, time proves creative, as many of the shapes and forms are brought into being by what philosophers in the school of phenomenology have called "passive synthesis," a constitution or construction of objects that happens to me and through me but without my intentions. How many times do we hear or read Goldsworthy exclaim something to the effect of "I could not have predicted what would happen." What comes to light in this way does not make up a stable and secure world where everything has its proper place because it was put there by some efficient causal agent, be it the divine agent or his successor, the self-assertive human subject. Rather, what comes into being through the time to which Goldsworthy lends a hand is created by a process of unsecuring and exposure that launches the unsettling journey that is what it means to be.

## Giving chance a chance

Watching Goldsworthy work on-site, one might be surprised by how many decisions he makes there while he is touching or in contact with the place—not from the disengaged perspective of an onlooker planning his actions in advance of being there, then creating by shaping or forming raw materials in accord with his conception. But Goldsworthy is no naïve intuitionist. He parodies such an image of himself in a scene shot at his house in the film *Rivers and Tides*, and he writes elsewhere and with more seriousness on the work of making a stone cairn in Iowa: "I have never calculated a sculpture as exactly as I have this one. The only way to connect physically the separate components of the sculpture is through mathematics." He intervenes in a place, rearranging it mathematically, by plan and calculation. His mastery is evident. However, "I find this approach challenging and creative, but only because I am not entirely sure of what I am doing and I know that, despite all my calculations, the final sculpture will still be a surprise. Some lack of control is essential to give tension and energy to a sculpture. If I were, through experience, to gain complete control of the sculpture through calculation then the process would become merely one of design—not growth."[39] Creation, for Goldsworthy, is not the realization of a well-designed plan, the execution of which he has total control over, but is rather allied with growth (the farmer again, or a loving parent). The thing that comes to light in such growth is not devoid of tension and keeps some energy of its own in reserve—a live load, as it were, energetic and energized.

## WORKING FOR CHANCE

What becomes quite clear in watching and listening to Goldsworthy is that the more he gets to work making something, the more chance to which he exposes himself. One can on this point revisit the classic essay "Science as a Vocation," wherein Max Weber offers the nearly canonic formulation of modern disenchantment. However much this essay speaks to the "increasing intellectualization and rationalization" of an age of technoscience in which "one can, in principle, master all things by calculation," one finds, on closer reading, that Weber also seems to admit chance and gifts into the disenchanted world of modern scientific life. Just before he names modern disenchantment, Weber addresses the need for "inspiration in the field of science." He observes that "what goes on in a factory or a laboratory," the institutions of human industry in which modern disenchantment was incubated, requires inspiration or "some idea to occur to one's mind." The question is how to get it. He goes on to say that no amount of work, no amount of science and planning, can guarantee that an idea will come, but at the same time, ideas do not come to us unless we roll up our sleeves and get to work. This idea on which the calculating enterprises of science and industry depend "has nothing to do with any cold calculation. . . . Ideas come when we do not expect them, and not when we are brooding and searching at our desks. Yet ideas would certainly not come to mind had we not brooded at our desks and searched for answers with passionate devotion."[40] The most famous theoretician of modern disenchantment here seems to suggest that brooding, serious calculation and work at a desk or other workplace, even in the most rationalized and intellectualized of modern endeavors, is no guarantee of achieving the sought-after effect but instead serves to increase our exposure to the incalculable arrival of the idea necessary to the creation of a work.

So too with Goldsworthy. His creative work invites chance and draws energy from events that do not come at his bidding. Lacking total control over the conditions responsible for a work, he leaves room where something incalculable might emerge, and only with the possibility of the incalculable can there be novelty and indeed a future that is truly future, not a projected past, determined in advance and assured by knowledge of present conditions and trajectories. However much Goldsworthy might

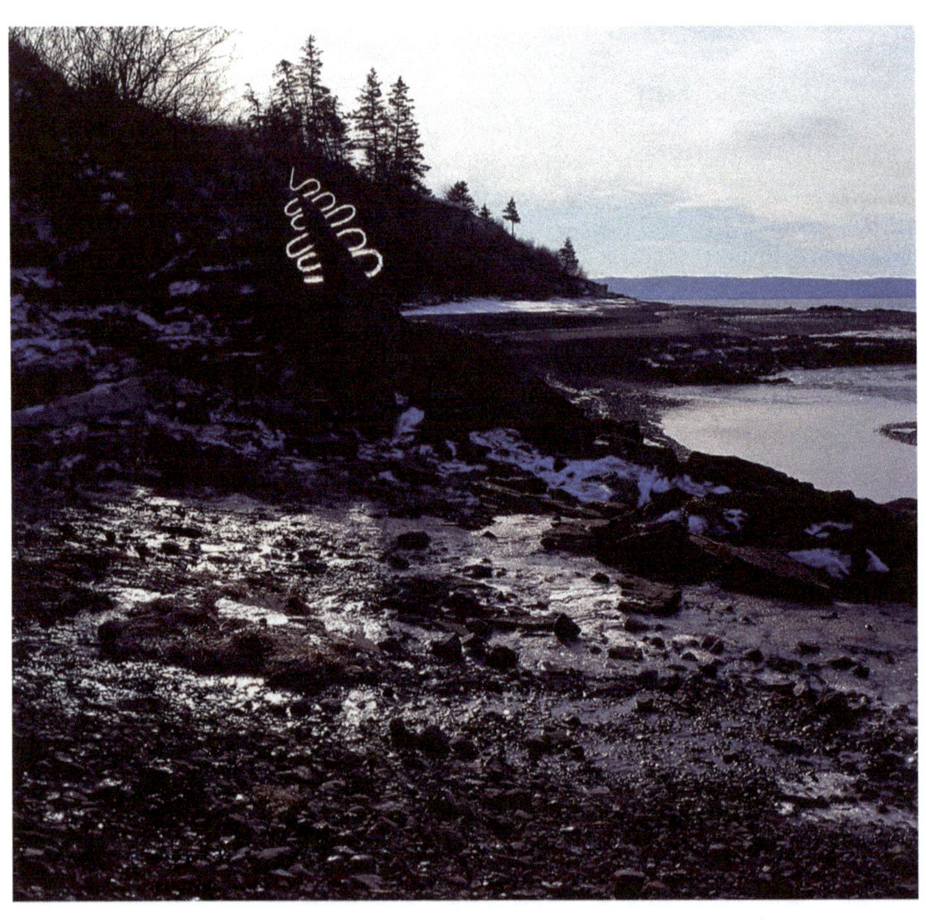

FIGURE 38. Andy Goldsworthy, *Reconstructed refrozen icicles / second attempt (first try thawed) / worked through the cold dark night into day / 9 February 1999*. Photograph by Andy Goldsworthy.

speak about knowing the potential of the place, being in touch with this potential does not let him predict what will come to pass. "I never had any idea that would happen," he remarks as the sun's emergence from behind a mountain illuminates an icicle sculpture (fig. 38). "So the potential here, the potential is fantastic... that the sun coming up would brighten it like that."[41] In the case of this icicle sculpture, it took the event of the sun's emergence from behind the mountain to bring this beautiful thing unexpectedly into the picture. The emergence of the thing remains partially dependent on something beyond the artist and therefore comes to pass as a surprising and wonderful event. All he knows, after all, is "the incredible potential of the place" and its energy. "I had no idea about the alignment of icicle, rock, place and sun before working. I was astonished that the sun rose directly behind the stone and illuminated the icicles perfectly on both sides while a shadow was cast by the cliff behind. It was a great moment."[42] Astonished and amazed himself, the master artist, it seems, is not master of the conditions or causes that lead to the thing's coming to light when he works *with* rivers and tides, wind and sky—even if he does still have a hand in the processes.

## THE EVENTFUL WORLD OF SCIENCE

Confounding those who want to impose a terse and simple equation of disenchantment and science, the world of contemporary science can be as unpredictable and full of unforeseen novelty as that opened by Goldsworthy's hand. Consider the groundbreaking work of the Nobel Prize–winning chemist Ilya Prigogine. Open, not closed, to the arrival of new things that might come to be, Prigogine's science makes possible a scientific account of wonderful world-systems in which responsibility for the emergence of things includes the intervention of creative events—as if to provide scientific confirmation of what Goldsworthy feels with his own hands.

Taking chaotic systems far from equilibrium as the norm, not the exception, Prigogine and his wife and fellow scientist Isabelle Stengers conceive of science not as gazing at a world brought to a stand motionless in a picture, but at an unsecured world where things emerge without adequate cause or sufficient reason. These systems are chaotic, first, because the large number of particles making them up makes it impossible to define initial conditions precisely and, second, because of the inherent impossibility of determining the position and velocity of any given particle at the same time. This lack of precision at the start results in uncertain knowledge of the future. When fixed laws of motion (classical mechanics and dynamics) are applied recursively over time to approximately defined initial conditions, the future looks not bright but blurred or fuzzy, even as it is known more and more lawfully. Finite observers, therefore, "have to rely on probabilities, renouncing the ability to foresee the behavior that a system will adopt, even if they know it as well as is possible." In other words, this world is one in which "statistical description has an irreducible character." Following Prigogine and Stengers's model of statistical accounting and calculation of the world, the scientific advance into the world—that is, the methodical, calculative work that knows more and more—takes place in a world of probabilities and potentials. This potentiality means that however much knowledge of a situation one might achieve (and considerable knowledge has indeed been amassed) the actual outcome remains uncertain and always surprising when it occurs because all one has mastered is probabilities and statistics. In this way the scientific advance into the world is detached from the project of dominating and controlling it, and becomes increasingly interested in "that which, by definition escapes manipulation or can only be subjected to it with ruses and losses . . . ; the tendency to escape from domination manifests the intrinsic activity of nature."[43] As nature becomes intrinsically active and incredibly potential, science becomes once again a human adventure, a relation with the unknown that grows with our knowledge, as the scientist welcomes the opportunity opened by "the end of certainty."[44]

Even as his increasing mass of knowledge means the loss of omniscience, the scientific man loses the privileged position from which he becomes master of the causal process and must admit other causes besides the efficient cause, causes over which he has little or no control. The more perfectly one might know the world of probabilities and the more mastery one might gain over the world of statistics, the less one can predict what will actually happen next, for, as Prigogine reminds us, the world as a statistical or probabilistic phenomenon is one in which the cause of what actually happens remains absent. This absent cause in excess of the reason or law is what Prigogine calls the event: "We need not only *laws*, but also *events* that bring an element of radical novelty to the description of nature."[45] Uncertainty and eventfulness is thus woven into the fabric of the processes responsible for something emerging into being. The oft-used phrase "objective nature" proves an untenable contradiction when uncertainty and approximation, defying objectivity, belong intrinsically to the nature of things.

Echoing this sense in which creativity exceeds efficient causality and the mastery of circumstances in order to welcome an unforeseen future, the theologian Gordon Kaufman writes, "There is a serendipitous feature in all creativity: more happens than one would have expected, given previously available circumstances, indeed, more than might have seemed possible."[46] A consideration of circumstances—or what critical philosophy might call "conditions for the possibility"—cannot deduce or anticipate the arrival of what wonders will get into the picture when creativity is a real, generative power. There is creativity and a wonderful world when conditions for possibility are not sufficient to account for the actuality of something happening. This is precisely what happens when one works *with* nature and admits the nature of things into the world one cultivates. The potentiality of the place is greater than one can conceive, and one has no certain idea what will happen.

### "LET'S HOPE IT WORKS"

As seen through the lens provided by a theologian like Kaufman, both Goldsworthy the artist and Prigogine the scientist assume the position of a very different subject than the disengaged onlooker who considers a picture he can see clearly and distinctly. They also assume the position of a very different god than the omniscient and omnipotent creator—the god in whose image the human subject of modern disenchantment is fashioned. Stengers reminds us inste ad of an old Jewish legend in which the unstable, unsecured world of Prigogine and Goldsworthy seems to resemble that of God's own creation:

> The world that seems to have renounced the security of stable, permanent norms is clearly a dangerous and uncertain world. It can inspire no blind confidence in us, but perhaps the feeling of mitigated hope that certain Talmudic texts have, it seems, attributed to the God of Genesis: "Let's hope it works" (*Halway Sheyaamod*), exclaimed God as he created the world, and this hope accompanies the subsequent history of the world and humanity, emphasizing right from the start that this history is stamped with the mark of radical insecurity.[47]

The hopeful creator referred to here is a creator who, according to Jewish legend, made twenty-six attempts at genesis, "all of which were destined to fail," and only on the last try brought this world to be out of what the French scholar of Judaism André Neher called the "chaotic heart of this previous rubble." Neher observes that such a world, haunted by a chaotic prehistory of recurrent dissipation and divine disappointment, possesses no "label or guarantee" of its own future permanence. Connecting this story with the biblical notion of a covenant that is the true subject of historical becoming, Neher observes that for Judaism the history of the world, the ongoing genesis of a world, is made by two partners, Yahweh and Israel, hand in hand, in relation with one another and engaged in the constant negotiation and renegotiation that comes with the irreducible plurality of a collaborative or covenantal work. Just as a God who creates hopefully after twenty-six tries implies the openness of the future, so too does the notion of a history making covenantal partnership between two parties imply that no single omnipotent agent determines or asserts by itself the progress from present to future. "History is traversed from one end to the other by a radical uncertainty. . . . History is not a continuous progression; it is eternal improvisation." Neher claims further that, "for the conception of a universe created in its entirety all at once, with all its elements, is substituted the vision of a world in which there are lacunae, holes. . . . This work [the creation of the world] was in no way meditated or realized according to a pre-established plan, but, quite to the contrary, it sprang from a radical unpreparedness . . . from an improvisation."[48]

The phrase Stengers renders as "Let's hope it works" is the Hebrew *halway sheyaamod*. To be more precise, *Halway* ("let's hope") is not in fact a verb; it is an exclamation—but yes, an exclamation expressing hope or a wish: "O that it would . . ." or "May it be the case that . . ." The phrase *halway sheyaamod* appears at least twice in connection with the creation of the world in the rabbinic commentary on the book of Genesis. In the first text, God exclaims, "Let's hope it works," after he begins the creation of the world not with the first letter of the alphabet but with the second, as if the fact that creation was from the very beginning displaced from its origin or ground (its alpha missing, as it were) rendered it unstable and uncertain. In the second, he exclaims, "Lets hope it works," after he decides to create the world on the basis of both judgment and mercy: "If I create the world on the basis of mercy alone, its sins will be great; on the basis of judgment alone, the world cannot exist. Hence I will create it on the basis of judgment and mercy"—which would seem to mean both that its sins will be great and that it cannot exist.[49] Hence, he exclaims, "Let's hope it works"—a world governed by twin yet irreconcilable principles, a world with both mercy and judgment is one whose working is a hope, not guarantee. In the text that Neher references, the rabbis are commenting on the biblical text claiming that God saw all creation to be very good. After creating the world, they explain, God calls out to the world, "O My world, O My world! mayest thou [*halway*, "let's hope you"] find favour in My eyes at all times."[50] It is as if God creates the world good but without the certainty or "blind confidence" that his creation will stay good. He creates with an exclamation of hope because he knows the world will run its own course, like the river.

Hope and creativity, together inseparably according to the Jewish legends, because creation comes to be in and as a process over which no one omnipotent agent has complete control from beginning to end and because without the uncertain future held open in hope nothing new would come to light under the sun—no matter how powerful one's will might be. Far from manifesting the glory or power of God, the universe manifests God's hope, a hope that might be one with the creativity of a being with hands, like Goldsworthy, who tries again and again, in multiple arts, to get the stones to lay right or the web to hold. The world is in God's hands, maybe even before his omniscient mind or his omnipotent will. Can we imagine a theology developed according to a model in which the creative act bringing all things into being was not speech or will that met not the least resistance but the divine hands setting to work *with*... ?

"Let's hope it works." The phrase marries urgency and patience, effort and desperation, in a way that characterizes living in time, what Stengers calls a history "stamped with the mark of radical insecurity." One can almost hear Goldsworthy on the beach saying the same thing as he puts his hands to the task of gently stacking stones to build a cairn in the brief span of time given to him before the tide returns and submerges the site: "Let's hope it works!" This is not just sitting back and praying. It is the expression of a creator who works when and where conditions are not known sufficiently to realize his own design, givens are not entirely under his control, and time is always running out before the end is reached. On the beach, the edge of the world, where the ground slides into the sea and the sea returns slowly but relentlessly to swallow the earth, the time given to Goldsworthy is short, but hurrying or working faster does not get him to the end any faster. He has a limited amount of time, and you sense the urgency in all that he does there; but little more will be achieved by rushing, and so we suffer with him through the extreme patience with which he gathers and stacks, measures and assesses rocks that soon will be swallowed by the rising tide. "The beach was, and still is, a great teacher.... There is a gamble and balance between what I want to make and the time available to achieve it. Rarely is there enough time to finish a work just as I want. This lesson reaches beyond work made on the beach."[51] When time is short and the end is near, "let's hope it works!"

## FAREWELL

The "dangerous and uncertain world... that can inspire no blind confidence in us," the world that comes to light through creative acts of unsecuring—this world is the one with a future, if one works to keep it open and to give chance a chance.

With the admission of uncertainty comes the chance that a more beautiful world might be created. Work that abandons total control invites the possibility of receiving the surprising gift of a work better than anything you might conceive on your own. Working, Goldsworthy moves into the

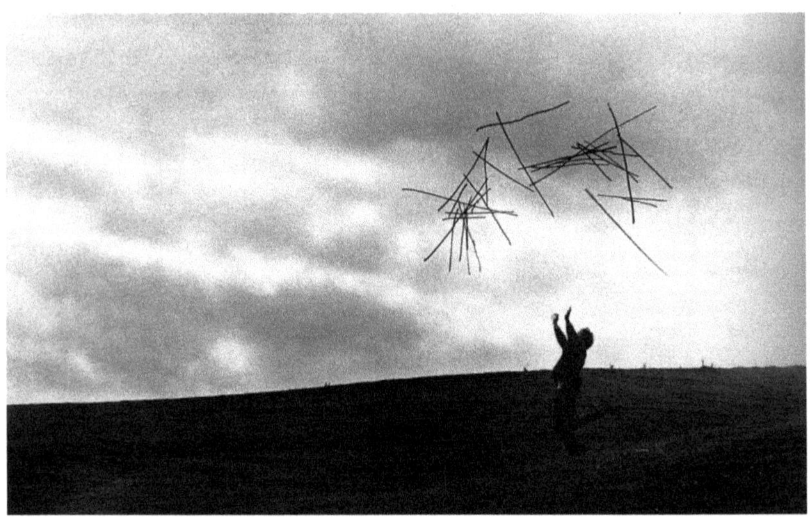

FIGURE 39. Andy Goldsworthy, *Hazel stick throws / Banks, Cumbria / 10 July 1980*. Photograph by Judith Goldsworthy.

clearing, the open, the outdoors or outside, where everything is up in the air, ever up for grabs, potentiality not actuality. What his work does is to leave it and keep it up in the air (fig. 39).

His hands are creative in that they let go, releasing and sending things on their uncertain, unsecure way of ongoing exposure in the clearing of a world. Here is a place not for keeping and retaining, not for burying so that a future might progress from the place of this grounded past and things be recovered. Rather, here is the place for throwing things to the wind (fig. 40), for scattering what remains and creatively letting go of things as they drift on and rise up to new forms unknown to me, most likely in a future never even retrieved by me—being in a creative dissipation toward the sea.

Its beauty is enchanting.

"Let's hope it works."

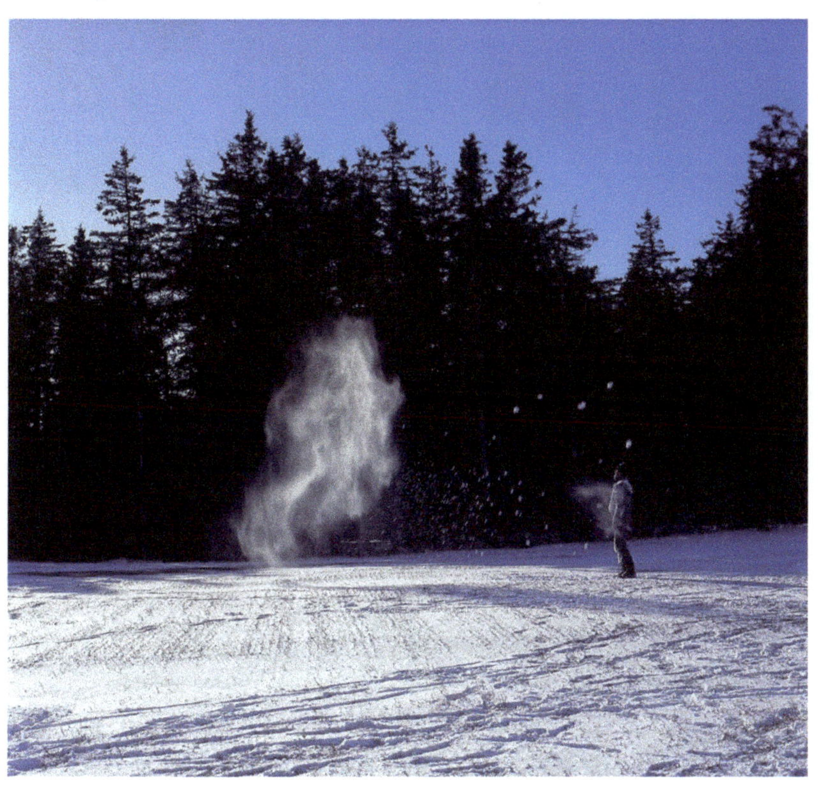

FIGURE 40. Andy Goldsworthy, *Snow / sun / wind / throws / 7 February 1999*. Photograph by Mark Austin.

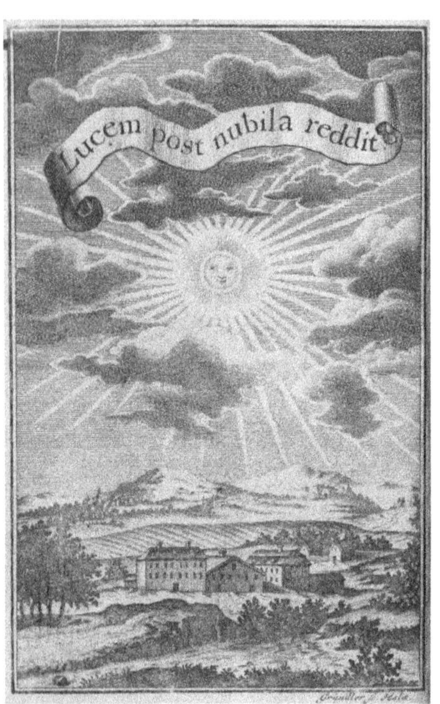


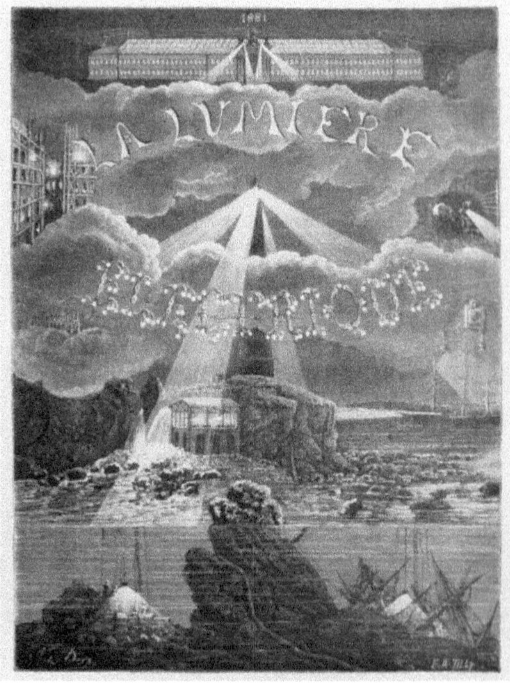


FIGURE 41. Frontispiece from Christian Wolff, *Vernünfftige Gedancken von Gott, der Welt und der Seele des Menschen auch allen Dingen überhaupt den Liebharen der Wahrheit* (1720). Rare Book Collection, University of North Carolina at Chapel Hill.

FIGURE 42. Title page from *La lumière électrique* (1882).

# Conclusions

This book began when, researching a class on religion and modernity, I happened upon two pictures that I took as emblems of modern disenchantment, two images of a light that clears the clouds and leads us to solid ground (figs. 41 and 42). Clouds dissipate, and things appear clearly and distinctly in the clearing. In the world made clear, we build our dwelling on solid ground.

## THINGS' APPEAL

My response to these pictures of modern disenchantment has been motivated by a sense, shared, I suspect, by many today, that the smile on the smiling sun has become less welcoming than it seems and more sinister in its saccharine cheer. We have grown disenchanted with the disenchanted world laid bare by the light of demystification and disenchantment. We suspect that something has gone missing from the world mastered by the apotheosis of electricity. Wilhelm Hausenstein, an art historian writing in his journal during World War II, put it this way: in the "electric light... objects (seemingly) appear much more clearly, but in reality [this light] *flattens* them. Electric light imparts too much brightness and thus things lose body." As things become more and more clear, all can be seen distinctly, yet this clarity entails a denaturing and growing lightness. Things and the world grow light... unbearably light. Having rendered themselves to the all-penetrating, "illusionless electric brightness,"[1] things surrender the shadows and the opacity that make them dark and mysterious but at the same time constitute their appeal. Darkness and the clouds are dispelled in the demystifying light of modern disenchantment, and yet the world laid bare seems less and less there, less and less appealing.

The poet Wallace Stevens (1879–1955) was sensitive to this disappearance of things in the light that was meant to lead them to ground. His poem "Looking across the Fields and Watching the Birds Fly" connects in interesting ways the metaphysics of Leibniz and Wolff, the image of *Lucem post nubila reddit*, and the conclusions reached by consideration of "The Apotheosis of Electricity." While visiting home, Mr. Homburg, the poem's main character, contemplates the following "irritating minor idea" as he looks at the birds outside flying in the clearing: "To think away the grass, the trees, the clouds / Not to transform them into other things, / Is only what the sun does every day."[2] The sun brings the world to light and at the same time carries it away. This thinking away that the sun does every day, or, inverting Mr. Homburg, this lighting away that disenchanted thinking does in an ongoing way, is assumed by the apotheosis of electricity. Saturated with a light that floods them with clarity, things dissolve, become light, and vanish. When thinking is like the sun, or the "second sun" of the electric factory, it makes a desert, solid ground where little to nothing grows.

What I have tried to do in this book is, like Mr. Homburg, to inhabit, instead and by contrast, places where we might adopt "a pensive nature" and discover a "daily majesty of meditation, / that comes and goes in silences of its own." I have tried to linger in the majesty of things that do not appear in the light of reasons rendered, as if I, like Mr. Homburg, could think, "then, as the sun shines or does not."

My efforts to reach the places where this "majesty of meditation" might happen have been organized by works of modern or contemporary art. These works question the way of constituting the appearance of things as it is depicted in the two pictures of modern disenchantment. They called for my response to what I see as the common structure governing the two pictures of bringing things to light in the condition of modern disenchantment. Chapter 1 addressed the source of light: the sun or the factory, in contrast with the lightning that vanishes, along with stormy skies, with the apotheosis of electricity. In this flickering light, things come to be without standing still, captured in a permanent presence, always accessible for the user or spectator. Chapter 2 addressed the need for clouds to part in order for the world to appear clearly and distinctly. By staging an encounter with a work of art that leads us into the cloud, it asked if we might affirm dwelling in a world where we encounter fuzzy, less definite things. Chapter 3 asked what happens when we see the light that must withdraw and be invisible to make the clearing clear. Chapter 4 looked into a clearing that stays so open that we see the distance out of which things come to be. What draws near in this clearing enters into this distance, where it is seen but not mastered, as if in the intimacy of the lovers' gaze. And chapter 5 encountered work that leads us to dwell in a clearing that includes not just solid ground but also the rivers and tides, winds and melt, against which the apotheosis of electricity struggles.

Together, the encounters with these artworks have pointed to another way to organize the picture, another format for lighting and illumination than the mode that leads to the world picture of modern disenchantment. Other things and other ways of human being get into the picture when things come to light in it differently.

## ART AND RELIGION: WORKING THROUGH

An important subtext of this book has concerned the relative neglect of contemporary art among students of religion and the inverse reticence concerning religion among art historians and art critics. "A certain kind of academic art historical writing," the noted art historian James Elkins observes, "treats religion as an interloper, something that has no serious place in scholarship." Very often this is the case because the art historian or critic assumes a particular narrative of history in general, and the history of art in particular, according to which the religious location of the image is precisely what is overcome when art and the art object emerge as autonomous, free realms of human creativity. This has resulted in an art history and criticism that tend toward strident forms of modern disenchantment, hearing anything that sounds religious or theological in the discussion of a work as a threat against the integrity of the art. Elkins himself feels compelled to offer an explicit declaration that his own book considering what he calls the "strange place of religion in contemporary art" should not be taken as "the confession of a closet religionist" or as "a crypto-conservative book aiming to re-instate old fashioned values"—as if an art historian risks losing his professional stature and reputation as an expert when he dares talk about religion.[3] Few artists, especially not young, unestablished ones, Elkins observes, want critics to address their work in religious or theological terms, since having a work labeled "religious" is often the fast track to insignificance or, at best, marginality in the art world.

The narrative of art history that such artists, historians, and critics assume is, in fact, indebted to a particular and particularly common version of secularization theory and the disenchantment thesis, a version that this book seeks to challenge. That narrative, according to Daniel Siedell's helpful account, goes something like this: modern art is art "produced in the modern era under the conditions of modernity"; it is, in short, "a product of modernism."[4] The conditions that constitute modernity are governed, according to the common narrative, by historical processes of secularization. Modernization equals secularization. But what then does secularization mean? The term is richly significant and embraces many realms (political or social-structural secularism, the secularization of consciousness, and so on), but what is important for us is that it includes the progressive emancipation of spheres of human activity and experience from the authority of religion so that each can attain autonomy. Religion is not a "sacred canopy" embracing, organizing, and legitimating every sphere of human life, but just one sphere of cultural activity among many others.[5] Indeed, to the degree that religion is defined as that which refuses to be located in just one sphere of culture, it is the very thing that must be quarantined or expelled if the modern differentiation of spheres of culture and human activity is to be maintained. According to this version of secularization theory, then, religion will be assigned to the realm of private or personal life, where it cannot impede the progressive autonomization of other spheres of culture and activity.

According to this narrative of secularization as the progressive differentiation of the spheres of cultural life, art achieves its secular end, autonomy, in conceptual or abstract works in which the subject of the artwork is the work of art itself. Referential content or traditional iconography would impugn the work's status as art, positioning it somewhere short of this modern liberation. Any purported religious significance in a work of art would be a regressive confusion of what should, to be modern, be autonomous spheres of cultural activity. When beholden to this narrative, modern art can be truly modern only if it considers religion as what it has put behind it.

* * *

This narrative has had unfortunate consequences for the mutual relations of religion and art. It has led much of post-Enlightenment religion to look upon modern art as decadent and soulless, and it has led art critics to be tongue-tied before much of what is interesting in modern art.

Accepting the secularization-as-disenchantment narrative, many of the religious can only look at modern art as indicative of a reality unaccepting of and hostile to it, one in which modern disenchantment has defeated religion. Pointing to polemics that emerged in the culture wars at the end of the twentieth century, Siedell laments, "The theory of secularization provided culturally conservative and Christian commentators on art a lens through which to view the history of modern art, a history that inevitably culminates with the decadence of the contemporary art world."[6] Scholars in religious studies similarly avoid modern and contemporary art, except when such art explicitly deploys traditional symbolism or iconography (confounding orthodox secularization theory), is in a medium such as film, or is a manifestation of popular culture (such as roadside votive shrines or black-velvet paintings). When art critics, in turn, accept the secularization-as-disenchantment model, they tend to remain mute before the aims and intentions of many of the artists about whom they are writing. Elkins has pointed this out, claiming "the virus of the fear of religion is virulent and contagious" and has led to an "absurd" situation in which religion "does not have a place in talk about contemporary art."[7]

Diagnosing this absurdity and the roots of the fear is another matter. According to the scholars I have been considering, its history appears to be rooted in a particular story we tell about art. That story is a version of the secularization narrative that sees modernity culminating in a disenchanted secularity.

In this book, I have tried to work against this narrative and break the necessary connection between secularity and disenchantment. My implicit contention has been that in denying themselves recourse to religious vocabulary or theological conceptuality, modern art critics give up what would be advantageous to a profound encounter with the works in question. Religion and theology has let me name what the art critic often names and addresses with only a limited vocabulary. In this sense, it lets me prolong the encounter with the work of art, deepening the event of its coming intimately over me and bringing its strangeness to light. When the work of art grows deep like this, the secular world it opens is far from disenchanted—which means that my encounters with these works of art also counter the tendency of religious critics, and even scholars of religion, to see secularity as shallow and soulless, disenchanted pure and simple.

* * *

The case of James Turrell provides a good example of the impasse between art and religion—and of how *Arts of Wonder* offers a way to work through it. Many admirers point to the "mystical" or "spiritual" dimension of his work without saying more. Yes, light has always been of interest to religious traditions, and Turrell's fascination with it surely evokes religion, but beyond that critics are often left speechless, and our encounter with the work ends there. As formal and technical discussions abound, the appeal is often deadened as the thing that happens in encountering the work is lost. One thing I have tried to accomplish is to educate contemporary art, gently, in religious and theological texts and forms of thought that, far from being alien to it, might be a great ally in giving voice to its encounter with works of art such as Turrell's.

Turrell's work should prove as relevant to scholars in religious studies as religious studies should to critics and admirers of his work, yet religious studies has not taken the opportunity it offers. A recent volume entitled *The Presence of Light*, for instance, aimed to consider the significance of light in a cross-cultural and transhistorical perspective. Its expressed intention was to test the hypothesis of "a universal basis for religious intuition and experience." Since "images of light hold pride of place" among those who argue for such a universal basis, the volume proposed considering theories and experiences of light as a means to "advance the larger comparative study of religious experience."[8] Now, I do not want to criticize a book for not addressing questions it never proposed, and I understand that a project must set limits in order to define itself, achieve success, and be valuable. It is worth remarking, however, that of the ten essays in this book, none contains a reference to the work of any contemporary artist, much less one such as Turrell who declares that "light . . . is itself the revelation." Indeed, including the work of a contemporary artist would go a long way toward supporting, or refuting, the purported universality of the experience in question by moving it out of the particularities of a tradition or specifically religious context. Perhaps these scholars of religion, too, have bought into a narrative of secularization that tells us that modern and contemporary art can only manifest a reality in which religion has been defeated.

* * *

Elizabeth Diller, of Diller + Scofidio, provides another good example of the impasse to which conversation between the disenchanted secularity of the art world and religion has come—and of how *Arts of Wonder* might work through it.

Her architectural firm organized a think tank of sorts in the early stages of its planning process for *Blur*. One participant quickly spotted the connection between *Blur* and mystical theology, only to be rejected by Diller. "[It's] a cloud of unknowing, for God's sake—the mystery of silence, the heightened presence of hushed sound, water lapping at the pylons, breezes wafting through girders, footfalls in the dim, the feel of fog on your face, shifting densities of opacity and translucency." This was the noted critic Lawrence Weschler. Weschler continued by observing that all the other layers that the design team wanted to attach—he referred chiefly to the media project of *Babble*—only served to distract from what he thought was the most amazing part of the work: "You're never going to top the primordial sensation of walking atop water—and into a cloud!"[9] Why put a media project at the heart of the cloud, the babble inside the blur? Rejecting Weschler, Diller insists that the media project, *Babble*, is not a distraction from or extraneous to *Blur*, but indeed what the project is about—the experience of inhabiting the global blur that is our world of nearly instantaneous communication. Diller's dismissal of a theological interpretation of the project reflects the supposedly insurmountable abyss between contemporary art and religion.

I think, however, that the dispute between Weschler and Diller, like that between contemporary art and religion, is drawn in terms that are too starkly opposed. Indeed, I'd like to think that Weschler was right: *Blur* was indeed a cloud of unknowing. And precisely because of that, it would, as Diller wants, creatively address today's world, where dwelling in a cloud seems to be what we are called upon to do. Rejecting the possibility of a response to modern art that comes out of religious considerations, the inhabitants of a disenchanted secularity see a theology and religion shaped by modern disenchantment, only to reject this religion. They see only a God who makes matters clear and distinct and only a religion that guarantees access to this divine light. Similarly, those among the religious who would reject the very project of making our blur habitable in favor of a supposed return to the clarity and certainty of belief would, I think, betray their own allegiance to the project of modern disenchantment. The devout religious believer who knows exactly the truth, a truth he believes that only a god brings, shares the disenchanted secular's conviction that seeing clearly and distinctly in an enlightening light is the only way to mastery and possession of the world.

With paired retrievals of the secular and the religious, *Arts of Wonder* addresses both parties. It says, on one hand, that considering the aesthetic experience of these secular artworks could liberate religion from definition by the modern project of disenchantment. And on the other hand, it says that the secular art world could find an unexpected resource in religion, provided it learns to see forms of religion other than those promoted in a disenchanted modernity. James Elkins's reluctant conclusion—"committed, engaged, ambitious, informed art does not mix with dedicated, serious, thoughtful, heartfelt religion. Wherever the two meet, one wrecks the other"—might very well be true of the art and religion shaped by modern disenchantment. But in this book, I have tried to show that this is not the only shape they can take.[10]

* * *

Saying this, I must distinguish my own project from Daniel Siedell's call for contemporary critics and curators "who have a rich vocabulary from which to revive the sacramental and liturgical identity of human practice and to demonstrate that this identity finds its most complete and profound embodiment in the Nicene Christian faith." I do not mean to answer his call for "critics, curators, and art historians who can creatively and critically bend and shape contemporary art toward Christ."[11] These statements bespeak Siedell's intention to show Christians how to embrace modern art; his book at times seems to suggest that contemporary culture might be better off if Christian commentators could lead it to embrace, in thought and practice, Nicene Christianity. Siedell thus speaks from a traditional religion and locates religion in a historical tradition. He addresses Christians, even if other elements of his book should be of significance to non-Christian members of the art community.

I do not believe that *Arts of Wonder* speaks in this way. It does not claim that the artists considered in this book are doing traditionally religious work, nor does it say that they are indebted to this or that religious tradition, symbol, or concept. And it certainly does not mean to claim that a disenchanted modernity could recover something it has lost if only it would again believe or return to the traditions that have traditionally located the religious.[12] This book has addressed people who are sensitive to human longings and experiences that might traditionally have been located in religious traditions, but I believe these longings exceed such a location and might also be encountered, and cultivated in, and by, contemporary works of art. These works appeal to the many disenchanted moderns who have grown disenchanted with modern disenchantment.

## AN ENCHANTING SECULAR

My decision to organize this book around encounters with works of art suggests that one need not look only to traditional religion or religious traditions to find occasion to question the set-up of reality in modern disenchantment. Beholden to media presentations of contemporary art as mocking religious symbolism and tradition, many of the religious would claim the only hope for escaping modern disenchantment comes from religious tradition. But the secular has, I contend, offered us other works, more appealing and more inviting to an encounter less stridently disenchanted. These works of art work to make up places where we encounter mystery and wonder, hopes for redemption and moments of epiphany, transcendence and creation, experiences that Michael Saler and Joshua Landy say are crucial parts of "*fully-secular and deliberate* strategies for re-enchantment." They go on to claim that "piece by piece, in a largely unwitting collaboration, modern intellectuals and creators have put together a panoply of responses to the Weberian condition, offering fully secularized subjects an affirmation of existence that does not come at the cost of naïveté, irrationalism, or hypocrisy." The artists I encounter here join ranks with those writers and thinkers that Landy and Saler consider, and I would like to think that *Arts of Wonder* shares their project of pursuing enchantments with "dignity" and "multiplicity."[13]

Where I depart from Landy and Saler, however, is in suggesting that if the "fully secular" has strategies for enchantment, then the religious past might also harbor anticipations of the future beyond of modern disenchantment. Freeing ourselves in this way from seeing the religious past according to the model developed for it by modern disenchantment, we might be prepared to open a future for a more appealing secularity, one full of charm. Our effort to hear the appeal of the secular might be supported by seeing it anticipated in religion's revelation of some god. This then would lead to a qualification of Saler and Landy's thesis: the notion of "fully" in the *"fully-secular"* would have to be abandoned if the fully secular bears the trace or echo of the religious past.

I have tried in this book to welcome the appeal of dwelling in this in-between, never fully enchanted, never fully disenchanted, never fully secular, never fully religious. Hence the effort to interpret my encounter with these secular artworks in and through reference to theological or religious texts. Each chapter juxtaposed religious or theological texts with the artwork. If it is not clear to the reader which is being reduced to which—is theology reduced to the experience of Diller + Scofidio's *Blur* or is *Blur* reduced to theological explanation? Is the raindance the significance of *The Lightning Field* or *The Lightning Field* the significance of the raindance?—then the reader has sensed my intention. He has experienced something of what I find wonderful in what comes or can come in the wake of modern disenchantment.

# NOTES

## Preface

1. Max Weber, "Science as a Vocation," in *From Max Weber: Essays in Sociology*, ed. H. H. Gerth and C. Wright Mills (New York: Oxford University Press, 1946), 155, 139.

## Introduction

1. Jonathan Crary, *Techniques of the Observer: On Vision and Modernity in the Nineteenth Century* (Cambridge, MA: MIT Press, 1990), 86.
2. Immanuel Kant, *Critique of Pure Reason* (New York: St. Martin's Press, 1965), 33.
3. Ibid., 284.
4. Arthur Schopenhauer, *On the Fourfold Root of the Principle of Reason* (La Salle, IL: Open Court, 1974), 6 (citing Wolff).
5. Martin Heidegger, *The Principle of Reason* (Bloomington: Indiana University Press, 1996), 27.
6. G. W. Leibniz, "A Résumé of Metaphysics," in *Leibniz: Philosophical Writings* (London: Dent, Rowman, and Littlefield, 1991), 145.
7. G. W. Leibniz, *Theodicy*, trans. E. M. Huggard (LaSalle, IL: Open Court Press, 1985), 128.
8. Donald Rutherford, *Leibniz and the Rational Order of Nature* (Cambridge: Cambridge University Press, 1995), 10.
9. Hans Blumenberg, *The Legitimacy of the Modern Age*, trans. Robert Wallace (Cambridge, MA: MIT Press, 1983), 149.
10. Ibid., citing Leibniz, *Theodicy* §338.
11. Ibid., 173.
12. Ibid., 137.
13. Wolfgang Schivelbusch, *Disenchanted Night: The Industrialization of Light in the Nineteenth Century* (Berkeley: University of California Press, 1988).
14. J. Lacassagne and R. Thiers, *Nouveaux système d'éclairage électrique* (Paris and Lyon, 1857), 25 (cited in Schivelbusch, *Disenchanted Night*, 55).
15. Schivelbusch, *Disenchanted Night*, 3.

## Chapter One

1. Michel Serres, *Angels: A Modern Myth* (Paris: Flammarion, 1995), 62.
2. Kenneth Baker, *The Lightning Field* (New Haven, CT: Yale University Press, 2008), 138.
3. Ibid, 14, 16.

4. Ibid., 26.
5. Camille Flammarion, *Les caprices de la foudre*, *Antigone* 20 (1994): 30, 220, 222.
6. Michel Serres, *La naissance de la physique dans le texte de Lucrèce* (Paris: Editions de minuit, 1977), 42.
7. Georges Didi-Huberman, "L'empreinte du Ciel," *Antigone* 20 (1994): 46.
8. Ibid., 40 (citing Flammarion, *Les caprices*, 65), 39.
9. Aby Warburg, *Images from the Region of the Pueblo Indians of North America* (Ithaca, NY: Cornell University Press, 1995), 53, 54.
10. Joseph-Leo Koerner, "Introduction," in Aby Warburg, *Le rituel de serpent: Récit d'un voyage en pays pueblo* (Paris: Macula, 2003), 39.
11. Giorgio Agamben, "Aby Warburg and the Nameless Science," in *Potentialities*, trans. Daniel Heller-Roazen (Stanford, CA: Stanford University Press, 1999), 98.
12. Aby Warburg, "On Planned American Visit (1927)," in Philippe-Alain Michaud, *Aby Warburg and the Image in Motion* (New York: Zone Books, 2007), 332.
13. Aby Warburg, "Memories of a Journey through the Pueblo Region," unpublished notes for the Kreuzlingen Lecture on the Serpent Ritual (1923), in Michaud, *Aby Warburg*, 301 (modified).
14. Koerner, "Introduction," in Warburg, *Le Rituel du serpent*, 23.
15. Ernst Gombrich, *Aby Warburg: An Intellectual Biography* (Chicago: University of Chicago Press, 1986), 229.
16. Sigrid Weigel, "Aby Warburg's *Schlangenrituel*: Reading Culture and Reading Written Texts," *New German Critique* 65 (Spring–Summer 1995): 136, 137.
17. These names are cited in Agamben, "Aby Warburg and the Nameless Science," 91, 94.
18. Ibid., 101, 100, 95.
19. Ibid., 101
20. Ibid.
21. Michaud, *Aby Warburg*, 27, 28 (citing Winckelman), 28, 27–28.
22. Warburg, "On Planned American Visit," 332.
23. Gombrich, *Aby Warburg*, 91.
24. Michael P. Steinberg, "Aby Warburg's Kreuzlingen Lecture. A Reading," in Warburg, *Images from the Region of the Pueblo Indians*, 103.
25. Warburg, "Memories of a Journey," 296, 302.
26. Elsie Clews Parsons, *Pueblo Indian Religion*, vols. 1 and 2 (Lincoln: University of Nebraska Press, 1966), 708ff.
27. Warburg, "Memories of a Journey," 320, 306, 306.
28. Michaud, *Aby Warburg*, 221.
29. Warburg, "Memories of a Journey," 322.
30. Ibid., pp. 312, 314.
31. Warburg, *Images from the Region of the Pueblo Indians*, 53, 53–54, 50.
32. Martin Heidegger, *Contributions to Philosophy (From Enowning)* (Bloomington: Indiana University Press, 1999), 76.
33. Ibid., 54, 54.
34. Rémi Brague, *The Wisdom of the World* (Chicago: University of Chicago Press, 2003), 212.
35. Laurance D. Linford, *Navajo Places: History, Legend, Landscape* (Salt Lake City: University of Utah Press, 2000), 235.
36. Ibid., 21, 204.
37. Ibid., 248 (citing Francis L. Fugate and Roberta B. Fugate, *Roadside History of New Mexico* [Missoula: Mountain Press Publishing, 1989], 394–95).

38. Ibid.
39. Michel Serres, *L'incandescent* (Paris: Ed. Le Pommier, 2003), 9.
40. Samuel Beckett, *The Unnameable*, in *Three Novels by Samuel Beckett* (New York: Grove Press, 1955), 293.
41. Serres, *L'incandescent*, 34.
42. Ibid., 12.
43. Ibid., 13, 14.
44. Michael Taussig, *My Cocaine Museum* (Chicago: University of Chicago Press, 2004), 49.
45. Ibid., 45.
46. Walter Benjamin, *The Arcades Project* (Cambridge, MA: Harvard University Press, 1999), 101–2 (cited by Taussig, *My Cocaine Museum*, 48).
47. Taussig, *My Cocaine Museum*, 45.
48. Andrew Ross, *Strange Weather: Culture, Science, and Technology in the Age of Limits* (London: Verso, 1991), 238, 240.
49. Michel Serres, *The Natural Contract* (Ann Arbor: University of Michigan Press, 1995), 28–29.
50. Parsons, *Pueblo Indian Religion*, 708.
51. Ibid., 333.
52. I am working from a French translation of Marbodius's *Liber de lapidibus*. Marbode, *Poème des pierres précieuses* (Grenoble: Ed. Jérome Millon, 1996), 48–49, 49.
53. Parsons, *Pueblo Indian Religion*, 178.
54. Ibid., 96, 457, 708.
55. Mircea Eliade, *Patterns in Comparative Religion* (Lincoln: University of Nebraska Press, 1958), 66.
56. Mircea Eliade, *The Sacred and the Profane* (New York: Harcourt Brace, 1959), 157, 158.
57. Serres, *La naissance de la physique*, 85 (English trans., p. 67).
58. Vladimir Janković, *Reading the Skies: A Cultural History of English Weather, 1650–1820* (Chicago: University of Chicago Press, 2000), 33, 3.
59. Ibid., 126, 127.
60. Ibid., 125, 130, 130.
61. Katherine Anderson, *Predicting the Weather: Victorians and the Science of Meteorology* (Chicago: University of Chicago Press, 2005), 1.
62. Janković, *Reading the Skies*, 34, 159.
63. Mark Monmonier, *Air Apparent: How Meteorologists Learned to Map, Predict, and Dramatize Weather* (Chicago: University of Chicago Press, 1999), 7.
64. Janković, *Reading the Skies*, 158.
65. Anderson, *Predicting the Weather*, 2.
66. Ibid., 1.
67. Monmonier, *Air Apparent*, 40, 31.
68. Janković, *Reading the Skies*, 130.
69. Ibid., 11.
70. Cited in Taussig, *My Cocaine Museum*, 231.
71. Arden Reed, *Romantic Weather* (Hanover, NH: University Press of New England, 1983), 28.
72. Brague, *Wisdom of the World*, 141. The citation is from the medieval theologian John Scotus Eriugena, *Periphyseon* 5.20.893d.
73. Baker, *Lightning Field*, 17, 24.
74. Sarah Iles Johnston, "Fiat Lux, Fiat Ritus," in *The Presence of Light: Divine Radiance*

and Religious Experience, ed. Matthew Kapstein (Chicago: University of Chicago Press, 2004), 8.

75. *Pseudo-Dionysios: The Complete Works* (New York: Paulist Press, 1987), 162.
76. Walter De Maria, "The Lightning Field," *Artforum* 18, no. 8 (1980).
77. Ibid.
78. Heidegger, *Contributions to Philosophy*, 84.
79. Erin Hogan, *Spiral Jetta: A Road Trip through the Land Art of the American West* (Chicago: University of Chicago Press, 2008), 124–25.
80. Ibid., 125, 129–30.
81. Baker, *Lightning Field*, 17.
82. John Beardsley, "Art and Authoritarianism: Walter De Maria's 'Lightning Field,'" *October*, no. 16 (Spring 1981), 37.
83. Plotinus, *Enneads*, VI, 3, 11, trans. Stephen MacKenna (London: Faber and Faber, 1956), 270. Plotinus speaks more often only disparagingly of such theurgic rituals, favoring instead a purely intellectual form of worship, contemplation, or spiritual practice.
84. Christopher Fynsk, *Language and Relation ... That There Is Language* (Stanford, CA: Stanford University Press, 1996), 274.
85. Massimo Cacciari, *The Necessary Angel* (Albany: SUNY Press, 1994), 11.
86. De Maria, "Lightning Field."

## Chapter Two

1. See most especially "The Question Concerning Technology" in The Question Concerning Technology and Other Essays (New York: Garland Press, 1977).
2. Hubert Damisch, *A Theory of / Cloud / : Toward a History of Painting* (Stanford, CA: Stanford University Press, 2002).
3. Ibid., 174.
4. *Blur: The Making of Nothing* (New York: Harry Abrams, 2002). Elizabeth Diller, "Blur / Babble," in *Anything*, ed. Cynthia Davidson (Cambridge, MA: MIT Press, 2001). Diller's text was written for the final event in a series of conferences gathering leading architectural theorists and practitioners, many of whom are quasi-celebrities: Peter Eisenman, Rem Koolhaas, Zaha Hadid, Stephen Holl, and Bernard Tschumi, among others.
5. Diller, "Blur / Babble," 133.
6. Good overviews of their work can be found in Hal Foster, "Architecture-Eye," *Artforum* 45, no. 6 (February 2007): 246–55, and Justin Davidson, "The Illusionists: How Diller Scofidio + Renfro Is Transforming New York," *New Yorker* (May 14, 2007), 126–37. Charles Renfro had been added as a partner in 2004.
7. Diller, "Blur / Babble," 135
8. Roger Anderegg, "Die Wunder-Wolke," *SonntagsZeitung*, May 19, 2002 (cited and translated in *Blur: The Making of Nothing*, 372).
9. *Blur: The Making of Nothing*, 15.
10. René Descartes, *Les météores*, in *Oeuvres de Descartes*, vol. 6 (Paris: Vrin, 1982), 231 (my translation).
11. René Descartes, *The Discourse on the Method*, in *Philosophical Writings of Descartes*, vol. 1 (Cambridge: Cambridge University Press, 1985), 121.
12. Hans Blumenberg, "Light as Metaphor for Truth," in *Modernity and the Hegemony of Vision*, ed. David Levin (Berkeley: University of California Press, 1993), 53.
13. Descartes, *Discourse on the Method*, 142–43.

14. Descartes, *Les météores*, 149.
15. Ibid., 231 (my translation).
16. Lorraine Daston, "Curiosity in Early Modern Science," *Word & Image* 11, no. 4 (October–December 1995): 397.
17. Ibid., 399.
18. *Blur: The Making of Nothing*, 162.
19. Diller, "Blur / Babble," 135.
20. *Blur: The Making of Nothing*, 162.
21. *Listening Post* (http://www.earstudio.com/projects/listeningpost.html) is referenced and discussed in Thomas Carlson, *The Indiscrete Image* (Chicago: University of Chicago Press, 2008).
22. See Paul Virilio, *Crepuscular Dawn* (Los Angeles: Semiotext(e), 2002).
23. Ibid., 72, 89.
24. Diller, "Blur / Babble," 135
25. *Blur: The Making of Nothing*, 162, 174.
26. Ibid., 175.
27. For a discussion of Diller's rejection of, or at least indifference to, the possibility of applying the notion of the cloud of unknowing to *Blur*, see "Conclusions" in this book.
28. *The Cloud of Unknowing* (New York: Paulist Press, 1981), 121.
29. Ibid., 139, 140.
30. Ibid., 127, 150.
31. Bernard McGinn, *The Foundations of Mysticism* (New York: Crossroads, 1992), 158.
32. Pseudo-Dionysius, "The Mystical Theology," in *Pseudo-Dionysius: The Complete Works* (New York: Paulist Press, 1987), 137.
33. *The Mystical Theology of St. Denis*, in *The Cloud of Unknowing and Other Works* (New York: Penguin, 2001), 1, 4.
34. *Cloud of Unknowing*, 121.
35. Gregory of Nyssa, *The Life of Moses* (New York: Paulist Press, 1978), 38–40, 42, 43, 46.
36. Ibid., 95.
37. One of the *Cloud* author's earliest works was a paraphrase of Richard's *Benjamin Minor (The Twelve Patriarchs)*, and important terms from Richard's *Benjamin Maior (The Mystical Ark)* appear throughout *The Cloud of Unknowing* itself.
38. Richard of St. Victor, "The Mystical Ark," in *Richard of St. Victor* (New York: Paulist Press, 1978), 303. The translation has been modified by consideration of the version offered in the introduction to *The Cloud of Unknowing*.
39. "Superlucenti divine incomprehensibilitatis caligne inclusa." This text from Gallus's Commentary on the Song of Songs is cited and commented on by Bernard McGinn in *The Flowering of Mysticism: Men and Women in the New Mysticism—1200–1350* (New York: Crossroads, 1998), 86.
40. Pseudo-Dionysius, "Mystical Theology," 137.
41. Jonathan Crary, *Techniques of the Observer: On Vision and Modernity in the Nineteenth Century* (Cambridge, MA: MIT Press, 1990), 86.
42. "The Celestial Hierarchy," in *Pseudo-Dionysisu: The Complete Works*, 183–84.
43. "The Celestial Hierarchy," 157, 187–88, 166.
44. Nicholas of Cusa, "On the Vision of God," VI.21 in *Nicholas of Cusa: Selected Spiritual Writings* (New York: Paulist Press, 1997), 244.
45. *Love and Other Technologies: Retrofitting Eros for the Information Age* is the title of a book by Dominic Pettman (New York: Fordham University Press, 2006).

46. *Cloud of Unknowing*, V, 128.
47. Ashley Schafer, "Designing Inefficiencies," in *Scanning: The Aberrant Architecture of Diller + Scofidio*, ed. Aaron Betsky (New York: Harry Abrams, 2003), 97.
48. Patrick Gilmartin, "Technological Landscapes: An Interview with Elizabeth Diller," *Praxis: Journal of Writing + Building* 4 (Fall 2002): 100.
49. "Designing Inefficiencies," in *Scanning: The Aberrant Architecture of Diller + Scofidio*, 100.
50. Gilmartin, "Technological Landscapes."
51. Schafer, "Designing Inefficiencies," 97.
52. Ibid., 101.
53. *Cloud of Unknowing*, 150–51.
54. Gregory of Nyssa, *Commentary on the Song of Songs* (Brookline, MA: Hellenic College Press, 1987), 131.
55. *Cloud of Unknowing*, 128, 140, 139.
56. Ibid., 130.
57. Ibid., 133, 139.
58. Ibid., 132, 130–31.

### Chapter Three

1. James Turrell, quoted in *James Turrell: Occluded Front*, ed. Julia Brown (Los Angeles: Lapis Press, 1985), 43.
2. Michel Serres, *Le Passage du Nord-Ouest. Hermès V* (Paris: Editions de Minuit, 1980), 43.
3. Ibid., 41.
4. Ibid., 41–42.
5. Turrell, in Brown, *James Turrell*, 43.
6. Bernard Stiegler and Ars Industrialis, *Réenchanter le monde: Le valeur esprit contre le populisme industriel* (Paris: Flammarion, 2006), 98, 99.
7. Turrell, quoted in Vicki Lindner, "An Interview with James Turrell," *Omni* 17, no. 9 (Winter 1995): 108.
8. Georges Didi-Huberman, *L'homme qui marchait dans la couleur* (Paris: Editions de Minuit, 2001), 29.
9. Ibid.
10. Ibid., 30.
11. Lindner, "Interview with James Turrell," 108.
12. Turrell, quoted in *Lux: Le monde en lumière* (Paris: Editions de Seuil, 2003), n.p.
13. Pseudo-Dionysius, "The Celestial Hierarchy," in *Pseudo-Dionysius: The Complete Works* (New York: Paulist Press, 1987), 146.
14. Commenting on Meister Eckhart's privileged divine predicate, one / unum, Bernard McGinn cites the following text: "The term 'one' is the same as 'indistinct' [i.e., not to be distinguished], for all distinct things are two or more, but all indistinct things are one." McGinn then summarizes Eckhart's position: "Since indistinction is the distinguishing mark of unum [i.e., divinity], what sets it off from everything else, to conceive of God as unum, or Absolute unity, is to conceive of him as simultaneously distinct and indistinct, indeed, the more distinct insofar as he is indistinct. While this may sound like mere wordplay, Eckhart's intention is totally serious." See McGinn, "Theological Summary," in *Meister Eckhart: The Essential Sermons, Commentaries, Treatises, and Defense* (New York: Paulist Press, 1981), 34.
15. Pseudo-Dionysius, "The Divine Names" and "The Celestial Hierarchy," in *Pseudo-Dionysius: The Complete Works*, 64, 146.

16. Walter Benjamin, "The Work of Art in the Age of Mechanical Reproduction," in *Illuminations* (New York: Schocken, 1968), 222.
17. Hans Urs von Balthasar, "Denys," in *The Glory of the Lord: A Theological Aesthetics*, vol. 2 (New York: Crossroad, 1984), 164.
18. Ibid., 164.
19. Ibid., 165.
20. Didi-Huberman, *L'homme qui marchait*, 31.
21. Ibid., 33, 34, 32.

### Chapter Four

1. Robert Pogue Harrison, *Forests: The Shadow of Civilization* (Chicago: University of Chicago Press, 1992), 245–46, 247.
2. Victor Turner, *The Ritual Process: Structure and Anti-Structure* (Ithaca: Cornell University Press, 1969), 128.
3. Giambattista Vico, *The New Science of Giambattista Vico* (Ithaca, NY: Cornell University Press, 1968), §564.
4. Harrison, *Forests*, 10. My reading is greatly indebted to Harrison's as it appears in this book.
5. Ernesto Grassi, *Vico and Humanism: Essays on Vico, Heidegger, and Rhetoric* (New York: Peter Lang, 1990), 100.
6. Vico, *New Science*, §369.
7. Harrison, *Forests*, 7.
8. Donald Philip Verene, *Knowledge of Things Human and Divine: Vico's New Science and Finnegan's Wake* (New Haven, CT: Yale University Press, 2003), 192.
9. Harrison, *Forests*, 4.
10. Vico, *New Science*, §377.
11. Harrison, *Forests*, 4.
12. Vico, *New Science*, §377.
13. Ibid., §§479, 391.
14. Harrison, *Forests*, 10.
15. Vico, *New Science*, §564.
16. Harrison, *Forests*, 4.
17. Vico, *New Science*, §§387, 370.
18. Ibid., §§372, 370.
19. Harrison, *Forests*, 57–58.
20. Rémi Brague, *The Wisdom of the World* (Chicago: University of Chicago Press, 2003).
21. Augustine, *Confessions*, 13.15.18.
22. Brague, *Wisdom of the World*, 212.
23. Marcel Minnaert, *The Nature of Light and Color in the Open Air* (New York: Dover, 1954), 153; cited in Craig Adcock, *James Turrell: The Art of Light and Space* (Berkeley: University of California Press, 1990), 181.
24. Georges Didi-Huberman, *L'homme qui marchait dans la couleur* (Paris: Editions de Minuit, 2001), 68.
25. Rebecca Solnit, *A Field Guide to Getting Lost* (New York: Viking, 2005), 29.
26. Ibid., 31, 33.
27. Ibid., 31. In contrast with Solnit, Jean-Luc Marion offers a theological interpretation, arguing that distance opens in the icon. Marion, *The Idol and Distance* (New York: Fordham University Press, 2001), esp. chap. 1, and *God without Being* (Chicago:

University of Chicago Press, 1995), esp. chap. 1. My own account of the theology of light in earlier sections of this book also connects medieval religion with the observance of distance. These differences notwithstanding, Solnit, Marion, and I all make a plea for not neglecting distance.

28. Ibid., 39.
29. Ibid., 29.
30. Ibid., 30.
31. Ibid., 31.
32. Vicki Lindner, "An Interview with James Turrell," *Omni* 17, no. 9 (Winter 1995): 110.
33. Friedrich Hölderlin, "In Lovely Blueness," in *Friedrich Hölderlin: Poems and Fragments* (London: Anvil Press Poetry, 2004), 796.
34. Martin Heidegger, "... Poetically Man Dwells ...," in *Poetry, Language, Thought* (New York: Harper & Row, 1971), 222.
35. Ibid., 223.
36. Ibid.
37. Mircea Eliade, *The Sacred and the Profane* (New York: Harcourt Brace, 1959), 119.

## Chapter Five

1. Martin Heidegger, *Nietzsche*, vol. 1 (San Francisco: Harper & Row, 1979), 81–82.
2. Martin Heidegger, "The Question Concerning Technology," in *The Question Concerning Technology and Other Essays* (New York: Garland Press, 1977), 13.
3. Michel Serres, *L'incandecent* (Paris: Ed. Le Pommier, 2003), 295. Thanks to Thomas Carlson for forwarding me this reference.
4. *Rivers and Tides: Andy Goldsworthy Working with Time*, dir. Thomas Riedelsheimer (DVD; New Video, 2004).
5. Ken Johnson, "Indoor-Outdoor Relations along the Hudson," *New York Times* (July 21, 2000).
6. Andy Goldsworthy, *Time* (New York: Harry Abrams, 2000), 8.
7. Johnson, "Indoor-Outdoor Relations."
8. Robert Pogue Harrison, *Forests: The Shadow of Civilization* (Chicago: University of Chicago Press, 1992), 201.
9. Karl Barth, *Protestant Theology in the Nineteenth Century* (Grand Rapids, MI: William B. Eerdmans, 2002), 41.
10. Jean-Paul Sartre, *Nausea* (New York: New Directions, 1964), 156; emphasis added. Quite fortuitously, I found the same text cited in Robert Harrison's more complete discussion of the city and the forest as viewed by Roquentin in his *Forests*.
11. Gregory of Nyssa, "On the Making of Man," in *Nicene and Post-Nicene Fathers of the Christian Church*, vol. 5, ed. Philip Schaff (New York: Christian Literature Co., 1893), 394–95. I found this text in Thomas Carlson, "Locating the Mystical Subject," in *Mystics: Presence and Aporia*, ed. Michael Kessler and Christian Sheppard (Chicago: University of Chicago Press, 2003).
12. André Leroi-Gourhan, *Gesture and Speech* (Cambridge, MA: MIT Press, 1993), 25, 89.
13. Richard E. Leakey and Roger Lewin, *Origins: What New Discoveries Reveal about the Emergence of Our Species and Its Possible Future* (New York: Dutton, 1977), 38, 45.
14. Ibid., 45.
15. Aristotle, "Parts of Animals" in *The Complete Works of Aristotle*, vol. 1 (Princeton, NJ: Princeton University Press, 1984), 1072. Aristotle is, of course, the source par excellence of that tradition which holds that human being is specified by reason and language.

A more dominant voice in his text and its interpretation holds that man has hands because he possesses reason: nature gave us hands because our mind equipped us to use them. And yet his assertion that man be defined as the rational animal is countered by this undercurrent in his text that considers the hands that make man specifically unspecific.

16. Ibid.
17. Bernard Stiegler, *Technics and Time*, vol. 1,*The Fault of Epimetheus* (Stanford, CA: Stanford University Press, 1998), 113.
18. Leroi-Gourhan, *Gesture and Speech*, 106.
19. Ibid., 91.
20. Aristotle, "Parts of Animals," 1072.
21. Leroi-Gourhan, *Gesture and Speech*, 116.
22. Sachiko Kusukawa, "A Manual Computer for Reckoning Time," in *Writing on Hands*, ed. Claire Richter Sherman and Peter M. Lukehart (Trout Gallery Dickinson College / Folger Shakespeare Library, 2000), 34.
23. Goldsworthy, *Time*, 8.
24. Ibid., 114.
25. Leakey and Lewin, *Origins*, 45.
26. Andy Goldsworthy, *Hand to Earth: Andy Goldsworthy Sculpture, 1976–1990* (New York: Harry Abrams, 1990), i.
27. Edward S. Casey, *Getting Back into Place: Toward a Renewed Understanding of the Place-World* (Bloomington: Indiana University Press, 1993), 229–30.
28. Michel Serres, *The Natural Contract* (Ann Arbor: University of Michigan Press, 1995), 48. These pages in Serres and the opposition religion / negligence are referenced by Thomas Carlson in *The Indiscrete Image* (Chicago: University of Chicago Press, 2008), 147.
29. John Sallis, "The Elemental Earth," in *Rethinking Nature: Essays in Environmental Philosophy*, ed. Bruce Foltz and Robert Frodeman (Bloomington: Indiana University Press, 2004), 142.
30. Goldsworthy, *Hand to Earth*, 116.
31. Ibid.
32. Ibid.
33. I borrow the term "unsecuring" from Samuel Weber, who proposes it as a translation of the Heideggerian *Entbergen*, rendered more commonly as "revealing." See Weber's "Upsetting the Setup," in *Mass Mediauras: Form, Technics, Media* (Stanford, CA: Stanford University Press, 1996).
34. Riedelsheimer, *Rivers and Tides*.
35. Goldsworthy, *Time*, 114.
36. Riedelsheimer, *Rivers and Tides*.
37. Andy Goldsworthy, *Passage* (New York: Harry Abrams, 2004), 63.
38. Riedelsheimer, *Rivers and Tides*.
39. Goldsworthy, *Passage*, 121
40. Max Weber, "Science as a Vocation," in *From Max Weber: Essays in Sociology* (New York: Oxford, 1948), 139, 136.
41. Riedelsheimer, *Rivers and Tides*.
42. Goldsworthy, *Time*, 113.
43. Isabelle Stengers, *Power and Invention* (Minneapolis: University of Minnesota Press, 1997), 27, 37, 36.
44. Ilya Prigogine, *The End of Certainty* (New York: Free Press, 1997).

45. Ibid., 5.
46. Gordon Kaufman, *In the Beginning... Creativity* (Minneapolis: Fortress Press, 2004), 56. Kaufman is an excellent example of a theologian for whom Christian notions of creation do not necessitate thinking of God as omnipotent or sole efficient cause.
47. Stengers, *Power and Invention*, 57. Stengers also refers to this text in a book co-authored with Prigogine, *Order Out of Chaos* (Boulder, CO: New Science Library, 1984), 313, where she adds an allusion to the rabbinic account of twenty-six attempts at Genesis. Stengers and Prigogine appear to have encountered the text in André Neher, "Visions du temps et de l'histoire dans la culture juive," in *Les Cultures et le temps* (Paris: UNESCO, 1979).
48. Neher, "Visions du temps," 178–79.
49. *Midrash Rabbah: Genesis* (London: Soncino Press, 1983), 1:10, 12:15. Professor Richard Marks, my colleague at Washington & Lee University, provided invaluable assistance in searching this collection and understanding its intricacies.
50. Ibid., 9:4.
51. Goldsworthy, *Time*, 7.

## Conclusions

1. Christoph Asendorf, *Batteries of Life: On the History of Things and Their Perception in Modernity* (Berkeley: University of California Press, 1993), 162 (citing Wilhelm Hausenstein, *Licht unter dem Horizon: tagbücher von 1942 bis 1946*, 273).
2. Wallace Stevens, *The Collected Poems* (New York: Vintage Books, 1990), 517.
3. James Elkins, *On the Strange Place of Religion in Contemporary Art* (New York: Routledge, 2004), xi.
4. Daniel A. Siedell, *God in the Gallery: A Christian Embrace of Modern Art* (Grand Rapids, MI: Baker Academic, 2008), 39, 36.
5. I allude here to a book by Peter Berger that has long been taken as a classic definition of religion and secularization theory. See Berger, *The Sacred Canopy* (Garden City, NY: Doubleday, 1967).
6. Siedell, *God in the Gallery*, 46.
7. Elkins, *On the Strange Place of Religion*, 115; James Elkins and David Morgan, eds., *Re-enchantment* (New York: Routledge, 2009), 111.
8. Matthew Kapstein, ed., *The Presence of Light: Divine Radiance and Religious Experience* (Chicago: University of Chicago Press, 2004), ix, x.
9. *Blur: The Making of Nothing* (New York: Harry Abrams, 2002), 172.
10. Elkins, *On the Strange Place of Religion*, 115.
11. Siedell, *God in the Gallery*, 130.
12. For the record, I am not claiming that Siedell make this claim to rescue disenchanted moderns.
13. "Introduction: The Varieties of Modern Enchantment," in *The Re-enchantment of the World: Secular Magic in a Rational Age*, ed. Joshua Landy and Michael Saler (Stanford, CA: Stanford University Press, 2009), 2, 14.

# *WORKS CITED*


Adcock, Craig. *James Turrell: The Art of Light and Space*. Berkeley: University of California Press, 1990.

Agamben, Giorgio. "Aby Warburg and the Nameless Science." In *Potentialities*. Stanford, CA: Stanford University Press, 1999.

Anderson, Katherine. *Predicting the Weather: Victorians and the Science of Meteorology*. Chicago: University of Chicago Press, 2005.

Aristotle. "Parts of Animals." In *The Complete Works of Aristotle*, vol. 1. Princeton, NJ: Princeton University Press, 1984.

Asendorf, Christoph. *Batteries of Life: On the History of Things and Their Perception in Modernity*. Trans. Don Reneau. Berkeley: University of California Press, 1993.

Atchley, J. Heath. *Encountering the Secular: Philosophical Endeavors in Religion and Culture*. Charlottesville: University of Virginia Press, 2009.

Augustine, Saint. *Confessions*. Vol. 2. Cambridge, MA: Harvard University Press, 1912.

Baker, Kenneth. *The Lightning Field*. New Haven, CT: Yale University Press, 2008.

Balthasar, Hans Urs von. "Denys." In *The Glory of the Lord: A Theological Aesthetics*, vol. 2. New York: Crossroad, 1984.

Barth, Karl. *Protestant Theology in the Nineteenth Century*. Trans. Brian Cozens and John Bowden. Grand Rapids, MI: William B. Eerdmans, 2002.

Beardsley, John. "Art and Authoritarianism: Walter De Maria's 'Lightning Field.'" *October*, no. 16 (Spring 1981).

Beckett, Samuel. *The Unnameable*. In *Three Novels by Samuel Beckett*. New York: Grove Press, 1955.

Benjamin, Walter. "The Work of Art in the Age of Mechanical Reproduction." In *Illuminations*. Trans. Harry Zohn. New York: Schocken, 1968.

Blumenberg, Hans. *The Legitimacy of the Modern Age*. Trans. Robert Wallace. Cambridge, MA: MIT Press, 1983.

———. "Light as Metaphor for Truth." In *Modernity and the Hegemony of Vision*, ed. David Levin. Berkeley: University of California Press, 1993.

*Blur: The Making of Nothing*. New York: Harry Abrams, 2002.

Brague, Rémi. *The Wisdom of the World*. Trans. Teresa Lavender Fagan. Chicago: University of Chicago Press, 2003.

Brown, Julia, ed. *James Turrell: Occluded Front*. Los Angeles: Lapis Press, 1985.

Cacciari, Massimo. *The Necessary Angel*. Trans. Miguel Vatter. Albany: SUNY Press, 1994.

Carlson, Thomas. *The Indiscrete Image*. Chicago: University of Chicago Press, 2008.

———. "Locating the Mystical Subject." In *Mystics: Presence and Aporia*, ed. Michael Kessler and Christian Sheppard. Chicago: University of Chicago Press, 2003.

Casey, Edward S. *Getting Back into Place: Toward a Renewed Understanding of the Place-World*. Bloomington: Indiana University Press, 1993.

*Cloud of Unknowing, The*. New York: Paulist Press, 1981.

Crary, Jonathan. *Techniques of the Observer: On Vision and Modernity in the Nineteenth Century*. Cambridge, MA: MIT Press, 1990.

Davidson, Justin. "The Illusionists: How Diller Scofidio + Renfro Is Transforming New York." *New Yorker* (May 14, 2007), 126–37.

DeMaria, Walter. "The Lightning Field." *Artforum* 18, no. 8 (1980).

Damisch, Hubert. *A Theory of /Cloud/: Toward a History of Painting*. Trans. Janet Lloyd. Stanford, CA: Stanford University Press, 2002.

Daston, Lorraine. "Curiosity in Early Modern Science." *Word & Image* 11, no. 4 (October-December 1995).

Descartes, René. *The Discourse on the Method*. In *Philosophical Writings of Descartes*, vol. 1. Trans. John Cotingham, Robert Stoothof, and Dugald Murdoch. Cambridge: Cambridge University Press, 1985.

———. *Les météores*. In *Oeuvres de Descartes*, vol. 6. Paris: Vrin, 1982.

Didi-Huberman, Georges. "L'empreinte du ciel." *Antigone* 20 (1994).

———. *L'homme qui marchait dans la couleur*. Paris: Editions de Minuit, 2001.

Diller, Elizabeth. "Blur/Babble." In *Anything*, ed. Cynthia Davidson. Cambridge, MA: MIT Press, 2001.

Elkins, James. *On the Strange Place of Religion in Contemporary Art*. New York: Routledge, 2004.

Elkins, James, and David Morgan, eds. *Re-enchantment*. New York: Routledge, 2009.

Eliade, Mircea. *Patterns in Comparative Religion*. Trans. Rosemary Sheed. Lincoln: University of Nebraska Press, 1958.

———. *The Sacred and the Profane*. Trans. Willard Trask. New York: Harcourt Brace, 1959.

Flammarion, Camille. *Les caprices de la foudre*. Extracts reprinted in *Antigone* 20 (1994).

Foster, Hal. "Architecture-Eye." *Artforum* 45, no. 6 (Feb 2007): 246–55.

Fynsk, Christopher. *Language and Relation . . . that there is language*. Stanford, CA: Stanford University Press, 1996.

Gilmartin, Patrick. "Technological Landscapes: An Interview with Elizabeth Diller." *Praxis* 4 (Fall 2002).

Goldsworthy, Andy. *Hand to Earth: Andy Goldsworthy Sculpture, 1976–1990*. New York: Harry Abrams, 1990.

———. *Midsummer Snowballs*. New York: Harry Abrams, 2001.

———. *Passage*. New York: Harry Abrams, 2004.

———. *Time*. New York: Harry Abrams, 2000.

Gombrich, Ernst. *Aby Warburg: An Intellectual Biography*. Chicago: University of Chicago Press, 1986.

Grassi, Ernesto. *Vico and Humanism: Essays on Vico, Heidegger, and Rhetoric*. New York: Peter Lang, 1990.

Gregory of Nyssa. *Commentary on the Song of Songs*. Trans. Casimir McCambley, OCSO. Brookline, MA: Hellenic College Press, 1987.

———. *The Life of Moses*. Trans. Abraham J. Malherbe and Everett Ferguson. New York: Paulist Press, 1978.

———. "On the Making of Man." In *Nicene and Post-Nicene Fathers of the Christian Church*, vol. 5, ed. Philip Schaff. New York: Christian Literature Co., 1893.

Harrison, Robert Pogue. *Forests: The Shadow of Civilization*. Chicago: University of Chicago Press, 1992.

Heidegger, Martin. *Contributions to Philosophy (From Enowning)*. Trans. Parvis Emad and Kenneth Maly. Bloomington: Indiana University Press, 1999.

———. *Nietzsche*, vol. 1. Trans. David Farrell Krell. San Francisco: Harper & Row, 1979.

———. "... Poetically Man Dwells ..." In *Poetry, Language, Thought*. Trans. Alfred Hofstadter. New York: Harper & Row, 1971.

———. *The Principle of Reason*. Trans. Reginald Lilly. Bloomington: Indiana University Press, 1996.

———. "The Question Concerning Technology." In *The Question Concerning Technology and Other Essays*. Trans. William Levitt. New York: Garland Press, 1977.

Hogan, Erin. *Spiral Jetta: A Road Trip through the Land Art of the American West*. Chicago: University of Chicago Press, 2008.

Hölderlin, Friedrich. "In Lovely Blueness." In *Friedrich Hölderlin: Poems and Fragments*. Trans. Michael Hamburger. London: Anvil Press Poetry, 2004.

Janković, Vladimir. *Reading the Skies: A Cultural History of English Weather, 1650–1820*. Chicago: University of Chicago Press, 2000.

Johnson, Ken. "Indoor-Outdoor Relations along the Hudson." *New York Times* (July 21, 2000).

Johnston, Sarah Iles. "Fiat Lux, Fiat Ritus." In *The Presence of Light: Divine Radiance and Religious Experience*, ed. Matthew Kapstein. Chicago: University of Chicago Press, 2004.

Kant, Immanuel. *Critique of Pure Reason*. Trans. Norman Kemp Smith. New York: St.Martin's Press, 1965.

Kapstein, Matthew, ed. *The Presence of Light: Divine Radiance and Religious Experience*. Chicago: University of Chicago Press, 2004.

Kaufman, Gordon. *In the beginning... Creativity*. Minneapolis: Fortress Press, 2004.

Koerner, Joseph-Leo, "Introduction." In Aby Warburg, *Le rituel de serpent: Récit d'un voyage en pays pueblo*. Paris: Macula, 2003.

Landy, Joshua, and Michael Saler, eds. *The Re-enchantment of the World: Secular Magic in a Rational Age*. Stanford, CA: Stanford University Press, 2009.

Leakey, Richard E., and Roger Lewin. *Origins: What New Discoveries Reveal about the Emergence of Our Species and Its Possible Future*. New York: Dutton, 1977.

Leibniz, G. W. "A Résumé of Metaphysics." In *Leibniz: Philosophical Writings*, ed. G. H. R. Parkinson. London: Dent, Rowman, and Littlefield, 1991.

———. *Theodicy*. Trans. E. M. Haggard. LaSalle, IL: Open Court, 1985.

Leroi-Gourhan, André. *Gesture and Speech*. Trans. Anna Bostock Berger. Cambridge, MA: MIT Press, 1993.

Lindner, Vicki. "An Interview with James Turrell." *Omni* 17, no. 9 (Winter 1995).

Linford, Laurance D. *Navajo Places: History, Legend, Landscape*. Salt Lake City: University of Utah Press, 2000.

*Lux: Le monde en lumière*. Paris: Editions de Seuil, 2003.

Marbode. *Poème des pierres précieuses*. Grenoble: Ed. Jérome Millon, 1996.

Marion, Jean-Luc. *God without Being*. Chicago: University of Chicago Press, 1995.

———. *The Idol and Distance*. New York: Fordham University Press, 2001.

McGinn, Bernard. *The Flowering of Mysticism: Men and Women in the New Mysticism—1200–1350*. New York: Crossroads, 1998.

———. *The Foundations of Mysticism*. New York: Crossroads, 1992.

———. "Theological Summary." In *Meister Eckhart: The Essential Sermons, Commentaries, Treatises, and Defense*. New York: Paulist Press, 1981.

Michaud, Philippe-Alain. *Aby Warburg and the Image in Motion*. Trans. Sophie Hawkes. New York: Zone Books, 2007.
*Midrash Rabbah: Genesis*. London: Soncino Press, 1983.
Minnaert, Marcel. *The Nature of Light and Color in the Open Air*. New York: Dover, 1954
Monmonier, Mark. *Air Apparent: How Meteorologists Learned to Map, Predict, and Dramatize Weather*. Chicago: University of Chicago Press, 1999.
*Mystical Theology of St. Denis, The*. In *The Cloud of Unknowing and Other Works*. Trans. A. C. Spearing. New York: Penguin, 2001.
Neher, André. "Visions du temps et de l'histoire dans la culture juive." In *Les Cultures et le temps*. Paris: UNESCO, 1979.
Nicholas of Cusa. "On the Vision of God." In *Nicholas of Cusa: Selected Spiritual Writings*. Trans. H. Lawrence Bond. New York: Paulist Press, 1997.
Parsons, Elsie Clews. *Pueblo Indian Religion*, vols. 1 and 2. Lincoln: University of Nebraska Press, 1966.
Plotinus. *Enneads*. Trans. Stephen MacKenna. London: Faber and Faber, 1956.
Prigogine, Ilya. *The End of Certainty*. New York: Free Press, 1997.
Pseudo-Dionysios. *Pseudo-Dionysios: The Complete Works*. Trans. Paul Rorem. New York: Paulist Press, 1987.
Reed, Arden. *Romantic Weather*. Hanover, NH: University Press of New England, 1983.
Richard of St. Victor. "The Mystical Ark." In *Richard of St. Victor*. Trans. Grover A. Zinn. New York: Paulist Press, 1978.
*Rivers and Tides: Andy Goldsworthy Working with Time*. Dir. Thomas Riedelsheimer. DVD. New Video, 2004.
Ross, Andrew. *Strange Weather: Culture, Science, and Technology in the Age of Limits*. London: Verso, 1991.
Rutherford, Donald. *Leibniz and the Rational Order of Nature*. Cambridge: Cambridge University Press, 1995.
Sallis, John. "The Elemental Earth." In *Rethinking Nature: Essays in Environmental Philosophy*, ed. Bruce Foltz and Robert Frodeman. Bloomington: Indiana University Press, 2004.
Sartre, Jean-Paul. *Nausea*. Trans. Lloyd Alexander. New York: New Directions, 1964.
Schafer, Ashley. "Designing Inefficiencies." In *Scanning: The Aberrant Architecture of Diller + Scofidio*, ed. Aaron Betsky. New York: Harry Abrams, 2003.
Schivelbusch, Wolfgang. *Disenchanted Night: The Industrialization of Light in the Nineteenth Century*. Trans. Angela Davies. Berkeley: University of California Press, 1988.
Schopenhauer, Arthur. *On The Fourfold Root of the Principle of Reason*. Trans. E. F. J. Payne. La Salle, IL: Open Court, 1974.
Serres, Michel. *Angels: A Modern Myth*. Trans. Francis Cowper. Paris: Flammarion, 1995.
———. *L'Incandescent*. Paris: Ed. Le Pommier, 2003.
———. *La naissance de la physique dans le texte de Lucrèce*. Paris: Editions de Minuit, 1977.
———. *The Natural Contract*. Trans. Elizabeth MacArthur and William Paulson. Ann Arbor: University of Michigan Press, 1995.
———. *Le Passage du Nord-Ouest. Hermès V*. Paris: Editions de Minuit, 1980.
Sherman, Claire Richter, and Peter M. Lukehart, eds. *Writing on Hands*. Trout Gallery Dickinson College/Folger Shakespeare Library, 2000.
Siedell, Daniel A. *God in the Gallery: A Christian Embrace of Modern Art*. Grand Rapids, MI: Baker Academic, 2008.
Solnit, Rebecca. *A Field Guide to Getting Lost*. New York: Viking, 2005.

Steinberg, Michael P. "Aby Warburg's Kreuzlingen Lecture: A Reading." In Aby Warburg, *Images from the Region of the Pueblo Indians of North America*. Ithaca, NY: Cornell University Press, 1995.

Stengers, Isabelle. *Power and Invention*. Minneapolis: University of Minnesota Press, 1997.

Stevens, Wallace. "Looking across the Fields and Watching the Birds Fly." In *The Collected Poems*. New York: Vintage, 1990.

Stiegler, Bernard. *Technics and Time*. Vol. 1, *The Fault of Epimetheus*. Stanford, CA: Stanford University Press, 1998.

Stiegler, Bernard, and Ars Industrialis. *Réenchanter le monde: Le valeur esprit contre le populisme industriel*. Paris: Flammarion, 2006.

Taussig, Michael. *My Cocaine Museum*. Chicago: University of Chicago Press, 2004.

Verene, Donald Philip. *Knowledge of Things Human and Divine: Vico's New Science and Finnegan's Wake*. New Haven, CT: Yale University Press, 2003.

Vico, Giambattista. *The New Science of Giambattista Vico*. Trans. Thomas Goddard Bergin and Max Harold Fisch. Ithaca, NY: Cornell University Press, 1968.

Virilio, Paul. *Crepuscular Dawn*. Trans. Mike Taormina. Los Angeles: Semiotext(e), 2002.

Warburg, Aby. *Images from the Region of the Pueblo Indians of North America*. Trans. Michael Steinberg. Ithaca, NY: Cornell University Press, 1995.

———. "Memories of a Journey through the Pueblo Region." Unpublished notes for the Kreuzlingen Lecture on the Serpent Ritual (1923). In Philippe-Alain Michaud, *Aby Warburg and the Image in Motion*. Trans. Sophie Hawkes. New York: Zone Books, 2007.

———. "On Planned American Visit (1927)." In Michaud, *Aby Warburg and the Image in Motion*.

Weber, Max. "Science as a Vocation." In *From Max Weber: Essays in Sociology*, ed. H. H. Gerth and C. Wright Mills. New York: Oxford University Press, 1946.

Weber, Samuel. *Mass Mediauras: Form, Technics, Media*. Stanford, CA: Stanford University Press, 1996

Weigel, Sigrid, "Aby Warburg's *Schlangenrituel*: Reading Culture and Reading Written Texts." *New German Critique* 65 (Spring-Summer 1995).

# *INDEX*

www.ingramcontent.com/pod-product-compliance
Lightning Source LLC
LaVergne TN
LVHW052352100826
845147LV00013B/819

* 9 7 8 0 2 2 6 4 1 1 8 0 4 *